BIBLICAL INTERPRETATION
IN AFRICAN PERSPECTIVE

Edited by
David Tuesday Adamo

University Press of America,® Inc.
Lanham · Boulder · New York · Toronto · Oxford

Copyright © 2006 by
University Press of America,® Inc.
4501 Forbes Boulevard
Suite 200
Lanham, Maryland 20706
UPA Acquisitions Department (301) 459-3366

PO Box 317
Oxford
OX2 9RU, UK

Library of Congress Control Number: 2005929542
ISBN 0-7618-3303-X (paperback : alk. ppr.)

™
⊖ The paper used in this publication meets the minimum
requirements of American National Standard for Information
Sciences—Permanence of Paper for Printed Library Materials,
ANSI Z39.48—1984

DEDICATION

To all Africanist Biblical Scholars all over the world who affirm African Biblical Interpretation as legitimate as Eurocentric Biblical Interpretation and who continue to write despite its non-acceptability in the academy.

TABLE OF CONTENTS

Historical Perspective

Contextual Interpretation of Texts

PREFACE

The decision to edit this book came in the year 2001 when I was on Sabbatical/Leave of Absence in the United States. This decision came as I received challenges on the condemnation of African Biblical Studies. It is a response to some Euro/American ideas that western method of biblical interpretation is the only legitimate interpretation.

The twelve articles are, to me, highly scholarly articles from reputable Africanist biblical scholars from all over the world. These are articles which demonstrate the nature of African Biblical Studies. The first part is on the historical perspective of biblical interpretation in Africa and the second part deals with specific interpretation of particular biblical texts. All the articles are fresh articles except Grant LeMarguand's article, "Siblings or Antagonists? The Ethos of Biblical Scholarship from the North Atlantic and African Worlds," which was originally published in the *African Journal of Biblical Studies* (vol. XIX, Nov. 2003, 2 pp.23-49) in an abridged version, and my article, "The Historical Development of Old Testament Interpretation in Africa" which was originally published in *Old Testament Essay* (16/1, 2003, 9-33). It is my hope that readers of this book will be able to familiarize themselves with the contextual nature of African Biblical Studies and thereby appreciate, if not accept it, as equally legitimate as any other method of biblical interpretations. Those who have read my previous publications (*Exploration in African Biblical Studies, Reading and Interpreting the Bible in African Indigenous Churches in Nigeria,* Africa *and The Africans in the Old Testament, Africa and Africans in the New Testament, and* other articles) on this aspect of biblical studies will appreciate the authors' contributions in this book.

Unfortunately, all my effort to get more female African Biblical scholars to contribute articles to this volume was abortive. Two scholars, Prof. Madipoane Masenya from the University of South Africa, Pretoria, and Dr. Oluronke Olajubu from the University of Ilorin, Ilorin, Nigeria however made valuable contributions. This is an evidence of dearth of female African biblical scholars. It is my hope that this will improve in the future.

It is gratifying to know that African biblical scholars are doing something concrete and are ever ready to continue the struggle of making African Biblical Studies known and acceptable to most western scholars who have hitherto closed their minds to it. I appreciate the effort of colleagues who took great pains to contribute articles to this book. Certainly, this is the beginning of good things to come.

David Tuesday Adamo PhD
Department of Religious Studies
Delta State University
Abraka, Delta State
Nigeria
Adamodt@yahoo.com
March 15, 2005

ACKNOWLEDGMENTS

I will like to acknowledge the following people: my colleague, Dr. Joseph Enuwosa, my doctoral student, Rev. Senne-Aya who read this manuscript and did some correction. I must also express my thanks to my cousin, Olorunshola Owoyele, who did the type-setting and most of the computer work involved. I appreciated my son, David Tuesday Adamo Jnr who also assisted in the computer work.

PART ONE

HISTORICAL PERSPECTIVE

CHAPTER I

INTRODUCTION

> When our own ways of understanding no longer work, it is
> essential to listen to others and learn from them. It seems to
> us that Western biblical scholarship suffers most from
> being "without context." It is carried out abstractly and
> therefore leads to abstract results and truths, which are not
> related to any context....Because of this, it is contextual
> Bible reading and contextual Bible hermeneutics that we
> need most.[1]

The above quotation reflects the situation in Europe and America where the Bible is mostly read and interpreted abstractly, that is, interpretation and reading that is uncommitted and that has nothing to do with the life and reading of ordinary people. In Africa, the situation is quite different. Reading and interpreting the Bible is done in the perspective of African culture and experience. It affects the present life situation of the African people. Reading and interpreting the Bible is not for aesthetic purpose or for fun. It is not for scholarship's sake but for application to daily life. The Bible is read and interpreted contextually. The Bible has no meaning, and no value, in Africa except when it is read and interpreted in African context. This is exactly what this book is all about. It is a collection of articles from various eminent biblical scholars who are committed to African biblical studies. The contributions are from scholars from various countries in the continent of Africa (Nigeria, South Africa, and Zimbabwe) and United States of America. Readers will notice that the majority of contributors are from Nigeria. The reason is not only because the editor is a Nigeria and teaches in Nigeria (Delta State University), but because Nigeria is the largest countries in Africa and has the greatest number of African biblical scholars in the continent. This is evident in the article of Knut Holter in this book, "Sub-Saharan African Doctoral Dissertation in Old Testament Studies 1967-2000: Some Remarks to their Chronology and Geography."[2]

Although this volume represents the latest trend in African biblical scholarship, it is not the final and complete authority in African Biblical studies. There are still more to be done by Africanist biblical scholars.

The book has two parts: historical perspective and contextual interpretation of texts. The historical perspective has six articles dealing with basic historical development of biblical interpretation in Africa, analysis of various African scholars' approaches to biblical interpretation and African presence in the Bible. David Tuesday Adamo's article traces the history of biblical interpretation from the biblical period to the present and emphasizes Africa and African contribution to biblical interpretation. Gerald West, in his article is concerned with how the Bible is used in South African Black Theology. It traces how the Bible is seen as having some divine power (the Bible as *Bola*) from the early time to the present in South Africa. Grant LeMarquand, focusing on African biblical scholars' method of interpretation, compares it with that of the Western interpretation. He discusses the work of Justin Ukpong more extensively and the differences between North Atlantic and African methods of interpretation. Madipoane Masenya discusses the use of the Bible among the Pentecostal churches in Northern Sotho, South Africa. According to her, there is still a need for liberation from the colonial ways in which the Bible is interpreted by women. Knut Holter is an Africanist biblical scholar who has been following the trend and nature of African biblical scholarship. He presented an analysis of doctoral dissertations written by Africans from 1967-2000. This analysis, done chronologically and geographically, is informative and highly valuable. Joseph Enuwosa examines the presence of Africa and Africans in the Acts of the Apostles, pointing out their contribution to the spread of Christianity in the New Testament.

The second part, the contextual interpretation of texts, has six articles dealing with interpretation of specific biblical passages in African context. David Tuesday Adamo's second article examines some imprecatory passages in the book of Psalms in African context. Unlike the view of most Western biblical scholars, these Psalms are not Psalms of curse or hate when approached in the light of African culture. Dapo Asaju, examines chieftaincy titles in African culture in light of biblical passages. Joseph Enuwosa also examines Ephesians 4:1-6 in light of African culture. The passage emphasises is on unity as it reflects African concept of community. Ukachukwu Chris Manus' article on Romans 12: 3-21 is a good piece on how intercultural hermeneutics can be utilized. When this method is applied to the book of Romans, the meaning of the passage comes to life and applicable to everyday life of Africans, especially Igbo and Yoruba persons. Oyeronke Olajubu examines the relevant biblical passages used to support celibacy and concludes that celibacy has no relevance in African culture. Robert Wafawanaka examines the concept of poverty in Africa in the light of the Bible. He compares and contrasts the Bible and African perspective and attitude to poverty.

Although this book may not be exhaustive in the field of African biblical studies, I hope that readers will find it informative and useful for further studies.

Considering the lack of contextual method of Western interpretation, I believe that readers of this book will discover that African biblical studies can be beneficial to the Western biblical interpretation.

Finally, the authors of various articles in this book do not suggest or claim that African biblical studies is the only legitimate method of biblical interpretation, rather they are saying that it is as equally legitimate as any other method. This is why they made use of both Western and African methods.

Endnotes

1. Walter Dietrich and Ulrich Luz (editors), *The Bible in the World Context: anExperiment in Contextual Hermeneutics* (Grand Rapids, Michigan/Cambridge,UK: William B Eerdmans Publishing Company, 2002), ix-x.
2. For further information see also, Knut Holter, *Old Testament Research for Africa* (New York, Washington D.C .Baltimore, Oxford: Peter Lang, 2002).

CHAPTER II

THE HISTORICAL DEVELOPMENT OF OLD TESTAMENT INTERPRETATION IN AFRICA[1]

Rev. Prof. David Tuesday Adamo

Introduction

The discussion of the history of Old Testament research in Africa is a difficult task. It is a difficult task not only because of the size of the continent, but also because of the diversity of the people. Yet I have taken it upon myself to conduct this research. The purpose of this essay is to trace in outline form the development of African Old Testament scholarship from the biblical period to the present. My emphasis is on different approaches employed by African biblical scholars in conducting Old Testament research. In order to achieve this purpose I examined the Bible and traced the presence of Africa and Africans to the various occasions when they read and interpreted the Bible in the Old and New Testament. In my discussion of the post biblical period I examined the interpretation of the Bible by African Church Fathers.

My focus is to examine the modern period, namely, the 1930s to the present. At the early period, the majority of African Old Testament scholars followed verbatim, the Western methods of interpretation. However, a new development in African Old Testament interpretation called African cultural hermeneutics arose. I plan to discuss what African cultural hermeneutics is and its divergent approaches, that is, African comparative approach, evaluative approach, African-in-the-Bible approach, the Bible as power approach, bibliographical approach, and contextual/reading with the ordinary people approach. The examinations of the progress made in these various approaches is followed by the future prospect of African Old Testament scholarship.

The Biblical Period

The discussion of the interpretation of the Bible during the biblical period is based on the fact that there is African presence in the pages of the Old and New Testaments. This fact has not been widely subscribed to in most western scholarship. I have discussed extensively African Presence in my books, *Africa and The Africans in the Old Testament*, and *Africa and Africans in the New Testament*.[2]

According to my finding, Africa and Africans was mentioned about 867 times in the Bible. Africa and Africans were mentioned more than any other nations in the Bible except Israel. In the history of the ancient Near East, various terms were used to refer to Africa and Africans. Such terms are Wawat, Kash, Kesh, by the Africans themselves (mainly the Egyptians), *Kushi, Kushu* by the Assyrians, Ethiopians by the ancient Greeks, Meluhhans by the Sumerians, and *Cush, Cushi, Cushit, Put* or *Punt* by the Biblical writers.[3]

One of the remarkable references to Africa and Africans in the Old Testament where African was reading and probably interpreting the Bible is in Jeremiah 36:1-23. There was a reference to one Yehudi, the son of Nathaniah, the son of Shelemaiah, the son of *Cushi*[4] who was a prince in the court of Jehoiakim. Of all the princes present, the prince, the son of *Cushi* with an African ancestry, was not only the one sent to retrieve the Jeremiah's scroll first, from Baruch and second from the chamber of Elishama, he was also the only one invited to read Jeremiah's scroll first, to the princes, and second, to the king. He was also the only one whose ancestry was traced to the third generation.

There are three important questions one needs to ask. (1) Why was he the only one among many princes whose ancestry was traced to the third generation? (2) Why was he the only one sent to retrieve the letter from Baruch and from Elishama? (3) Why was he the only one invited to read the letter to the princes and to the king? The answer to the first question is that the author of the book of Jeremiah wanted the readers to know that he has an African ancestry (Cushi). The answer to the second question is that he was the most trusted among the princes. The answer to the third question is that he was the only one who was literate among the princes.

Although there is no unanimous agreement concerning the identification of that particular letter of Jeremiah in the book of Jeremiah, I hold very strongly the opinion that the script was included in the Bible and more likely, in the book of Jeremiah. Yehudi, the son of Nathaniah, the son of Shelemaiah, the son of

Cushi, read that letter two consecutive times before the princes and before the king. I presume that the reading of that letter of Jeremiah was followed by interpretation hence the content of that scroll and the Yehudi's interpretation made the king so furious. This was probably why the other princes advised Baruch and Jeremiah to hide. This may also be the reason why the king was so furious and decided to tear the roll and punish Jeremiah. They were not prepared to handle the content of such letter and Yehudi's interpretation.

Another reference to Africans reading and interpreting the Old Testament in the pages of the Bible was in the New Testament. In Acts 8, the so-called "Ethiopian eunuch" was coming from Jerusalem where he went to worship as part of his annual pilgrimage. Although many Western scholars doubted the authenticity of most of the passages, which refer to Africa and Africans, there is no contention among biblical scholars that this so- called "eunuch" was an African. He was in possession of and reading part of the Old Testament scripture, namely, the book of Isaiah. He was probably reading and reflecting on the passage but he was reading and perhaps, was not able to understand it. Note that Philip, the evangelist asked, "Do you understand what you are reading?" The fact is not that he did not understand the Hebrew language in which the Old Testament was written, but after some reflections, he could not understand the passages. In other words, the evangelist was asking whether or not the African understood the meaning of the text.

The implication of this according to my reflection is that Africa and African presence in the Bible is no more a dispute and that before many nations, including the Western nations ever got possession of the pages of the Old Testament, Africans were already in possession, reading and interpreting it.

The Post Biblical Period

The history of the interpretation of the Old Testament during the early Christian Church began with African interpreters. I believe that no well-informed biblical scholar would dispute the fact that Africa is the cradle of systematic biblical interpretation. Justin Ukpong rightly confirmed this fact when he traced biblical interpretation to the University of Alexandria in Africa.[5]

Clement of Alexandria who was a pulpit of Pantaenus was an African scholar whose nativity most Western scholars attributed to Greece instead of Africa. There was no clear evidence to support Athens as his place of nativity. Although he travelled extensively to East and West, he spent most of his fruitful life in the city of Alexandria and as the head of the African University in Alexandria. He did extensive exegetical work on both the Old and New Testaments.

Origen was an African scholar born in Egypt in about 185 CE. At the age of 18 he was appointed to succeed Clement of Alexandria as the head of the University of Alexandria. Among the ante-Nicene scholars, he was the greatest as a theologian and biblical scholar. He was a biblical scholar per excellence. He later moved to Caesarea and established a new biblical and theological school as a result of persecution in Alexandria. He was a textual critic. Apart from his textual work on the Old Testament, Hexapla, he commented on almost all the books of the Bible.

Quintus Septimus Florence Tertullianus was one of the outstanding early African theologians. He was born in Carthage, North Africa. He was one of the most prolific Latin Fathers of his period who regarded the Old Testament scriptures as divinely given. He did much exegetical work on the books of the Old Testament.

Caecilius Cyprianus of Carthage became bishop of Carthage two years after his conversion by the acclamation of his people. He was "a rich master of eloquence in Carthage" before he was converted to Christianity.[6] He was eventually placed to be the head of the whole North African clergy. He administered, very brilliantly, the Episcopal office in Carthage. He seems to have memorized the entire scriptures. Of the 7,966 verses in the New Testament, he quoted 886 verses (about one-ninth of the entire New Testament). His New Testament, according to his reconstruction, contains the four Gospels, the Pauline Epistles, I Peter, I John and the Apocalypse.[7] He cited 934 biblical quotations from both Old Testament and New Testament and used them about 1,499 times in various contexts.[8]

Athanasius was born between 296-298 CE in Egypt. He was educated in the African University in Alexandria. He was one of the "key ecclesiastical and theological leaders of the church in the 4th century who read and commented on every book of the Bible. He later became the bishop of Alexandria. His major contribution is his commentary on every book of the Bible and his polemical work against the Arians who taught that the Son was different in essence from the Father. According to him, the Son was a created being.[9] His commentary on the books of the Bible also assisted the church in authenticating which books of the New Testament is to be regarded as canonical.

Augustin of Hippo was born in North Africa to a Christian Mother called Monica who fervently prayed for his conversion because of her belief that a child of many prayers can never be lost. He lost his father at the age of eighteen. He became the bishop of Hippo in Africa and later became one of the greatest interpreters of the scriptures.

Cyril was a bishop of Alexandria and was also vast in Scriptural interpretation. He later succeeded his uncle who was a local patriarch. He discussed scriptural passages with "pathos." He commented on the books of the Bible verse by verse, especially the books of Isaiah, Psalms, John, and Matthew. His acceptance of the books also helped in the process of the formation of the Christian Scripture.

Despite the fact that the method of interpretation by this eminent African scholar is allegorical, the undisputed truth is that Africa retained its pioneering role of a well-established rhetorical and biblical interpretative tradition during the 2nd and 3rd centuries of the Christian era. The early Christian church was forced to draw up a list of authoritative and acceptable books of the Bible. Upon this basis, the Christian church accepted the present books of the protestant Bible as canonical and authoritative books of the Bible.[10]

The Modern Period

The modern periods of African biblical scholarship have been discussed by two eminent scholars- Justin Ukpong and Knut Holter. While Justin Ukpong who is deeply committed to African biblical studies, divides the development of biblical interpretation in Africa into three phases: "Reactive and apologetic," "Reactive-Proactive," and "Proactive periods,"[11] Knut Holter divides it into "thematic and institutional perspectives."[12] I will rather divide this essay into the Biblical, post biblical, and modern periods. The modern period is the period from 1930 to the present.

The Period of 1930 to 1960s

The period, 1930 to 1960 reflects the colonial period in Africa. I will like to call this the missionary period. The 19th and 20th centuries were the time the missionaries in Africa condemned African indigenous religion as "demonic and immoral." As such, the only way for Christianity to grow is to wipe out this indigenous religion and culture. Thus, the early missionaries employed the policy of "come-ye-outism" for the indigenous people who were converted to Christianity. The basic method of interpretation in this period is mainly literal interpretation with the underlying motive of interpreting the Bible to stamp out African Indigenous Religion and culture. The indigenous Bible interpreters followed the same line of the missionary literal method of interpretation. In the missionary schools, seminaries, and Bible colleges, African Indigenous religion and culture were not worth studying. It was an abomination for such to be put in the curriculum. An example of this was that up till 1968 when I entered a Bible college in my home country, there was no place for the teaching of African Indigenous Religion and culture. The interpretation of the Bible was characterized by conservatism or evangelicalism. The Bible became a proof text to eradicate African Indigenous Religion and culture. This reminds me of an incident when Professor Omoyajowo, a Professor at the University of Ife (now Obafemi Awolowo University) was invited to give a Kato Lecture at an ECWA Theological Seminary and Bible College on the "Value of African Indigenous Religion and culture. He was almost chased out of the chapel before he could finish his lecture. The lecturers and students did not like his emphasis that there is any value in African indigenous religion and culture. I remember very vividly that student insulted him with the type of questions they asked him openly. The lecturers, mostly missionaries hurriedly had meetings to discuss and condemn his lecture. The students throughout that week condemned such lecture as unchristian.

Both the Westerners and Africans who were sympathetic to African indigenous religion and culture reacted to this condemnation. In this reaction to the missionary condemnation of African religion and culture, sympathetic scholars began to compare African religion and culture with Ancient Israel and culture. During this period emerging African biblical scholars interpreted the Bible with caution however. This was because of fear of being ostracized from the church, which the missionaries actually controlled. During this period there was no freedom of biblical interpretation. Emerging African scholars were not given freedom in their interpretation of the biblical text. They were forced to interpret the Bible like the Western missionaries.

I will like to commend the courage of scholars like J. J Williams, J. S Mbiti, K. Dickson, E.B Idowu, Awolalu, S. Kibicho, and others who had the courage to interpret the Bible comparatively and apologetically. They did some pioneering work on the comparative study of African culture and religion and the Old Testament. J.S Mbiti, E.B Idowu and O Awolalu, and Kibicho called the attention of the African public, and of course, the Western society to the relevance of African Indigenous religion. J.J. William, as early as 1930, had the courage to write Hebrewism *of West Africa: From Nile to Niger with the Jews.*[13] Raephel Patai, published "Hebrew Installation Rites: A Contribution to the Study of Ancient Near Eastern-African Culture Contact," in 1947[14] and "The Ritual Approach to Hebrew-African Culture Contact," in 1962.[15] In 1962 Prince E. S Thompson published, *"*The Approach to the Old Testament in an African Setting*," in Ghana Bulletin of Theology.*[16] J.S. Mbiti wrote a PhD dissertation, "Christian Eschatology in Relation to Evangelization of Tribal Africa," for Cambridge University in 1963. In 1964, E. Isaac published an article, "Relations Between the Hebrew Bible and Africa" in *Jewish Social Studies.*[17] G.Kibicho wrote an article titled, "Interaction of the Traditional Kikuyu Concept of God with the Biblical Concept.[18] As early as 1967, B. A. Osuji wrote a doctoral dissertation in Rome with the title, "The Hebrew and Igbo Concept of Religion and Sin Compared in the Light of Biblical and Rabbinic Material."[19] K. A Dickson and P. Elingworth edited a very valuable book in 1969, *Biblical Revelation and African Beliefs.*[20]

The main conclusion by these authors of the comparative study is that African indigenous religion and culture is *praeparatio evangelica.* The importance of the study of African indigenous religion and culture was stressed as a means by which the Old Testament Scripture could be appropriately understood. It was contended that rather than adopting a militant attitude to exterminate African indigenous religion, Christians and scholars should seek to understand it since it is a crucial part of the life of Africans. The majority of this publication employed Eurocentric methodology in their interpretation of the Old Testament. This is understood because by 1960 it was reported that there were only six universities in Sub-Sahara Africa.[21] Imagine how far one can go with only six universities in the entire continent of Africa. Most of the writing done at that period was done from the Eurocentric perspective since the majority of the people who had higher studies in Old Testament Studies were trained in Europe or America. However, one cannot deny the fact that the comparative approach to the Old Testament and African Indigenous Religion was an acceptance and a positive response to the challenge posed by the missionaries and the Eurocentric education provided for the Africans. Even though Nigerian universities (University of Ibadan and University of Nigeria) took the lead in initiating graduate degree program, none of these institutions awarded any graduate degree especially doctorate until 1980s.[22]

Unfortunately, technological advancement was not as it is today. Thus, scholars' interaction in these few institutions was almost nil at this period. Journals were scarce and the few available ones were not well circulated. Among the well-known and leading journals of this period were *Orita* published in 1967 by the Department of Religious Studies, University of Ibadan and *Africa Theological Journal*, which was published in 1968 in Tanzania. But these journals are not totally devoted to the study of Old Testament in African setting. Up till now there are no single biblical journals devoted to the study of Old Testament in African setting. There is, of course, *Old Testament Essays* in South Africa, but it is not totally devoted to the interpretation of Old Testament in African context. Although there have been some articles written in African context, the concentration has been very Eurocentric in its approach. There is also some kind of sketchy interlibrary loans in Africa today, but from 1930 to 1960s such was non- existent.

A close examination of the trend of Old Testament scholarship from the 1930s to 1960s, shows that the literature produced were scanty. This situation was due to some problems facing the African scholars and missionaries. This period was indeed a period of serious struggle and preparation for serious African Old Testament scholarship. While Knut Holter has earlier described the period of 1960s to 70s as a period of background of African Old Testament Scholarship,[23] Prof. Justin Ukpong described it as reactive and apologetic period. I describe it as a period of challenges to African biblical scholars.[24] Although Professor Ukpong was right in describing this period as reactive and apologetic, such description goes beyond this period. It characterizes the entire period of African Biblical studies till the present time. Of course, a brief history of biblical interpretation and theology in Africa shows that biblical interpretations and theologies, whether Eurocentric or Africentric, are in a sense reactive and apologetic. They started with a basic disagreement with the existing Eurocentric interpretations and theologies. Search for more satisfactory methods of interpretations and theologies that would be reflective of and relevant to African experience at that particular time in history began. In other words, all these interpretation were contextual.

Despite all these problems facing African scholars in this early period, the foundation of real African Old Testament scholarship had been well laid. The subsequent progress in African Old Testament scholarship owes its existence to these earlier African biblical scholars.

1970 to 1980s Periods

The period from the 1970 to 1980s was the real emergence of African biblical Studies. During this period, African Scholars began to have more access to Western postgraduate education. The natural reaction to more exposure to Euroncentric interpretation of the biblical text and the further condemnation of not only African Indigenous Religion, but African comparative methods of biblical interpretation was further publications and a search for authentic African hermeneutics in biblical interpretation. While comparative methodology continued, contextual or inculturation hermeneutic was sought vigorously. This happened in every area of Christian interpretation of Christianity in Africa. There were indignation and blatant rejection of Eurocentric condemnation of African biblical interpretation. Unfortunately, the Western publishers rejected most of the articles and books published during this period because they thought that such methodologies were illegitimate or inappropriate.[25] African biblical writers were blamed for not following verbatim the Eurocentric methods of interpretations-Historical Critical, Form Critical, Redactional, Textual Critical methods. Despite this persistent rejection of African scholarship, African biblical scholars continued to forge ahead to do their own things. They started publishing in the local journals, most of which were not circulated beyond the shores of the country. Training of more African Old Testament scholars was also encouraged.

Apart from the comparative method of interpretation that went on during this period, African Cultural Hermeneutics in biblical interpretation began to take shape. The various aspects of African cultural hermeneutics included Africa and African in the Bible, using Africa to interpret the Old Testament and Old Testament to interpret Africa.

First, let us discuss what is African Cultural Hermeneutics that became a serious and important method at this period. I have given the definition of African cultural hermeneutic in one of my books as follows:

> African cultural hermeneutics in biblical studies is an approach to biblical interpretation that makes African social cultural context a subject of interpretation. Specifically it means that analysis of the text is done from the perspective of African world-view. African Cultural hermeneutics is rereading the scripture from a premeditated Africentric perspective.[26]

The definition above, if understood in its proper context, means that African cultural hermeneutics is contextual like any other Third World interpretation and theology. It is liberative, inculturative, evaluative, and of course, Africentric. This methodology is employed for specific purposes:

1.   To understand God in the light of the Bible and African culture and experience.
2.   To reappraise the ancient biblical tradition, African culture, and experience.
3.   To correct the effect of current ideological conditioning which Eurocentric biblical scholars have subjected Africa and Africans.
4.   To break "the hermeneutical hegemony and ideological stranglehold that Eurocentric biblical scholars have long enjoyed.
5.   To tell the world of biblical scholarship that African cultural hermeneutics is as legitimate as any other hermeneutic, especially Eurocentric hermeneutic.
6.   To tell the biblical academia that it is therefore appropriate to use this hermeneutic in conjunction with other hermeneutics to arrive at a proper understanding of the scripture.

Professor Justin Ukpong calls the period between 1970-1990s "the most dynamic and rewarding periods in biblical studies in Africa."[27] There were many published articles in journals and books with the sole purpose of making biblical studies relevant to Africa and Africans. African comparative method increased immensely in published articles, books, and dissertations. This comparative method took a new shape in that most of the scholarly work done went beyond mere comparison and included some relevance of African culture to the Bible, the Bible to African culture, and the ways to move forward. For example in 1973 and 1979, Kwensi Dickson wrote "The Old Testament and African Theology," and "Continuity and Discontinuity between the Old Testament and African Life and Thoughts," respectively.[28] In 1980, Renju published, "African Traditional Religions and Old Testament: Continuity or Discontinuity?,"[29] African comparative methods were employed in many dissertations written at this period: Francis Oko Ugwueze, "Igbo proverbs and biblical proverbs: Comparative & thematic research", Th.D., Pontifical Urban University, Rome, Italy, 1976; .John Onaiyekan, "The priesthood among the Owe-Yoruba of Nigeria and in Pre-monarchical Ancient Israel: A comparative Study", Th.D., Pontifical Urban University, Rome, Italy, 1976; Justin S. Ukpong, "Ibibio Sacrifice and Levitical Sacrifice: A Comparative Study of the Sacrificial Systems of the Ibibio People of Nigeria and of Ancient Israel as recorded in the Book of Leviticus", Th.D., Pontifical Urban University, Rome, Italy, 1980;[30] George Latunji Lasebikan, "Prophecy or schizophrenia? A Study of Prophecy in the Old Testament and in selected Aladura churches", Ph.D., University of Ibadan, Ibadan, Nigeria, 1983; Charles Osume, "A study of the Okpe Theophanises and their Correspondences in the Old Testament", Ph.D., University of Aberdeen, Aberdeen, United Kingdom, 1984; Joseph Arulefela, "An analysis of the biblical and Yoruba Concepts of Covenant with Implications for the Christian Education of Yoruba Christians",

Ph.D., New York University, New York, USA, 1980;[31] Joseph W.Apuri, "Human sacrifice, Isaac and Jesus: A Study of Human Sacrifice in the Ancient Near East and Ashante and related Tribes, in the Light of the Blood of Jesus in the Epistle to the Hebrews", Th.D., Pontifical Urban University, Rome, Italy, 1983; Rulange K. Rwehumbiza, "A comparative Study between the Development of Yahwistic Monotheism and the Concept of God among the Bantu people of Africa South of the Sahara: A biblico-theological Evaluation", Th.D., Pontifical Lateran University, Rome, Italy, 1983; [32]

Samuel Simbandumwe, "Israel in Two African Prophet movements," Ph.D., University of Edinburgh, Edinburgh, United Kingdom, 1989;[33]

Africa and Africans in the Bible

Apart from the comparative studies, another important attempt by African biblical scholars to employ African cultural hermeneutics was through the researches that recognized the presence of Africa and Africans in the Old Testament. Justin Ukpong calls this "Africa-in-the-Bible-studies."[34] For so many years Eurocentric biblical scholars have dominated biblical studies and many have followed the policy of de-Africanization of the Bible by dismissing the idea of African presence in the Bible. In their exegesis they located Cush (Africa) in everywhere else but Africa. E. A Spencer in his book, *Genesis*, considered the identification of Cush with Africa "a mistaken identity."[35] George Rawlinson, Claus Westermann and G.Ch Aalders and C.T Francisco believed that Cush in Genesis could not be located in Africa but Mesopotamia.[36] Few who recognized Africa and African presence believed that they have not made any contribution to the history of ancient Israel. They were all regarded as slaves in ancient Israel. Thus, W. Mckane in his commentary on I-II Samuel considered the Cushite man in King David's army a slave from Africa.[37] Hammershaimb in his commentary on Amos said that the dark-skinned people from Africa were held in contempt by the ancient Israelites.[38] James Luther Mays holds the opinion that Ancient Israelite people only knew Africans as slaves.[39] Many African biblical scholars, inspired by the African American scholars also began the search for the presence of Africa and Africans, as a response to some Eurocentric deAfricanization of the Bible. "Africa in the Bible Studies" does not only seek to establish African presence in the Biblical record, but also ascertain their religious, economic, social, military, and political contribution to ancient Israel. This methodology aims at correcting such negative image of Africa and Africans in Eurocentric biblical studies. Many African biblical scholars, including African Americans, began to work diligently in this line. In fact, the African Americans in their Africentric approach to biblical interpretation have had a great influence on other African biblical scholars who adopted this method.[40]

I got involved in this research methodology as early as 1984 with my PhD dissertation, "Africa and Africans in the Old Testament and Its Environment," which was later published in 1998 as *Africa and The Africans in the Old*

Testament. During this period, I published "The Black Prophet in the Old Testament," [41] and "The African Wife of Moses: An Examination of Numbers 12:1-9,"[42] T. L .J Mafico has also written "Evidence for African Influence on the Religious Customs of the Patriarchs" What I have done (with other African American Africentric biblical scholars) in the above Africentric approach to biblical studies is that I have successfully established the historical and geographical link with the biblical world and have also corrected the negative image of Africa and Africans prevalent in the Eurocentric interpretation of the biblical text.

Using Africa to interpret the OT and OT to Interpret Africa

Another method in African Cultural Hermeneutics that was employed at this period was the methodology of using Old Testament to interpret Africa and African to interpret the Old Testament.[43] In this approach, a combination of historical critical method and anthropological/sociological methods is used. While the historical critical method was used to analyze the biblical text, the anthropological/social method was used for the analysis of the African culture and situation for the purpose of understanding a biblical text in the light of African tradition and culture. The purpose is also to arrive at authentic Christianity that is both biblical and African.[44] Sometimes the African biblical scholars try to evaluate the Old Testament in the light of African culture, religious belief, and practices. An example of this type of approaches can be seen in E.A McFall's *Approaching the Nuer through the Old Testament.*[45] Fiensy's work also reflects this type of methodology, "Using Nuer Culture of Africa in Understanding the Old Testament: Evaluation."[46]

African biblical scholars also tried to use the biblical text to judge a particular issue in African or church society. In other words, the biblical text was used as a critic of a particular theme or issue in African society. After the use of historical critical method to analyze a particular biblical text, the relevance of that text to African issues was drawn. Challenges to particular African issues were made clear also. Example of such studies is clear from the work of several African biblical scholars such as Gabriel Abe's work, "Berith: Its impact on Israel and Its Relevance to the Nigerian Society.[47] Andrew Igenoza's article is another perfect example of the above methodology. He wrote an article, "Medicine and Healing in African Christianity: A Biblical Critique," in *African Ecclesial Review.*[48] J.J Burden's article, "Magic and Divination in the Old Testament and Their Relevance for the Church in Africa," in *Missionalia* is another good example.[49]

1990 to the Present

I consider this period and not the 1980s, as the very period of boom in African biblical scholarship. Comparative approach, the Africa and Africans in the Old Testament, and using Africa to interpret the Old Testament and using the Old Testament to interpret Africa continued more extensively. African Old Testament scholars added more realistic approaches such as the Bible as Power, evaluative studies, bibliographical approach, and "reading with the ordinary readers.

Comparative Approach[50]

During this period comparative approach continued but with a different dimension that reflects African cultural hermeneutics. It included some element of critical evaluation of both African culture and the Old Testament. Real hermeneutics of suspicion was at work. After comparing African culture and Christianity or the Old Testament, the relevance of African culture to the study of the Old Testament or the relevance of Old Testament to African culture is added to the comparison. In 1990 M.G Swanpoel wrote "An Encounter Between Old Theology and African Concepts of God."[51] S.O Fadeji, wrote in 1990, "Biblical and African Names of God: A Comparison,"[52] J.A Van Rooy also wrote in 1994 an article, "God's self Revelation in the Old Testament and African Concept of God."[53] From 1990 to the present, there are many publications with this comparative method. The following are further examples of such work. Dr. Kris Owan wrote in 1994 and 1997, "Manifestations of Wisdom in the Old Testament and in African Religious Traditions" and "African proverbial Wisdom and Biblical Proverbial Wisdom: Wholesome Bedfellows and more."[54] I have done some substantial writing using the comparative method. In 1989 I wrote, "Understanding the Genesis Creation Account in An African Background," In 1997 I also published "Peace in the Old Testament and in the African Heritage."[55]

During this period, there were also many doctoral dissertations in Old Testament that refleced this type of comparative methodology. Samson Njuguna Gitau wrote in 1994, "A comparative Study of the Transmission, Actualization and Stabilization of Oral Traditions: An Examination of Traditions of Circumcision in Africa and Ancient Israel."[56] John Ademola Aworinde wrote in 1997 "A Comparative Analysis of Destiny in the Old Testament and in Yoruba Philosophy of Life." [57] Robert Wafawanaka, "Perspectives on the Problem of Poverty in traditional Africa and in Ancient Israel."[58] Raphael Winston Kawale also wrote "God and Nature in Genesis 1:1—2:4a and Chewa Cosmogony." [59] Edwin Zulu, "A Ngoni assessment of the Role of Ancestors within Israelite World-views and Religion in Genesis 11:28—50:26." [60] Shola Ademiluka, wrote a doctoral thesis in 1998, "The Genesis Accounts of Creation and the Fall in an African Setting."[61]

The Bible As Power Approach

An important development in African Cultural Hermeneutics during the period between 1990 to the present is the Bible as Power approach to the interpretation of the Old Testament. This approach gradually started in 1980s but became prominent in the 1990s. This is an "existential" and "reflective" approach to the interpretation of the Bible. Unlike the Eurocentric conservative biblical scholars who were preoccupied with the subject of inerrancy and infallibility of the Bible, African Christians believe and respect the Bible without any attempt to defend it and apologize for it. The Bible, to them, is the Word of God and is powerful and that its power is relevant to everyday life of Africans.[62] The Bible is used as a means of protection, healing and success. This method is mostly prevalent among the African Indigenous Churches in Africa and the Diaspora. African Indigenous churches became dissatisfied with the Eurocentric methods of biblical interpretation employed by the missionary mainland churches. They were also dissatisfied with Western oriented churches self-imposition of the structure of Western institution at the expense of African culture. They recognized that many of the Eurocentric biblical interpretation and theologies nourished in the Western biblical intellectualist context had no root in the life of the African community. Western approach to the interpretation of the Bible became unprofitable. They therefore had to form their own African indigenous churches that would meet the needs of the African community. They made the Bible relevant to the African communities by employing African culture in their interpretation of the Bible. Our studies have revealed that African Indigenous churches have used the Bible as the WORD OF GOD and recognized the power inherent in it. The Bible has been used for healing, protection and success in life.[63] Unfortunately, there was very little interest by missionaries and their churches to study these churches and their effectiveness.

Many scholars have employed these methods in their interpretation of the Bible. Musa Gaiya published an article "The Bible in Aladura Churches" in 1991.[64] Shola Ademiluka also wrote an article in 1995 titled, "The Use of Therapeutic Psalms in Inculturating Christianity in Africa."[65] In 1997 Nahashon Ndungu wrote, "The Bible in an African Independent Church,"[66] Zablon Nthamburi and Douglas Waruta also wrote "African Hermeneutics in African Instituted Churches."[67] I have made some important contribution in this area of the Use of the Bible in African Indigenous Churches. My emphasis is the existential use of the Bible to solve everyday problems, namely for healing, protection, and success in life. I have published the following articles that reflect such studies. "African Cultural Hermeneutics,"[68] "The Use of Psalms in African Indigenous Churches in Nigeria,"[69] and "The Use of Medicine in African Indigenous Churches in Nigeria,"[70] and Distinctive Use of Psalms in African Independent Churches in Nigeria.[71] I have also published *Reading and Interpreting the Bible in African Indigenous Churches*[72] and *Exploration in African Biblical Studies*.[73]

Africa and Africans In the Bible Approach

Africa and Africans in the Bible approach reached its peak in the period before 1990 to the present. As said earlier Africa and Africans were mentioned more than any other foreign nations in the Old Testament. They were mentioned in every strand of biblical literature. During this time the search for African presence in the Bible went beyond mere presence. Their economic, religious, military, social, political contribution and major influence in Ancient Israel were discussed in detail. African Old Testament scholars have continued to demonstrate that the Old Testament would have not been in the shape it is now without the African presence and contribution. Although this approach does not attempt to present the theological importance of Africa and Africans in the Old Testament, it is an important study that demonstrates the importance and influence of Africa and Africans in the Old Testament. It also demonstrates that the Bible is not only an ancient Jewish document; it is also an African document. It also seeks to demonstrate that there is no record of prejudice against Africa and Africans in the Bible.[74] Africa and Africans were held in high esteem.[75] However, African biblical scholars have also done some substantial work in this area. In 1996 Teresa Okure wrote a paper titled, "Africans in the Bible: A Study of Hermeneutics."[76] I have also made some important contribution between 1990 to the present. The following are some of my publication during this period. "The African Queen: An Examination of I Kings 10:1-13;"[77] "The Table of Nations in an African Context;"[78] "Ethiopia in the Bible;"[79] "Ancient Africa and Genesis 2:10-14;" "Jehudi's African Identity in Jeremiah 34:14,21-23;"[80] *Africa and The Africans in the Old Testament;*[81] "Images of Cush in the Old Testament: A Reflection on African Hermeneutics;"[82] and "Africanness in the Bible."[83]

Apart from some scholars of African Diaspora, many Western Old Testament scholars have not shown and are not showing any interest in the research on African presence in the Old Testament. An exception to this fact however, is a Norwegian Old Testament scholar, Knut Holter, who has done some credible work on the Presence of African and Africans in the Old Testament. A whole section of his book, *Yahweh in Africa*, contains several articles with the following subtitles, "Africa in the Old Testament," "Should Old Testament Cush be Rendered 'Africa'," and "Is Israel Worth More to God than Cush? An Interpretation of Amos 9:7."[84]

African Bibliographical Studies[85]

Between 1930s and 80s one could hardly talk of the African bibliographical studies apart from John Mbiti's book, Bible and Theology in African Christianity, which contains some bibliographical materials in 1986,[86] and biographical reference work, *Theology in Context: Information on Theological Contributions from Africa, Asia, Oceania and Latin America* which contains "Annotated Bibliography (1984)." It was not until 1990s that serious African bibliographical work began.

The credit of the actual serious African Old Testament bibliographical studies goes to a colleague, Norwegian scholar, and Africanist, Prof. Knut Holter who is seriously concerned with this problem of absence of coordinated Old Testament bibliographical materials in Africa. He published a book, *Tropical Africa and the Old Testament: A Selected and Annotated Bibliography.* As far as I know this is the first serious African Old Testament bibliographical index. It listed about 232 works on Old Testament and Africa South of the

Sahara. This book also has abstracts of each Old Testament publication on Africa.

His "Old Testament Studies in Africa: Resource Page" on the internet at **www.misjons.no/res/ot** *Africa* is an electronic bulletin Board for African Old Testament Studies. The availability of his article "Sub-Saharan African Doctoral Dissertations in Old Testament Studies, 1967-2000: Some remarks to their Chronology and Geography," is valuable.

Another renowned scholar on African bibliographical studies is Grant LeMarquand at Trinity Episcopal School for Ministry, Ambridge, Pennsylvania. In 1995 he published "A Bibliography of the Bible in Africa: A Preliminary Publication," in *A Bulletin for Contextual Theology in Southern Africa.*[87] In the same year he published another valuable and more extensive bibliographic article, with the same title, in the *Journal of Inculturation Theology.* It has approximately 1,000 references to African biblical studies materials.[88] He published his most recent outstanding bibliographical work in The Bible in Africa with the title, "A Bibliography of the Bible in Africa."[89] Containing 167 pages, it is by far the most voluminous bibliographical index known to me in African biblical studies. Although they are general materials on biblical studies, hermeneutics and translation, but there are also materials on the Old Testament.

Evaluative Approach[90]

Evaluative approach refers to the essays on books produced by African or non-African Old Testament scholars for the purpose of criticizing the work of African Old Testament scholars. This criticism may be constructive, negative, or both. Somebody said that if one does not want to be criticized such a person should not publish. For progress, correction, and readjustment in African Old Testament scholarship, there is a need for evaluation of our work. Some scholars stand out in their evaluation and criticism of the work of African Old Testament scholars. Dr. Knut Holter and his student Marta Hoyland Lavik seem to be at the forefront of such work. Dr. Holter in his book, *Yahweh in Africa* which contains many of his articles earlier published in many academic journals reflects his concern for excellence in African Old Testament studies.[91] In his articles, he gave a survey of the trend of African Old Testament scholarship from 1960 to 1990s. He discussed the thematic, institutional, and contextual perspectives in African Old Testament Studies. He also decried the marginalization of African Old Testament scholars. He emphasized that Western Old Testament scholars have something to learn from African Old Testament scholars.[92] He also criticized my work. In the process of appraising the work, which he thinks is the "most prolific" and "productive" African Old Testament scholarly work, he criticized my rendering of Cush as Africa. Like other Western biblical scholars, he thinks some Cush passages should not be translated as Africa.[93]

Marta Hoyland Lavik, is not less critical of any other work either. She wrote a critique of my publications for her master's thesis (unfortunately I could not read the thesis since it was written in Norwegian). However, she wrote some articles "The 'African' Texts of the Old Testament and Their African

Interpretations,"[94] and "An African Presence in the Old Testament? David Tuesday Adamo's interpretation of the Old Testament Cush passages,"[95] After summarizing and presenting the work of "four contrasting scholars"- E. Mveng, G.A Mikre_Selassie, Sempore and David Adamo and crediting me with the honor of "probably being the African scholar who has made the single most important contribution to the field" of African presence in the Old Testament, she saw the possible "danger in" my interpreting some biblical texts existentially since it "may potentially divorce us from the original historical setting of the text."[96] According to Marta Hoyland Lavik, there should be more emphasis on the negative roles of Africa and Africans in the Old Testament.[97] She also agrees with Dr. Holter that all Old Testament *Cush* should not refer to African continent.[98]

These criticisms are valuable in that they drew our attention to the opinions of other scholars. The criticisms do not only help us to know the area for further research, they assist us to know how other Western Old Testament scholars who are concerned about African Old Testament scholarship understand us.

"Reading with the Ordinary Reader's" Approach.

This is the latest approach to African Biblical Studies championed by two African biblical scholars-Professors Justin Ukpong and David West. They advocate doing biblical studies with the ordinary people. By ordinary people they mean, the poor, the oppressed, the underprivileged, and the untrained in the art of biblical interpretation. They refer to the common people in the community. Professor Ukpong calls this reading "Inculturation Hermeneutics."[99] Gerald West calls this a "contextual bible reading."[100] This hermeneutics is contextual in nature and it "seeks to make any community of ordinary people and their sociocultural context the *subject* of interpretation of the Bible."[101] What this means is that biblical scholars sitting down with untrained biblical scholars and studying the Bible without directing the reading. It means that the reading agenda becomes that of the community. The trained biblical scholars do not control the reading process.[102] Instead the trained biblical scholars read as part of the community. They only facilitate the reading process. It means that the ordinary people read in their own socio-cultural perspective. It means that the community of ordinary people makes use of their African cultural resources as "hermeneutical tools for interpretation of the Bible." These hermeneutical tools include African socioreligious and cultural institutions, thought system, and practices, African oral narrative genre, and African arts and symbols. This methodology helps the people interpret the Bible in their own sociocultural perspectives. The interpretation therefore reflects their concerns, values, and interests. One of the advantages of this reading is that it does not only create critical reading masses but also builds "the community of faith that reads the Bible critically."[103] It empowers them to read the Bible critically in the light of their specific situation and societal transformation. This procedure helps to provide an interface between the ordinary readers and the academic Bible readers and bridge the wide gap between them.[104]

This approach is one of the hermeneutics that Western readers can learn from the African approach. This is because many ordinary people read the Bible more than scholars. If the Western academic readers refuse to learn this African method, the Bible would eventually become meaningless for the ordinary people as it now seems to be in most part of Europe.

The Future of African Biblical Study

Before discussing what I see as the future of African biblical studies, I will like to mention the actual problems facing African Old Testament studies in Africa. Certainly, most of these problems are also true of African biblical scholarship in general.

Oppressive government policies in African countries constitute one of the problems that African Old Testament scholars face. Military rulers who are of very low education become leaders of most African countries. They have no regard for education and research.[105] They cry about researches in sciences, but do not provide the means for such research. Most universities in Africa are dilapidated and manpower is inadequate because most competent Old Testament scholars have migrated to Western countries for survival.

Close to the above problems is the lack of current journals and books from the outside world. Very few of us have access to current Old Testament journals and books from the Western world because the cost of subscriptions is too high. Unfortunately, most African biblical scholars in Africa barely have enough to eat. It is absolutely important to be familiar with the current trend in Old Testament scholarship from around the world so as to receive challenges. Most of our libraries are devoid of current materials. Most African Old Testament scholars do not have the fund to attend international conferences because their universities are not able to sponsor them.

There is extensive reliance on the West for our training. The truth is that due to our limited facilities in the field of biblical studies, the majority of our churches, theological seminaries and universities still rely very heavily on the Western scholars for training. Incompetent scholars in the field of Old Testament scholarship supervise few students who are being trained in African institutions.

Related to the above problem is that the majority of African biblical scholars who are trained in the art of Old Testament scholarship take up ecclesiastical work and have no time to do academic research.

With the above problems there are few African Old Testament scholars in Africa. Generally very few students have interest in studying religion at all because they think there is no future prospect. Most of them believe that only those who want to be pastors are the only ones supposed to study religion. Few students who are forced to study religion, especially at the undergraduate level, refuse to undertake Old Testament Studies in their research because of the languages involved.[106] They prefer other courses in church history, theology, and philosophy and African Indigenous religion.

Further more, one of the major problems of African Old Testament studies in Africa is the marginalisation of African Old Testament scholars by the West. Without taking into special consideration the condition under which we do research in Africa, whatever article and books written by African scholars in Africa are regarded as inferior and unsophisticated. This is based on the Eurocentric culture and standard of scholarship, which they claim to be universal standard. The Old missionary idea that African culture is barbaric, fetish, paganistic, magical, and as such of no value, still influences modern Eurocentric biblical scholars. Our works are not published in reputable journals of Eurocentric biblical scholars or publishers. Many of our articles written in Africa by African biblical scholars are published locally. Most Western biblical scholars do not bother themselves to glance through African Old Testament essays and books to read what we are saying.

Refusal of some of our Western Old Testament colleagues in West to understand the above situation and assist anyway they can has not encourage many of the few African Old Testament colleagues to be committed to the profession. Such ways would be through cooperation in research and exchange of scholars and students. Sponsorship of outstanding scholars in Africa to attend academic conferences around the world would help.

With African Old Testament scholars grappling with so many problems as outlined above, is there any future in African Old Testament research?

However, going through the history of African biblical scholarship shows that there is a future hope for African Old Testament scholarship. African Old Testament scholarship has come a long way. The story of African Old Testament scholarship from the time of the biblical/post-biblical periods to the present is evidence that there is hope in the future. Despite the huge problems that Africa and Africans are encountering, distinctive African Old Testament scholarship is still well alive. Few of us who are Old Testament/biblical scholars are determined to continue this distinctive African biblical scholarship despite the presence of the huge problems facing us in Africa. Outstanding biblical scholars who are involved in this struggle include myself from Delta State University, Nigeria, Justin Ukpong of Catholic Institute of West Africa, Nigeria, Gerald West of the University of Natal, South Africa, Samuel Oyin Abogunrin and few others. Although Knut Holter[107] of the School of Mission and Theology, Norway, is not an African, his interest and determination in doing and publishing in the field of African Old Testament scholarship is encouraging and serves as evidence that one day our Western colleague will hear, understand, and recognize that our African cultural hermeneutics is as legitimate as theirs.

Certainly, the future is also bright for African Old Testament scholarship if our colleagues in the Western world would relieve themselves of the scholarship prejudice against African Old Testament scholarship and accept the fact that their methodology is not universal or the only recognized hermeneutics in the world. They need to recognize that "African cultural hermeneutic" or "inculturation hermeneutic" or "contextual hermeneutic" is equally legitimate methods in biblical studies in Africa. Even though African cultural hermeneutic does not claim universality, it is a legitimate hermeneutics and there is much that the Western and the world biblical scholars can learn.

The future of African Old Testament scholarship will be most bright if there could be cooperation between African Old Testament and the Western Old Testament scholars in term of exchange of students, research, and colleagues. This cooperation could also include financial assistance to attend international academic conferences.

Whether we are recognized or not, the struggle continues. We shall continue to write and publish our materials in journals and books that give us the privilege to do so.

ENDNOTES

1. This article was originally published in *Old Testament Essay* 16/1 (2003), 9-23. I appreciate the permission given to reprint it in this book.
2. David Tuesday Adamo, *Africa and Africans in the Old Testament* (San Francisco: Christian University Press, Press, 1998). Reprinted Eugene, Oregon: WIPF and Stock Publishers, 2001). See also *Africa and Africans in the New Testament* (Lanham, Maryland: University Press of America, to be published).
3. For detail discussion of these terms see my book, *Africa and The Africans in the Old Testament*.
4. Note that the Hebrew word *Cush* in modern Hebrew still means " black."
5. Justin Ukpong, "Developments in Biblical Interpretation in Africa," *The Bible in Africa*, Gerald O. West and Musa Dube eds. (Boston: Brill, 200), 11.
6. Donald K. McKim, *Historical Handbook of Major Biblical Interpreters (henceforth Historical Handbook)* (Downer Groves: Intervarsity Press, 1998), 8.
7. *Historical Handbook*, 161.
8. *Historical Handbook*, 162.
9. Donald K McKim, Ed. *Historical Handbook*, 17-21.
10. What is most interesting is that most of these African biblical scholars and theologians of the early church have their own canon and the list of the books of the New Testament they accepted as authoritative. Origen and Athanasius are few examples with clear list of acceptable books. Apart from individual list, one of the most important documents for the study of the early history of the canon of the New Testament, Muratorian Canon, was found in the monastery of Bobo in Africa. The first council that accepted the present canon of the books of the New Testament took place in Africa that is in the Synod of Hippo Regius in North Africa.
11. Justin Ukpong, Professor of New Testament Studies, Catholic Institute of West Africa. "Developments in Biblical Interpretation in Africa: A Historical and Hermeneutical Directions," *The Bible in Africa*, eds. Gerald O West and Musa W. Dube (Boston: Brill, 2000), 11-28.
12. Knut Holter, "Current State of Old Testament Scholarship in Africa Where is we at the Turn of the Century?" *Interpreting the Old Testament in Africa*," (eds) Mary Getui, Knut Holter, and Victor Zinkuratire, (New York: Peter Lang, 2001).
13. J.J Williams, *Hebrewism of West Africa: From Nile to Niger with the Jews* (London: George Allen and Unwin, New York: Lincoln Macveach/ The Dial Press, 1930.
14. *Hebrew Union College Annual* 20:143-225.
15. *Jewish Social Studies*,24:86-96. A Doctoral Dissertation Pontifical Urban University, Rome.
16. 2:3, 1-11
17. 26(1964):87-98.
18. S.Kibicho, "The Interaction of the Traditional Kikuyu Concept of God with the Biblical Concept," *Cahiers des Religions Africaines*, 2:4 (1968).
19. B.A Osuji
20. (London: Lutherworth, 1969).
21. J.K Marah, *Pan African Education: The last Stage of Educational Developments in Africa* (City: The Edwin Mellen Press, 1989). See also Knut Holter, *Yahweh in Africa: Essay on Africa and the Old Testament* (New York: Peter Lang, 2000), 10-11.

22. Knut Holter, "Current State of Old Testament Scholarship in Africa: Where are We at the Turn of the Century?" *Interpreting the Old Testament in Africa: Papers from the international Symposium on Africa and the Old Testament in Nairobi, Oct.1999*, eds. Mary Getui, Knut Holter, Victor Zinkuratire (New York:Peter Lang,2001), 30; "Old Testament Scholarship in Sub-Sahara Africa," *The Bible in Africa*, 36; *Yahweh in Africa: Essays on Africa and the Old Testament* (New York: 2000), 10-11.

23. Knut Holter, *Yahweh in Africa: Essay on Africa and the Old Testament* (New York: Peter Lang, 2000), 10-11. Holter described this period.

24. Eric Anum, "Comparative Readings of the Bible in Africa: Some Concerns," *The Bible in Africa*, 457.

25. I have mentioned above the accusation that I was trying to smuggle Africa into the Bible when I sent my article to one reputable Western journal.

26. D.T Adamo, *Exploration in African Biblical Studies* (Eugene, Oregon: WIPF and Stock Publishers, 2001), 8-9. See also "African Cultural Hermeneutics," *Vernacular Hermeneutics* (Sheffield: Sheffield Academic Press, 1999), 66-90.

27. Justin Ukpong, "Developments in Biblical Interpretation in Africa," *The Bible in Africa*, 14.

28. *Ghana Bulletin of Theology*, vol.4, no. 4 (June 1973); *African Theology En Route* eds. Koffi Appiah-Kubi and S. Torres (Maryknoll: Orbis Books, 1979).

29. Atal sa Angang, et al., eds 113-118.

30. It was later published with the title, *Sacrifice – African and Biblical: A Comparative Study of Ibibio and Levitical Sacrifices* (Rome: Urbaniana University Press, 1987).

31. It was later published as *Covenant in the Old Testament and in Yoruba land* (Ibadan: Daystar Press, 1988).

32. It was later published as *A Comparative Study Between the Development of Yahwistic Monotheism and the Concept of God Among the Bantu People of Africa South of the Sahara: A Biblico-Theological Evaluation* (Rome: Pontifical Lateran University, 1983).

33. It was later published as *A Socio-Religious and Political Analysis of the Judeo-Christian Concept of Prophetism and Modern Bakongo and Zulu African Prophet Movements*. Lewiston: Edwin Mellen Press, 1992 (African Studies; 28).

34. Ukpong, "Developments in Biblical Interpretation in Africa," *The Bible in Africa*, 14.

35. *Genesis, The Anchor Bible*. 3rd edition (Garden City, New York: Doubleday and Co., 1979), 14-20.

36. G. Rawlinson, Origin of Nations (New York: Charles Scribners' Son, 1894); Claus Westernmann, Genesis 1-11, Translated by J.J Sculling (Minneapolis: Augsburg Pub. House, 19), 208-220; B.Ch. Aalders, Genesis, Vol I. Translated by W. Heynen (Grands Rapids: Zondervan Publishing House, 1981); C.T Francisco, Genesis, Broadman Bible Commentary, Vol.1. Gen. Editor Clifton Allen (Nashville: Broadman Press, 1973), 127.

37. I and II Samuel (London: SCM Press, 1963),267.

38. The Book of Amos: A Commentary, Translated by John Sturdy (New York: Shockin Books, 1970), 134.

39. Amos (Philadelphia: Westminster Press, 1969), 157

40. The following are some of the African American Scholars who conducted early researches along this line: As early as 1971, Robert Bennett, Jr. wrote a pioneering article, "African and the Biblical Period," Harvard Theological Review 64 (971): 484-485. In 1974, Alfred Dunston wrote a book, *The Black Man in the Old Testament and Its World* (Philadelphia: Dorrance R. Company, 1974). As early as 1974, Charles Copher who wrote an article, "The Black Man in the Biblical World,"

Journal of Interdenominational Theological Center 1 (1974), wrote extensively more than other African Americans of this period. Eventually, all his articles were collected together in a book, *Black Biblical Studies*: An Anthology, Chicago: Black Light Press, 1993). I will like to consider him the Father of Africans in the Bible Studies. He was also instrumental in my accepting and following this line of research. In 1989 Cain Hope Felder has a section in his book, *Troubling Biblical Waters* (Maryknoll, New York: Orbis Press, 1989).

41. *Journal of Arabic and Religious Studies (JARS)*, Vol. 4 (Dec. 1987), 1-8.
42. *Africa Theological Journal (ATJ)* Vol. 18 no 3. (1989) 230-237.
43. Justin Ukpong, "Developments in Biblical Interpretation in Africa," *The Bible in Africa (henceforth "Developments")*,16-17. Dr. Ukpong calls this methodology evaluative approach.
44. Ukpong, "Developments..." 16.
45. (Pasadena: William Carey Library, 1970).
46. *Journal of the Society of the Old Testament* (1987) 38:73-83
47. *African Journal of Biblical Studies* 1 (1986): 66-73.
48. *African Ecclesial Review* 30 (1988): 12-25.
49. *Missionalia* 1(1973)103-112.
50. Ukpong.
51. *Theologia Viarorum*, 18: (1990), 20-30.
52. *Ogbomosho Journal of Theology* 5 (1990): 29-36.
53. In Die Sikriflig, 28/2: 261-74.
54. Kris Owan, *Journal of Inculturation Theology*, 1/1:54-72; *Bible Bhashyam* 23/3: 151-73
55. In The Bible in African Christianity eds. Hannah Kinoti and John Waliggo (Nairobi, Kenya: Acton Press,1997), 99-111.
56. Ph.D., Boston University, Boston, Massachusetts, USA, 1994.
57. Ph.D., University of Jos, Jos, Nigeria,
58. Th.D., Boston University, Boston, Massachusetts, USA, 1997.
59. Th.D., University of Stellenbosch, Stellenbosch, South Africa, 1998
60. Th.D., University of Stellenbosch, Stellenbosch, South Africa, 1999.
61. Ph.D, University of Ilorin, Ilorin, Nigeria, 1998.
62. Zablum Nthaburi and Douglas Waruta, "Biblical Hermeneutics in African Instituted Churches," in The Bible in African Christianity edited by Hanna Kinoti and John Waliggo (Nairobi, Kenya: Acton Press, 1997), 40-57.
63. See my books, David Adamo, Reading and Interpreting the Bible in African Indigenous Churches (Eugene, Oregon: WIPF and Stock Publishers, 2001).
64. *African Journal of Biblical Studies* 6/1 (1991): 105-113.
65. *Africa Ecclesia Review* 37/4 (1995) :221-227
66. *The Bible in African Christianity* eds. HW. Kinoti and J. M Waliggo Nairobi, Kenya: Acton Press, 1997), 58-67.
67. *The Bible in African Christianity*, 40-57.
68. *Vernacular Hermeneutics* edited by Surgitherajah (Sheffield: Sheffield Academic Press, 1999), 67-91.
69. *The Bible in Africa*, 336-349.
70. *Journal of Urgent Anthropological Research*, Vienna, Austria, 1999.
71. *Melanesian Journal of Theology*, Vol.9 No 2 (1993), 94-111.
72. (Eugene, OR: WIPF and Stock Publishers, 2001).

73. (Eurgene, OR. WIPF and Stock Publishers, 2001).
74 . The present prejudice is a modern invention.
75. See Grant Lemarquand, "A Bibliography of the Bible in Africa," *The Bible in Africa*, 662-667 for the list of African American contribution in this important area of research.
76. Unpublished paper presented to the Annual Meeting of the Society of Biblical Literature, New Orleans, Louisiana, and Nov. 24, 1996.
77. Journal of Arabic and Religious Studies (JARS), (1990),14-24
78. Journal of African Religion and Philosophy, (JARP) Vol. 2 (1993):14-24.
79. *African Christian Studies*, Vol.8, No 2. (1992), 51-54.
80. *Bible Bhashyam* 18/3(1992), 153-162.
81. Eugene, OR. 2001)
82. *Interpreting the Old Testament in Africa*, 65-74.
83. *African Journal of Biblical Studies*, (2001)
84. (New York: Peter Lang, 2000). He has published many other essays on Old Testament scholarship in Africa with the aim of calling attention of the Western scholars to what African Old Testament scholars have to offer.
85. Ukpong, *The Bible in Africa.*
86. (Nairobi: Oxford University Press, 1986).
87. *A Bulletin of Contextual Theology*, 2/2:6-40. I will like to acknowledge the fact that these bibliographical essays have been very crucial to the success of this article.
88. *Journal of Inculturation Theology*, 2/1:39-139.
89. *The Bible in Africa*, 633-800
90. Ukpong, *The Bible in Africa*
91. (New York: Peter Lang, 2000).
92. See his articles, "The Current State of Old Testament Scholarship in Africa: Where Are We at the Turn of the Century?" in Knut Holter, Mary Getui, and Victor Zinkuratire, Eds., *Interpreting the Old Testament in Africa* (New York: Peter Lang,1999), 27-39; Knut Holter, "Old Testament Scholarship in Sub-Sahara Africa," "It's not Only a Question of Money! African Old Testament
Scholarship between the Myths and Meanings of the South and the Money and Methods of the South," "The Institutional Context of Old Testament Scholarship in Africa," and "Popular and Academic Contexts for Biblical Interpretation in Africa," in *Yahweh in Africa.*
93. Knut Holter, "Should Old Testament Cush Be Rendered 'Africa'? in *Yahweh in Africa*, 107-114. Despite his criticism, I certainly belief that his interest in African Old Testament scholarship, and his publication has done more service to African Old Testament, especially as he spends his energy in bringing African Old Testament scholarship to the attention of the Old Testament Scholars in the Western World.
94. *Interpreting the Old Testament in Africa*, 43-54.
95. *Old Testament Essays*, 11 (1998), 50-58.
96. Marta Hoyland Lavik, The 'African' Texts of the Old Testament and their African Interpretations" *Interpreting the Old Testament in Africa*, 50. She is a doctoral student at School of Mission and Theology, at Stavanger, Norway.
97. *Interpreting the Old Testament in Africa*, 50.
98. *Interpreting The Old Testament in Africa, 50.*
99. "Inculturation Hermeneutics: An African Approach to Biblical Interpretation, Walter Dietrich and Ulrich Luz, *The Bible in a World Context: An Experiment in*

Contextual Hermeneutics (Grand Rapids: Wm. B. Eerdmans Publishing Co., 2002), 17-32.

100. The Contextual Bible Study (Pietermaritzburg: Cluster Publications, 1993).

101. Ukpong, *The Bible in the World Context*, 18.

102. Ukpong, *The Bible in the World Context*, 21.

103. Ukpong, *The Bible in the World Context*, 22.

104. Ukpong, "Developments in Biblical Interpretation in Africa," *The Bible in Africa*, 23.

105. Nigerian is an example of these African countries. Since independence in 1960, the majority of the rulers were military dictators who had no regard for human values and the rule of law. They did not care for education and research. The Nigerian treasury was frequently looted.

106. David Adamo, "Doing Old Testament Research in Africa, "*Bulletin of African Old Testament Scholarship*, vol.

107. He teaches Old Testament at the School of Mission and Theology, Stavanger, Norway. He is the most productive Western Old Testament scholars in the field of distinctive African Old Testament scholarship that I know. It is gratifying that he has published many articles and books on African Old Testament scholarship and have personally took it upon himself to seek funds to assist African scholars to publish their materials and attend international Old conferences. There may be other African and non- African Old Testament scholars around that are not known to me that are determined to continue this struggle.

CHAPTER III

THE BIBLE IN SOUTH AFRICAN BLACK THEOLOGY: THE BIBLE AS *BOLA* AND OTHER FORMS OF AFRICAN BIBLICAL INTERPRETATION

Gerald West

Introduction: the Bible as *Bola*

Following the death of Dr van der Kemp, "that valuable man who [pioneered and] superintended the African missions" on behalf of the London Missionary Society.[1]

> the Directors thought it expedient to request one of their own body, the Rev. John Campbell, to visit the country, personally to inspect the different settlements, and to establish such regulations, in concurrence with Mr. Read and the other missionaries [already in Southern Africa], as might be most conducive to the attainment of the great end proposed-the conversion of the heathen, keeping in view at the same time the promotion of their civilization.[2]

John Campbell, a director of the London Missionary Society, had been commissioned and sent to the Cape in 1812 in order "to survey the progress and prospects of mission work in the interior."[3] Campbell made his way from mission post to mission post in the Colony, and when he came to Klaarwater, which was then some distance north of the boundary of the Cape Colony, though the boundary was to follow him some years later (in 1825) almost as far as Klaarwater, he heard that Chief Mothibi of the Tlhaping people, a hundred miles further to the north, had expressed some interest in receiving missionaries.[4] With barely a pause in Klaarwater, spending no more than a week there, Campbell and his party set off for Dithakong ("Lattakoo"), which was then the capital of Chief Mothibi, on the 15th June 1813.

Though not the first whites or missionaries to make this trek, theirs is the first sustained visit. During this visit, there was the first documented engagement with the Bible by the Tlhaping.[5] We pick up the missionary trail and tale as they arrive on the outskirts of Dithakong in the afternoon of 24th June 1813. Having crested a hill, "Lattakoo came all at once into view, lying in a valley between hills, stretching about three or four miles from E. to W."[6] As they descended the hill towards "the African city," they were "rather surprised that no person was to be seen in any direction, except two or three boys," and the absence of an overt presence continued even as the wagons wound their way between the houses, save for a lone man who "made signs" for them to follow him. The stillness continued ("as if the town had been forsaken of its inhabitants"), until they came "opposite to the King's house." They "were then conducted" into the Chief's circular court (*kgotla*), "a square, formed by bushes and branches of trees laid one above another, in which,….several hundreds of people assembled together, and a number of tall men with spears, draw[n] up in military order on the north side of the square." And then the silence was broken! "In a few minutes the square was filled with men, women, and children, who poured in from all quarters, to the number of a thousand or more. The noise from so many tongues, bawling with all their might, was rather confounding, after being so long accustomed to the stillness of the wilderness."[7] All was not as it had seemed to the missionaries!

Signed upon and conducted into a dense symbolic space[8] not of their choosing or understanding, Campbell and company become the objects of Tswana scrutiny. With a feeling of being "completely in their power," Campbell confesses in a letter written some days later, "They narrowly inspected us, made remarks upon us, and without ceremony touched us . . . "[9] The Tlhaping "see," "feasting their eyes," they "examine," and they "touch."[10] Having been momentarily "separated," and having "lost sight of each in the crowd," the missionaries soon gathered themselves, though they "could hardly find out each other," and devised "a scheme, which after a while answered our purpose; we drew up the wagons in the form of a square, and placed our tent in the centre."[11] Being led into a round "square" not of their own making, they construct a square which they (only partially) control.[12] From this site of some control they plot and execute "the real object" of their visit, which they explain in the following terms to the nine local leaders, representing Chief Mothibi in his absence from the city, who gather in their tent "a little after sun-set."[13]

> Through three interpreters, viz. in the Dutch, Coranna, and Bootchuana languages, I informed them that I had come from a remote country, beyond the sun, where the true God, who made all things was know-that the people of that country had long ago sent some of their brethren to Klaar Water, and other parts of Africa, to

tell them many things which they did not know, in order to do them good, and make them better and happier- . . . . [that] I had come to Lattakoo to inquire if they were willing to receive teachers-that if they were willing, then teachers should be sent to live among them.[14]

The leadership reply that they cannot/may not give an answer until Mothibi returns, after which there is an informal, it would appear, exchange of gifts: tobacco and milk.[15] A number of observations, interactions, and transactions are recorded over the next few days as Campbell (impatiently) waits for the arrival of Mothibi. But in the evening of the 27th, when the uncle of the Chief, "Munaneets," comes to their tent with an interpreter, there was "much interesting conversation," during which the Bible is explicitly designated in discourse. Two days earlier, on the first morning after their arrival (the 25th June) Campbell and his party hold worship in their kitchen—a house in "the square, used by them for some public purpose" but assigned to the missionaries as their kitchen—which is attended by "some of the people." It is hard to imagine the Bible not being present and not being used as either an unopened sacred object or an opened text during this time of worship. Similarly, during worship in the afternoon of the 27th, at which "About forty of the men sat round us very quietly during the whole time,"[16] the Bible too must have been present. But the first explicit reference to the Bible in this narrative, where it is separated out from the normal practice and patterns of the missionaries, is in the discussion with the Chief's uncle.

In their constant quest for information and opportunities to provide information, scrutinising as they are scrutinised, the missionaries "enquired of him their reason for practising circumcision."[17] It is not clear what prompts this question, but quite possibly what appear to be a series of ritual activities each day involving women, perhaps the initiation of young women,[18] may, by association, have generated a question to do with male initiation.[19] The Chief's uncle replies that "it came to them from father to son." Sensing, no doubt, an opportunity "to instruct," the missionaries persevere, asking "Do you not know why your fathers did it?" The Chief's uncle and his companions answered, "No." Immediately the missionaries respond, Campbell reports, saying: "We told them that our book informed us how it began in the world, and gave them the names of Abraham, Ishmael, and Isaac, as the first persons who were circumcised."[20] The illocutionary intent of this information is clearly to establish an earlier, and therefore superior, claim of origin. Origins were becoming increasingly important to the emerging modernity of missionary England, and so the Bible was seen as particularly potent, containing as it did 'the Origin' of all origins.[21] However, what impressed the Chief's uncle and his colleagues was not this claim to an all-encompassing origin, but the naming of the missionaries' ancestors, Abraham, Ishmael, and Isaac, which is why "This appeared to them very interesting information, and they all tried to repeat the names we had mentioned, over and over again, looking to us for correction, if they pronounced any of them wrong. Munaneets, and the others who joined the company, appeared anxious to have them fixed on their memories."[22] The book-the Bible-appeared, from the perspective of the Tlhaping, to contain the names of the missionary ancestors, and perhaps, if they picked up the intent of the missionaries proclamation, the ancestors of their ancestors. This was, indeed, interesting, and potentially powerful, information. The missionary's attempt to subsume the Tlhaping's oral account of circumcision under their textual, biblical account may have marked the Bible, in the eyes of the Tlhaping, as a site worth watching, and perhaps even occupying; or it may have demonstrated the dangers of this strange object of power.

Impressed, but probably also a little perplexed by this intense interest in the names of Abraham, Ishmael, and Isaac, the missionaries persist, asking next "if they knew any thing of the origin of mankind, or when they came." The people reply, "saying they came from some country beyond them, pointing to the North which is the direction in which Judea lies.[23] Those two men came out of the water; the one rich, having plenty of cattle, the other poor, having only dogs. One lived by oxen, the other by hunting. One of them fell, and the mark of his foot is on a rock to this day." With no apparent attempt to probe the African origin of the story in more detail, but with a clear indication of it's (and their circumcision story's) inadequacy, the missionaries immediately "endeavoured to explain to them how knowledge, conveyed by means of books, was more certain than that conveyed by memory from father to son."[24] The Chief's uncle, "Munaneets," is quick to realise the source of this "knowledge," knowing long before Michel Foucault theorised it, the articulations of power and knowledge on each other;[25] for he asks "if they should be taught to understand books." The use of the modal "should" perhaps, convey, as it often does in English, a sense of asking permission; Campbell's reconstruction and representation of this dialogue (via three other languages!) may accurately capture a concern on the part of the Chief's uncle that, given the evident power of the book(s), so openly exhibited by the missionaries, they the Tlhaping may not be granted access to the book(s).[26] That the missionaries and the Chief's representatives have in mind 'the Book,' in particular, is clear from missionaries' answer: "We answered, they would; and when the person we should send (provided Mateebe consented), had learned their language, he would change the Bible from our language into theirs."[27]

One of the local participants was clearly worried about this portent of outside instruction, including perhaps the presence of the Bible a new (outside) site and source of power/knowledge, though this is less clear, for during the conversation, Campbell reports, "an old man who is averse to our sending teachers, asked how we made candles, pointing to that which was on our table. He also said," Campbell continues, "he did not need instruction from any one, for the dice which hung from his neck informed him of every thing which happened at a distance; and added, if they were to attend to instructions, they would have no time to hunt or to do any thing."[28] This fascinating exchange, re-presenting as it is a complex exchange, seems to suggest a profound grasp by

this "old man," possibly an *ngaka* (an indigenous doctor/diviner/healer), because
he is wearing a "dice," one of the elements among the bones, shells, and other
materials making up the *ditaola* used in divining,[29] of the dangerousness of non-
indigenous instruction. The context of the discussion, and the centrality of the
Bible in the discussion, if not also centrally positioned on the table in the
meeting space,[30] makes it likely that he assumes that the missionaries' book(s)
are their equivalent of his "dice." My conjecture finds some support from Robert
Moffat's account of an incident in which he says, "My books puzzled them," he
wrote. "They asked if they were my 'Bola,' prognosticating dice."[31] Whether his
aversion to "instruction" is an aversion to both the source (the Book) and the
interpreter (the missionaries) of the source is not clear, but is a question that sits
at the centre of my study. We must not assume that this "old man" shares the
assumption of the missionaries that the book and its instruction are one and the
same thing. His concern that "if they were to attend to instructions, they would
have no time to hunt or to do any thing," may reflect rumours of the time
schedules and modes of production of established mission station church and
school routines to the south[32] in which case the focus of his aversion is the
instruction regime rather than the source of power/knowledge itself, the Book.

But I may be imagining a fissure where there is none, for this insightful "old
man" may be making a simpler point; by pointing to the candles, and asking
how missionaries made them, he may be demonstrating an important difference
between knowledge that he and his people would find useful-how to make
candles-and knowledge that is potentially damaging and dangerous-instruction
about what happens "at a distance," such as circumcision, ancestors, and origins.
The book, the source of the latter, but not, it would seem from his analysis, of
the former, is as much a problem as the instruction.

Thus ends my lengthy introduction, with the beginning of biblical
interpretation among the Tlhaping people. Biblical interpretation among this
(pre-Christian) southern African people begins with the Bible as *bola*. But why
do I begin with the Bible as *bola*? I have been led to this beginning by my
dialogue with South African Black Theology, and in the rest of this essay I will
chart my journey and the companions who have (re)directed my way.

Biblical Hermeneutic Signposts

My account of my journey towards the Bible as *bola* begins with an
anecdote that I first heard from Takatso Mofokeng:[33]

> When the white man came to our country he had the Bible and we
> (Blacks) had the land. The white man said to us "let us pray." After
> the prayer, the white man had the land and we had the Bible.

Mofokeng was my first tutor in matters to do with the Bible and black
South Africans. And I return to his article again and again as a guide. Mofokeng

made two things absolutely clear: first, the Bible is both a problem and a solution in South Africa, and, second, the Bible is a problem not only because of ideologically racist interpretations but also because of ideologically oppressive socio-historical production. Having been introduced to this dilemma by Mofokeng, Itumeleng Mosala then took me deeper in analysing this dilemma. His work allowed me to listen in on a discussion taking place in Black Theology between himself and a host of other Black theologians, and this discussion has strongly shaped my path ever since.

A Hermeneutics of Trust

Allow me to return now, for rhetorical and hermeneutical effect, to the anecdote told by Mofokeng, though this time the teller is not Mofokeng, but a fellow Black theologian, Desmond Tutu.

> When the white man came to our country he had the Bible and we (Blacks) had the land. The white man said to us "let us pray." After the prayer, the white man had the land and we had the Bible.

To which, having retold the anecdote, Desmond Tutu has on occasion responded, "And we got the better deal!"[34] This response is typical of a hermeneutics of trust with respect to the Bible that characterises much of South African Black Theology, and in particular the biblical hermeneutics of Black theologians like Tutu and Allan Boesak.[35]

I have discussed the biblical hermeneutics of Tutu and Boesak in detail elsewhere, both from an emic approach—using the categories and concepts internal to the discourse of Black Theology—and from an etic approach—using concepts and categories from discourses outside of Black Theology. Here I will briefly delineate some of the key characteristics of this particular orientation to the Bible and biblical interpretation in South African Black Theology, again using both emic and etic concepts and categories.

Their overall interpretative orientation towards the Bible is one of trust. A hermeneutics of trust is evident in a number of respects. First, as in much of African Theology (and African American Black Theology and Latin American Liberation Theology), the Bible is considered to be a primary source of Black Theology.[36] The Bible belongs to Black Theology in the sense that doing theology without it is unthinkable. Second, the Bible is perceived to be primarily on the side of the black struggle for liberation and life in South Africa. The Bible belongs to Black Theology in the sense that the struggle for liberation and life is central to them both.[37]

While there is definitely awareness that there are different, sometimes complementing and sometimes contradicting, theologies in the Bible, this is understood as evidence of the thoroughly contextual nature of the Bible, but because the pervasive theological trajectory is one of liberation, the plurality of theologies in the Bible is unproblematic for Black Theology.[38] Those who use the Bible against black South Africans are therefore misinterpreting the Bible, because the Bible is basically on the side of Black Theology.

In terms of interpretative interests,[39] the dominant interests among Black theologians who work within a framework of a hermeneutics of trust can be characterised as a combination of a focus on the literary dimensions of the biblical text together with a focus on the central symbolic and thematic semantic axis (or trajectory) of the final canonical form. A relatively careful and close reading of particular texts is used in conjunction with a generally accepted sense of the liberatory shape of the final Christian canonical form, culminating as it does in Jesus, "the ultimate reference point."[40]

Although race may not be an obvious dimension of biblical texts—and South African Black Theology has not shared the same passion as Black Theology in the USA for recovering an African presence in the Bible or of bringing racial analysis to bear on the Bible itself[41]—Tutu and other black theologians found numerous lines of connection between their struggle and the struggle of God's people in the pages of the Bible. Mofokeng too makes the claim that,

> when many Black Christians read their history of struggle carefully, they come upon many Black heroes and heroines who were inspired and sustained by some passages and stories of the Bible in their struggle, when they read and interpreted them in the light of their Black experience, history and culture. They could consequently resist dehumanization and the destruction of their faith in God the liberator. It is this noble Black Christian history that helps to bring out the other side of the Bible, namely, the nature of the Bible as a book of hope for the downtrodden.[42]

A Hermeneutics of Suspicion

But, according to Mofokeng, this is not the whole story. In a direct response to the anecdote already recounted above about Bibles, white men and African land, he asserts that this story expresses more precisely than any statement in the history of political science or Christian missions the ambiguity of the Bible and "the dilemma that confronts black South Africans in their relationships with the Bible."

> With this statement, which is known by young and old in South Africa, black people of South Africa point to three dialectically related realities? They show the central position which the Bible occupies in the ongoing process of colonization, national oppression and exploitation. They also confess the incomprehensible paradox of being colonized by a Christian people and yet being converted to their religion and accepting the Bible, their ideological instrument of colonization, oppression and exploitation. Thirdly, they express a

historic commitment that is accepted solemnly by one generation and
passed on to another—a commitment to terminate exploitation of
humans by other human.[43]

That the Bible is both a problem and a solution is, as I have indicated, at the
centre of Mofokeng's analysis. His dominant orientation is one of suspicion
towards the Bible. Again, here I can only sketch the contours of the biblical
hermeneutics of his analysis, using wherever possible the emic categories and
concepts of Black Theology itself.[44]

While the "external" problem of the misuse of the Bible by oppressive and
reactionary white South African Christians remains, Mofokeng identifies a more
fundamental problem—the "internal" problem of the Bible itself. Mofokeng is
critical of those who concentrate only on the external problem, those who accuse
"oppressor preachers of *misusing* the Bible for their oppressive purposes and
objectives" and "preachers and racist whites of not practising what they preach."
It is clear, Mofokeng maintains, that these responses are "based on the
assumption that the Bible is essentially a book of liberation." While Mofokeng
concedes that these responses have a certain amount of validity to them, the
crucial point he wants to make is that there are numerous "texts, stories and
traditions in the Bible which lend themselves to only oppressive interpretations
and oppressive uses because of their inherent oppressive nature." What is more,
he insists, any attempt "to 'save' or 'co-opt' these oppressive texts for the
oppressed only serve the interests of the oppressors."[45] Young blacks in
particular, Mofokeng continues, "have categorically identified the Bible as an
oppressive document by its very nature and to its very core" and suggest that the
best option "is to disavow the Christian faith and consequently be rid of the
obnoxious Bible." Indeed, some "have zealously campaigned for its expulsion
from the oppressed Black community," but, he notes, with little success.[46]

Unfortunately, Mofokeng does not offer further reflection on those who
would "be rid of the obnoxious Bible;" instead he focuses on the reason for their
lack of success, which, he argues, is

> largely due to the fact that no easily accessible ideological silo or
> storeroom is being offered to the social classes of our people that are
> desperately in need of liberation. African traditional religions are too
> far behind most blacks while Marxism, is to my mind, far ahead of
> many blacks, especially adult people. In the absence of a better
> storeroom of ideological and spiritual food, the Christian religion and
> the Bible will continue for an undeterminable period of time to be the
> haven of the Black masses par excellence.

Given this situation of very limited ideological options, Mofokeng
continues, "Black theologians who are committed to the struggle for liberation
and are organically connected to the struggling Christian people, have chosen to
honestly do their best to shape the Bible into a formidable weapon in the hands
of the oppressed instead of leaving it to confuse, frustrate or even destroy our

people."[47]

But on just how the Bible is to become "a formidable weapon in the hands of the oppressed" Mofokeng is not too clear. For this we will have to turn to the work of Itumeleng Mosala. Mosala is clearer in his analysis, and takes me considerably further in my journey. In an early essay on "The Use of the Bible in Black Theology" he is the first Black theologian to question in print the ambiguous ideological nature of Bible itself.[48] Mosala's basic critique is directed at the exegetical starting point of Black Theology, particularly as this starting point is expressed in the work of Boesak and Tutu. In Mosala's analysis the problem is that their exegesis begins with "the notion that the Bible is the revealed 'Word of God.'"[49] He traces this view of the Bible as "an absolute, non-ideological 'Word of God'" back to the work of James Cone.[50] He finds it even in the work of the "most theoretically astute of [African American] black theologians," Cornel West. Whatever the origin, what matters to Mosala is that "South African black theologians are not free from enslavement to this neo-orthodox theological problematic that regards the notion of the "Word of God" as a hermeneutical starting point underlines the pervasiveness of this view of the Bible by subjecting Tutu, Boesak, as well as Sigqibo Dwane, Simon Gqubule, Khoza Mgojo, and Manas Buthelezi to a similar critique.[51]

Mosala's contention is that most of the Bible "offers no certain starting point for a theology of liberation within itself." For example, he argues that the biblical book of Micah "is eloquent in its silence about the ideological struggle waged by the oppressed and exploited class of monarchic Israel." In other words, "it is a ruling class document and represents the ideological and political interests of the ruling class." As such there "is simply too much de-ideologization to be made before it can be hermeneutically straightforward in terms of the struggle for liberation."[52] The Bible, therefore, cannot be the hermeneutical starting point of Black Theology. Rather, those committed to the struggles of the black oppressed and exploited people "cannot ignore the history, culture, and ideologies of the dominated black people as their primary hermeneutical starting point." [53]

However, this does not mean that Mosala totally rejects the Bible. While the Bible cannot be the primary starting point for Black theology "there are enough contradictions within the book [of Micah, for example] to enable eyes that are hermeneutically trained in the struggle for liberation today to observe the kin struggles of the oppressed and exploited of the biblical communities in the very absences of those struggles in the text." Because the Bible is "a product and a record of class struggles,"[54] Black theologians are able to detect "glimpses of liberation and of a determinate social movement galvanized by a powerful religious ideology in the biblical text." But, he continues, the "existence of this phenomenon is not in question; rather, the problem here is one of developing an adequate hermeneutical framework that can rescue those liberating themes from the biblical text."[55]

Mosala goes on in his work to offer his analysis of an adequate hermeneutical framework for Black Theology, proposing dialectic between an appropriation of black culture and experience and an appropriation of the Bible.[56] "Black Theology has roots in the Bible insofar as it is capable of linking the struggles of oppressed people in South Africa today with the struggles of oppressed people in the communities of the Bible," but because the oppressed people in the Bible "did not write the Bible," and because their struggles "come to us *via* the struggles of their oppressors," "Black Theology needs to be firmly and critically rooted in black history and black culture in order for it to possess apposite weapons of struggle that can enable black people to get underneath the biblical text to the struggles of oppressed classes." However, Black Theology must also be "firmly and critically rooted in the Bible in order to elicit from it cultural hermeneutical tools of combat" with which black people can penetrate beneath both the underside of black history and culture and contemporary capitalist settler colonial domination to the experiences of oppressed and exploited working class black people. [57]

While the forms of Black Theology inherited by Mosala are, he recognises, "firmly . . . . rooted in the Bible" they are not "critically rooted in the Bible." This is the fundamental problem of Black Theology for Mosala, and because his understanding of what it means to be "critically rooted in the Bible" is so important in its contribution to South African Black Theology I will discuss his contribution in some detail.

Mosala contends that the impotence of Black Theology as a weapon of struggle comes from the enslavement of Black Theology "to the biblical hermeneutics of dominant ideologies."[58] More specifically, Black Theology's impotence comes from embracing "the ideological form of the text"[59]—"the oppressor's most dangerous form."[60] Existential commitment to the struggle against apartheid in South Africa, insists Mosala, was no substitute "for scientific analysis of the valence of a tradition in the class struggle."[61] While Mosala accepts that "texts that are against oppressed people may be co-opted by the interlocutors of the liberation struggle," he insists that "the fact that these texts have their ideological roots in oppressive practices means that the texts are capable of undergirding the interests of the oppressors even when used by the oppressed. In other words, oppressive texts cannot be totally tamed or subverted into liberative texts."[62]

Mosala rejects a "fundamentalism of the Left,"[63] that "attempts to transplant biblical paradigms and situations into our world without understanding their historical circumstances." Like Norman Gottwald, and using his analysis, Mosala criticises liberation theologians who invoke biblical symbols of liberation but who "seldom push those biblical symbols all the way back to their socio-historic foundations" and consequently are not able to "grasp concretely the inner biblical strands of oppression and liberation in all their stark multiplicity and contradictory interactions." Not only does this "picking and choosing" of biblical resources by some liberation theologians "not carry sufficient structural analysis of biblical societies to make a proper comparison with the present possible," a lack of interest in and knowledge of "the history of social forms and ideas from biblical times to the present" results in the risk that "unstructural understanding of the Bible may simply reinforce and confirm unstructural understanding of the present."[64] It is "a risky business," says Gottwald, "to 'summon up' powerful symbolism out of a distant past unless the symbol users are very self-conscious of their choices and applications, and fully aware of how their social struggle is both like and unlike the social struggle of the architects of the symbols."[65] Efforts to draw "religious inspiration" or "biblical values" from, for example, early Israel "will be romantic and utopian unless resolutely correlated to both the ancient and the contemporary cultural material and social organizational foundations."[66]

Mosala agrees with Gottwald; he is concerned at "a thinness of social structural analysis and a thinness of biblical analysis" in Black Theology.[67] His fundamental objections against the biblical hermeneutics of Black Theology are that not only does it suffer from an unstructural understanding of the Bible, but, both as a consequence and as a reason, it also suffers from an unstructural understanding of black experience and struggle. Central to Mosala's hermeneutics of liberation is the search for a theoretical perspective that can locate both the Bible and the black experience within appropriate socio-historical contexts. Historical-critical tools (to delimit and historically locate texts), supplemented by sociological resources (especially historical materialist forms of analysis) provide the theoretical perspective for Mosala's treatment of texts. Historical-materialism, particularly its appropriation of 'struggle' as a key concept, provides the categories and concepts necessary to read and critically appropriate both black history and culture and the Bible. "The category of struggle becomes an important hermeneutical factor not only in one's reading of his or her history and culture but also in one's understanding of the history, nature, ideology, and agenda of the biblical texts."[68]

In order to undertake this kind of analysis, Mosala argues, black interpreters must be engaged in the threefold task of Terry Eagleton's "revolutionary cultural worker": a task that is projective, polemical, and appropriative. While Mosala does not doubt that Black Theology is "projective" and "appropriative" in its use of the Bible, it is "certainly *not* polemical—in the sense of being critical—in its biblical hermeneutics."[69] Black Theology has not interrogated the text ideologically in class, cultural, gender, and age terms. Black Theology has not gauged the ideological 'grain' or asked in what code the biblical text is cast and so has read the biblical text as an innocent and transparent container of a message or messages.[70] By not using socio-historical modes of interpretation, Black Theology continues to spar "with the ghost of the oppressor" in its most powerful form—the ideological form of the text.[71]

The Bible, according to Mosala's analysis, is a complex text best understood as a "signified practice." "It cannot be reduced to a simple socially and ideologically unmediated 'Word of God.' Nor can it be seen merely as a straight forward mirror of events in Ancient Israel. On the contrary it is a *production*, a remaking of those events and processes."[72] Using the language of redaction criticism, Mosala argues that the different "layers" historical-critical work detects each have a particular ideological code. Some layers of the Bible are cast in "hegemonic codes," which represent social and historical realities in ancient Israel in terms of the interests of the ruling classes. Other parts of the Bible are encoded in "professional codes," which have a relative autonomy, but which still operate within the hegemony of the dominant code. Then there are layers that are signified through "negotiated codes," which contain a mixture of adaptive and oppositional elements, but which still take the dominant codes as their starting point. Finally, there are a few textual sites that represent "oppositional codes" which are grounded in the interests and religious perspectives of the underclasses of the communities of the Bible. [73]

A critical and structural analysis of the biblical text requires that Black Theology identify the ideological reference code in which a particular text is encoded. For it is only by recognizing the particular ideological encoding of a text that an interpreter can prevent herself or himself from colluding with the dominant and hegemonic. Moreover, it is only by recognizing the particular encoding of a text that the interpreter can then interpret the text 'against the grain.' In other words, the polemical task of the interpreter is vital because it enables the appropriative task. A critical analysis of the biblical text ensures that Black Theology is able to appropriate the text against the grain. Such an approach would not be selective, nor would it engage in 'proof-texting.' Rather, a critical and structural ideological mode of reading "advocates an analytic approach to the text of the Bible that exposes the underlying literary and ideological plurality in the text without denying the hegemonic totality or shall we say unity of the final product." [74]

This phrase of Eagleton's, "against the grain," seeks to remind us, Mosala argues, "that the appropriation of works and events is always a contradictory process embodying in some form a 'struggle.' The interpretive struggle consists of, depending on the class forces involved, "either to harmonize the contradictions inherent in the works and events or to highlight them with a view to allowing social class choices in their appropriation." [75] The concern of Mosala is not that black theologians *cannot* read any text, no matter what its encoding, against the grain, but that they *ought not* to do this without *recognising* what they are doing.

The Bible "is the product, the record, the site, and the weapon of class, cultural, gender, and racial struggles. And a biblical hermeneutics of liberation that does not take this fact seriously can only falter in its project to emancipate the poor and the exploited of the world. Once more, the simple truth rings out that the poor and exploited must liberate the Bible so that the Bible may liberate them." [76] "One cannot," Mosala maintains, "successfully perform this task by denying the oppressive structures that frame what liberating themes the texts encode. [77] So, only a *critical* appropriation of the Bible along socio-historical and ideologically socialist lines, systematically and critically (re)located in the broad black working-class struggle, [78] will enable the Bible to be a resource with which Black Theology will be to "get the land back and get the land back without losing the Bible."[79]

I have dwelt on Mosala's work at some length, both because it is one of the clearest analytical contributions of Black Theology to reflection on the Bible and because his work has indelibly shaped my own. If Mofokeng was my first tutor, then Mosala has been my mentor. By constantly returning to his work I have continued to find resources with which to move forward in my own reflections on the place of the Bible in South Africa. Even when his work, and that of Mofokeng's, has not offered direct guidance to the path I have taken, their work has provided signposts for my journey. My interest in ordinary black biblical interpretation is a case in point.[80]

A number of theoretical and praxiological impulses have directed my work in the direction of the biblical interpretation of ordinary poor and marginalised Bible users,[81] but the most important of these many impulses have come from South African Black Theology.[82] First, there is Mofokeng's provocative assertion that young blacks "have categorically identified the Bible as an oppressive document by its very nature and to its very core" and have therefore gone on to suggest that the best option "is to disavow the Christian faith and consequently be rid of the obnoxious Bible."[83] Second, there is Mosala's claim that Black theologians like Boesak and others "have been surpassed by the largely illiterate black working class and poor peasantry who have defied the canon of Scripture, with its ruling class ideological basis, by appropriating the Bible in their own way using the cultural tools emerging out of their struggle for survival."[84] Though neither of these scholars has pursued these points in any depth, Mosala has done some preliminary description and analysis of the reading practices of ordinary African Bible 'readers' in an African Independent church.[85] His attempt has inspired me, though his conclusion that "the only identifiable hermeneutics" among these black Bible interpreters is "the hermeneutics of mystification,"[86] has left me unsatisfied and determined to probe more deeply. But third, and perhaps most importantly, the practice of a significant number of Black theologians has informed and constantly (re)directed my studies.

A range of work in local black churches and communities with ordinary black Bible interpreters by black theological practitioners such as Dumisani Phungula, McGlory Speckman (Speckman 1993a; Speckman 1993b; Speckman and Kaufmann 2001a; Speckman and Kaufmann 2001b), Bafana Khumalo, Malika Sibeko, Sipho Mtetwa, Martin Mandew, Alpheus Masoga (Masoga 2001), Phumzile Zondi and Solomuzi Mabuza, among others, is the basis for much of my recent research and reflection.[87] My engagement with these Black theologians and with them with local communities of ordinary black biblical interpreters has pushed me down the path I now walk. However, my dialogue with another Black theologian, Tinyiko Maluleke, has caused me to constantly probe and (re)examine this path.

A Post-Biblical (?) Hermeneutics

As a way into Maluleke's contribution to my understanding of the place of the Bible in the South African context let us return to the anecdote I began this section with:

> When the white man came to our country he had the Bible and we (Blacks) had the land. The white man said to us "let us pray." After the prayer, the white man had the land and we had the Bible.

Tinyiko Maluleke puts a profound question to this anecdote,[88] asking what precisely it means to say that black people "have the Bible." Although Maluleke does not formulate the question in this way, his frequent and insightful reflections on the Bible and biblical interpretation in South African Black Theology (and African Theology) push in this direction.

In a brief 'concept' paper, Tinyiko Maluleke categorizes three phases of South African Black Theology. Though Maluleke's phases follow a chronological periodisation, he stresses the continuity between the phases:

> The first phase starts with the formation of the Black Theology Project by the University Christian Movement in 1970, while the second starts in 1981 with the establishment of the Institute for Contextual Theology. In phase one, Black Theology, though acknowledging Blackness to be a state of mind, nevertheless took objective Blackness as its starting point in such a way that all Black people were the focus of liberation and the whole Bible (Christianity) could be used for liberation. In phase two, objective Blackness, in and of itself, is no longer sufficient. Not all Black people are the focus of Black Theology. Not all theology done by Black people is Black Theology and not all the Bible (Christianity) is liberating. Furthermore, while phase one Black Theology was closely linked to the Black Consciousness philosophy, phase two Black Theology recognized a wider ideological ferment within the Black Theology movement. Most distinctive of the second phase has been the increasing introduction of Marxist historical materialism in the hermeneutic of Black Theology.[89]

The contours of the third phase are more difficult to discern, says Maluleke, because "we are living in and through it" (61). Nevertheless, he does offer a tentative sketch of the third phase. Repudiating allegations of Black Theology's death, Maluleke argues that the third phase of Black Theology draws deeply on resources within earlier phases of Black Theology, and elaborates these formative impulses into the future.

First, while the plurality of ideological positions and political strategies in the construction of Black Theology has been acknowledged since the early 1980s, the ideological and political plurality within Black Theology in the 1990s is more marked and brings with it a new 90s temptation that must be refused.[90] Ideological and political plurality in post-apartheid (and post-colonial)[91] South Africa must avoid both the temptation of an uncommitted play with pluralism and the temptation of a despairing paralysis (perhaps even abandonment) of commitment. Despite the pressures of ideological and political plurality, commitment remains the first act in Black Theology, whatever the particular brand.

Second, if race was the central category in the first phase of Black Theology, and if the category of class was placed alongside it in the second phase of Black Theology, then gender as a significant category has joined them in the third phase of Black Theology. But, once again, the tendency to minimise the foundational feature of Black Theology, namely, race, must be resisted. Gender, like class, in South Africa always has a racial component. Furthermore, warns Maluleke, in a context "where race is no longer supposed to matter," racism often takes on different guises and becomes "more 'sophisticated,'"

The third and final feature of phase three Black Theology has three related prongs, each of which might be considered as a separate element. Here, however, I want to stress their connectedness, as does Maluleke, and so will treat them as sub-elements of a formative feature of the third phase of South African Black Theology. The formative feature of phase three Black Theology is the identification of African Traditional Religions (ATRs) and African Independent/Instituted/Initiated Churches (AICs) as "significant" (perhaps even primary?) dialogue partners.[92]

Subsumed under this general feature, the first of the three prongs has to do with culture. Whereas phase one Black theology "ventured somewhat into cultural . . . . issues," phase two "became more and more concerned with the struggle of black people against racist, political and economic oppression."[93] However, "At crucial moments connections with African culture would be made-provided that culture was understood as a site of struggle rather than a fixed set of rules and behaviours." Culture remains problematical in phase three, but the envisaged rapprochement with ATRs and AICs that characterises phase three foregrounds culture in a form not found in phase two.

The second prong has to do with solidarity with the poor. In each of its phases, Black Theology "has sought to place a high premium on *solidarity with the poor* and not with the state or its organs—however democratic and benevolent such a state might be."[94] While such a position "must not be mistaken with a sheer anti-state stance . . . Black Theology is first and foremost not about the powerful but about the powerless and the silenced." And, and I stress this conjunction, "serious interest" in ATRs and AICs affords Black Theology in phase three "another chance of demonstrating solidarity with the poor—for ATRs is [sic] the religion of the poor in this country."[95]

Closely related to the first and second prong, but particularly to the first, is a third. By making culture a site of struggle, Black Theology "managed to relativise the Christian religion sufficiently enough to encourage dialogue not only with ATRs but with past and present struggles in which religions helped people to take part, either in acquiescence or in resistance." If, as Mosala has argued,[96] African culture can be a primary site of a hermeneutics of struggle for African Theology, supplemented only with a political class-based hermeneutics, then Christianity is not a necessary component in a Black Theology of liberation.[97] A key question, therefore, for the third phase of South African Black Theology is, "Have black and African theologies made the necessary epistemological break from orthodox or classical Christian theology required to effect 'a creative reappropriation of traditional African religions'?"[98]

Speaking to his own question, Maluleke argues that South African Black Theology has tended to use "classical Christian tools, doctrines and instruments—for example the Bible and Christology" for its purposes. Black Theology has used Christianity (and what follows is Mosala's take on the anecdote we have repeatedly reflected on) to "get the land back and get the land back without losing the Bible."[99]

> Realising that Christianity and the Bible continue to be a "haven of the Black masses" (Mofokeng 1988:40), black theologians reckoned that it would not be advisable simply "to disavow the Christian faith and consequently be rid of the obnoxious Bible." Instead the Bible and the Christian faith should be shaped "into a formidable weapon in the hands of the oppressed instead of just leaving it to confuse, frustrate or even destroy our people" (Mofokeng 1988:40). Preoccupation with Christian doctrines and ideas was, for black theology therefore, not primarily on account of faith or orthodoxy considerations, but on account of Christianity's apparent appeal to the black masses.[100]

Given this analysis, Maluleke goes on to argue,

> What needs to be re-examined now [in phase three] however, is the extent to which the alleged popularity of Christianity assumed in South African black theology is indeed an accurate assessment of the religious state of black people. If it were to be shown that ATRs are as popular as Christianity among black South Africans then in not having given much concerted attention to them, black theology might have overlooked an important resource. There is now space for this to be corrected by making use of alternative approaches.[101]

As I have shown, via Maluleke's analysis, one of the important features of phase three Black Theology is the recognition, recovery, and revival of its links with ATRs and AICs, and in so doing renewing its dialogue with African Theology in its many and various forms.[102] In other words, Maluleke could be said to be revisiting and questioning Mofokeng's assertion that "African traditional religions are too far behind most blacks."[103] Is this actually the case, asks Maluleke? Gabriel Setiloane asks the question even more starkly: "why do we continue to seek to convert to Christianity the devotees of African traditional religion?"[104] "This," says Maluleke, "is a crucial question for all African theologies [including South African Black Theology] as we move into the twenty-first century."[105]

Alongside this question, of course, looms the related question, prompted by Maluleke's analysis, of whether Black Theology can be done without the Bible.[106] If it is true, as is claimed by both Mofokeng and Mosala, that the Bible is primarily of strategic, not substantive,[107] importance to Black Theology, a claim that is vigorously rejected by Tutu (see above) Boesak, and Simon Maimela,[108] and many other Black theologians, then there are good grounds for a Black Theology without 'the Book.'

However, Maluleke, like Mofokeng, doubts whether "pragmatic and moral arguments can be constructed in a manner that will speak to masses without having to deal with the Bible in the process of such constructions."[109] The Bible remains in the 1990s, and probably into the millennium, "a 'haven of the Black masses.' And as long as it is a resource, it must be confronted, "precisely at a hermeneutical level." Quite what Maluleke means by this is not yet clear, but he does offer some clues, which emerge in his dialogue with the biblical hermeneutics of African Theology.[110]

He agrees with Mercy Amba Oduyoye, who speaks with many African women,[111] when she says that the problem with the Bible in Africa is that "throughout Africa, the Bible has been and continues to be absolutized: it is one of the oracles that we consult for instant solutions and responses."[112] "However," continues Maluleke, while many African biblical scholars and theologians are locked into a biblical hermeneutics that makes "exaggerated connections between the Bible and African heritage," "on the whole, and in practice, [ordinary] African Christians are far more innovative and subversive in their appropriation of the Bible than they appear."[113] They "may mouth the Bible-is-equal-to-the-Word-of-God formula, they are actually creatively pragmatic and selective in their use of the Bible so that the Bible may enhance rather than frustrate their life struggles."[114] The task before Black Theology, then, is "not only to develop creative Biblical hermeneutic methods, but also to observe and analyse the manner in which African Christians 'read' and view the Bible."

Indeed, an important task confronting Black and African theologies in South Africa is "to observe and analyse the manner in which African Christians 'read' and view the Bible." As the work of Mofokeng and Mosala has hinted, ordinary black South Africans have adopted a variety of strategies in dealing with an ambiguous Bible, including rejecting it[115] and strategically appropriating it as a site of struggle.[116] But, as I have argued,[117] neither Mofokeng nor Mosala provide the kind of detail required for Maluleke's project. Even my own attempts to reflect on and conjure concepts that elucidate the way in which ordinary black South Africans 'read' the Bible are not detailed enough,[118] and my scant comments on how black Christians "view" the Bible are equally inadequate.[119]

With reference to the latter—how black African Christians "view" the Bible—Maluleke pushes us to be more precise and asks us biblical scholars to question our inherited understandings of African biblical scholarship.

Unpacking African biblical hermeneutics

Having used the term 'African biblical scholarship,' I must hasten to acknowledge that I am chastened by my colleague Tinyiko Maluleke's critique of my use of terms like this.[120] Maluleke is right,

> there cannot and should not be such a thing as "African Biblical Scholarship" if this is envisaged in terms akin to that produced by western-type training. Both African Christians and African Christian theologians have not been able to relate in any exclusive way to the Bible-as a singular collection of texts-in the way that both the historical critical and latter day sociological hermeneutics have done. Except for a small minority, very few Black and African Biblical scholars have been able to do discipline-specific textual biblical studies.[121]

Maluleke goes on to suggest that like ordinary African Christians, African biblical scholars relate to the Bible has been as "part of a larger package of resources and legacies which include stories, preaching and language mannerisms, songs, choruses, ecclesiologies, theodicies, catechism manuals and a range of rituals and rites." We must not be misled, says Maluleke, by the overt presence of the Bible among African Christians; while it is "one of the few 'tangible' things" in African Christianity, "The Bible," insists Maluleke, "has been appropriated and continues to be appropriated as part of a larger package of resources." And 'African biblical scholars' cannot escape this reality; indeed they are examples of this reality.

> Most, if not all African 'biblical' scholars operate as philosophers, missiologists and quasi-systematic theologians (e.g. Dickson, Mbiti and Fashole-Luke). Indeed, it seems that the more Mbiti insisted on the centrality of the Bible in African Theology, the more of a philosopher, missiologist and systematic theologian he became.[122]

Clearly then we need to keep the term 'African biblical scholarship' in inverted commas as a signpost that we cannot take the content of this term as self-evident. Elsewhere I have chartered some of the contours of 'African biblical scholarship' and together with Musa Dube provided a glimpse of 'African biblical scholars' at work.[123] In a recent essay I have also employed these terms (in their accompanying inverted commas) as a means of teasing out and understanding more clearly the forms of engagement between African scholars and the Bible. In this essay, however, I simply want to acknowledge the legacy of Black Theology in problematising these terms. In particular, Maluleke's insistence on 'African biblical scholarship' as something quite different from "that produced by western-type training" requires probing. We African biblical scholars, all of us, assume that the Bible is central to the lived faith of ordinary African Christians. As we have noted, it is commonly assumed, even argued, by Black and African biblical scholars and theologians that the Bible is a significant resource for African Christians.[124] Maluleke himself acknowledges this, pointing to the many ways in which the Bible is a resource in Africa: as the most widely translated book it makes a contribution to the construction of indigenous grammars and texts, it is a basic textbook in primary and higher education, literacy has been closely tied to Bible reading and memorization, it is the

> most accessible basic vernacular literature text, a storybook, a compilation of novels and short stories, a book of prose and poetry, a book of spiritual devotion (i.e. the 'Word of God') as well as a 'science' book that 'explains the origins of all creatures. In some parts of Africa, the dead are buried with the Bible on their chests, and the Bible is buried into the concrete foundations on which new houses are to be built. In many African Independent Churches it is the physical contact between the sick and the Bible that is believed to hasten healing.[125]

Clearly African Christians relate to the Bible in various ways, *and this is Maluleke's point (and mine), that we recognize the diverse ways in which ordinary Africans actually engage with the Bible.* In fact, Maluleke goes further, insisting that we probe beneath the apparent place of the Bible in the lives of ordinary indigenous Africans. Leaning on the work of those Black theologians who have gone before him, particularly Mosala and Mofokeng, Maluleke asks us to re-examine the relationship between black Africans and the Bible.

Back into the Future

It is not only Maluleke who leans on those Black theologians who have gone before him; I too, a white South African, have only found my way in the field of South African biblical hermeneutics because of the profound legacies left by early generations and current proponents of South African Black Theology.[126] But significant as the contributions of Black Theology have been over the past thirty years, the ancestors of Black Theology lay further back, as Maluleke's recent work on the importance of ATRs and AICs suggests. In fact, Maluleke's recent studies have played an important role in pushing my own work back into the past, back toward the Bible as *bola*.

We have been right to concentrate, as Maluleke's formulation indicates, on the *present*, placing our focus on an observation and analysis of "the manner in which African Christians 'read' and view the Bible." Now, perhaps, is an appropriate time to follow Maluleke's gaze to the past, to the interpretative ancestors of Black Theology. We cannot do justice to Maluleke's task, I would argue, unless we also observe and analyse the manner in which indigenous Africans, both before and after 'Christianity,'[127] *have 'read'* and *have viewed* the Bible. Implicit in Maluleke's summoning of (or being summoned by) African Traditional Religion(s) and the African Independent Churches, is the pull of the past, a past that includes the Tlhaping and other indigenous southern Africans. The Bible as *bola* is a signpost reminding us that we must go back as we move into the future of biblical hermeneutics in South Africa.

Endnotes

1. John Campbell, *Travels in South Africa: undertaken at the request of Missionary Society*. Third Edition, Corrected ed. (London (Reprint, Cape Town): Black, Parry, & Co. 1815) (Reprint, C. Struck 1974), v. (henceforth Campbell).
2. Campbell 1815 (Reprinted 1974):vi
3. Jean Comaroff, *Body of power, spirit of resistance: the culture and history of a South African people* (Chicago: University of Chicago Press, 1985).
4. Jean Comaroff, and John L. Comaroff, *of revelation and revolution: Christianity, colonialism and consciousness in South Africa*. Vol. 1. (Chicago: University of Chicago Press., 1991), 178.
5. I am of course aware that I am here relying on missionary documentation and therefore on missionary narrative constructions of such encounters, but socially engaged biblical scholars (and anthropologists [see \Comaroff, 1991 #3276:xi, 171, 189]) have become adept at "reading against the grain," particularly in contexts like South Africa where, Itumeleng Mosala reminds us, "the appropriation of works and events is always a contradictory process embodying in some form a 'struggle'" [Mosala, 1989 #2967:32].
6. Campbell, 180.
7. Ibid, 180
8. The "square" would have been round (see references cited above); that it is described as "a square" demonstrates both some recognition of the political space into which they had been brought and the desire to re-vision what they found [see Comaroff, 1991 #3276:182-183; Comaroff, 1997 #3449:287-293].
9. J.Campbell, Klaarwater, 26 July 1813 [CWM. Africa. South Africa. Incoming correspondence. Box 5-2-D].
10. J.Campbell, Klaarwater, 26 July 1813 [CWM. Africa. South Africa. Incoming correspondence. Box 5-2-D].
11. Campbell, 180
12. Campbell never quite copes with the way in which local people, mainly the leadership, just walk into "our tent," 181, 184.
13. Ibid, 181)
14. Ibid, 182).
15. Ibid.
16. Ibid, 191)
17. Ibid.
18. Ibid, #3526:185-186, 188, 191, 194-195; Comaroff, 1985 #3411:114-118].
19. see Comaroff 1985:85-115.
20. Campbell, 191-192.
21. The English were, of course, about to have their views on origins thoroughly shaken and stirred by an English explorer and naturalist Darwin, Charles Darwin, *The origin of species: by means of natural selection of the preservation of favoured races in the struggle for life*. New York: Washington Square Press, 1859; the beginnings of this paradigm shift (in the Kuhnian sense can be detected

in the missionary message (see below); Thomas Kuhn *The structure of scientific revolutions*. Second Edition ed. (Chicago: University of Chicago Press, 1970).

22. Campbell , 192.

23. This is a puzzling reference; could it mean biblical Judea, and if so, might the missionaries have here 'seen' confirmed the origin of all peoples, even these 'sons of Ham,' from this distant land in and of the Bible? That Campbell thought in such categories is evident from a letter to Mr David Langton dated 27th July 1813, in which Campbell apologises for not having written sooner, saying that he has "written much from this land of Ham." Campbell then goes on to present him with an account of his visit to Dithakong [J. Campbell, Klaar Water, 27 July 1813 [CWM. Africa. South Africa. Incoming correspondence. Box 5-2-D].

24. Campbell, 192

25. I use the terms power and knowledge in close conjunction here and the term power/knowledge a little later deliberately, realising the hardworking hyphen (in the French *pouvoir-savoir*) and slash (in the English) bear a heavy load of theory. Accepting Foucault's invitation "to see what we can make of" his fragments of analysis (79), my use is intended to allude to this theory, especially to the fragmentary nature of Foucault's theory (79), to the implicit contrast of "idle knowledge" (79) with local forms of knowledge and criticism, subjugated knowledge (81-82), and their emergence as sites of contestation and struggle over against "the tyranny of globalising discourses" (83) and their appropriation as genealogies which wage war on the effects of power of dominant discourses (84), whether scientific (Foucault's focus) or other forms of dominating discourse. In particular, my use picks up on Foucault's analysis of the articulation of each on the other, namely, that "the exercise of power itself creates and causes to emerge new objects of knowledge and accumulates new bodies of information," that the "exercise of power perpetually creates knowledge and, conversely, knowledge constantly induces effects of power," and that it "is not possible for power to be exercise without knowledge, it is impossible for knowledge not to engender power" (52), Michael Foucault, *Power/knowledge: selected writings and other interviews 1972-1977*. Edited by C. Gordon. (New York: Pantheon, 1980).

26. William J. Burchell's earlier stay among the Tlhaping, and his more secretive employment of text generally and the Bible specifically, may have contributed to this question (see William Burchell, *Travels in the interior of Southern Africa.* With a new Introduction by A. Gordon-Brown ed. Vol. 2. (London, 1824) (Reprint, Cape Town): Longman, Hurst, Rees, Orme, Brown, and Green (Reprint, C. Struik, 1967), 391.

27. Campbell, 192).

28. Ibid, 193).

29. I am grateful to Mogapi Motsomaesi and Mantso 'Smadz' Matsepe for elucidating and helping me to interpret elements of this encounter.

30   Some days later during a visit from Mothibi's senior wife, Mmahutu, the Bible is clearly positioned on the table in the missionaries' tent.

31.   see Comaroff and Comaroff 1991:345; R. Moffat, *Missionary labours and scenes in Southern Africa.* (London (Reprint, New York ,1824): John Snow (Reprint, Johnson Reprint Corporation, 1969), 384.

32.   This entire volume of the Comaroff's might be described as a detailed study of such routines and regimes.

33.   Mofokeng, T. 1988. Black Christians, the Bible and liberation. *Journal of Black Theology* 2(1988) : 34-42.

34.   I have been unable to find a published source for this comment, but I personally have heard him make the comment on two public occasions.

35.   I am not sure that the upper case is accurate in designating Tutu as a Black theologian; a lower case 'black' may be more appropriate because I am not sure that either Tutu or Boesak would still refer to themselves as 'Black' theologians, that is, proponents of Black Theology.

36.   Mbiti, John S. 1977. The Biblical Basis for present trends in African Theology. In *African theology en route: papers from the Pan-African conference of Third World theologians, Accra, December 1977,* edited by K. Appiah-Kubi and S. Torres (Maryknoll, NY: Orbis, 1977).

37.   See Desmond Tutu, *Hope and suffering: sermons and speeches.* (Johannesburg: Skotaville, 1983), 124-129.

38.   Tutu, 106.

39.   Norman K.Gottwald, *The Tribes of Yahweh: a sociology of the religion of liberated Israel, 1250-1050 B.C.* (Maryknoll, New York: Orbis, 1979).

        G. Fowl, The ethics of interpretation; or, what's left over after the elimination of meaning. In *The Bible in three dimensions: essays in celebration of the fortieth anniversary of the Department of Biblical Studies,* University of Sheffield, edited by D. J. A. Clines, S. E. Fowl and S. E. Porter (Sheffield: JSOT Press, 1990).

40.   J. Draper, "Was there no-one left to give glory to God except this foreigner?": breaking the boundaries in Luke 17:11-19, In *Archbishop Tutu: prophetic witness in South Africa,* edited by L. Hulley, L. Kretzschmar and L. L. Pato. (Cape Town: Human and Rousseau, 1996). Gerald West, *Biblical hermeneutics of liberation: modes of reading the Bible in the South African context.* Second Edition ed. (Maryknoll, NY and Pietermaritzburg: Orbis Books and Cluster Publications, 1995), 64-70, 146-173; Tutu 1983:106;

41.   Felder, Cain Hope, ed. *Stony the road we trod: African American biblical interpretation.* Minneapolis: Fortress, 1991).

42.   T. Mofokeng, "Black Christians, the Bible and liberation," *Journal of Black Theology* 2 (1988):34-42.

43.   Ibid, 1998:34.

44.   For more detail see West 1995.

45.   Mofokeng, 37-38.

46.   Ibid, 40.
47.   Ibid, 40.
48.   Mosala, "The Use of the Bible;" 197; I. Mosala, *Biblical hermeneutics and black theology in South Africa*. Grand Rapids: Eerdmans, 1989, 1-42
49.   I. Mosala, Biblical hermeneutics and black theology in South Africa (Grand Rapids: Eerdmans, 1989), 15.
50.   For a discussion of the role of James Cone in South African Black Theology see the important book by Per Frostin (Frostin 1988:89-90).
51.   Itumeleng Mosala, "Black theology:" (Unpublished paper, 1989). More recently, Tinyiko Maluleke has extended this critique to African theologians north of the Limpopo river, including Lamin Sanneh, Kwame Bediako, John Mbiti, Byang Kato, and Jesse Mugambi [Maluleke, 1996 #3457:10-14].
52.   Mosala, "The Use of the Bible." 196; Mosala, Biblical *Hermeneutics*, 120-121).
53.   Mosala, "The Use of the Bible," 197.
54.   Ibid, 196
55.   Mosala, *Biblical Hermeneutics,* 40.
56.   Itumeleng Mosala, 1986a. "Ethics of the economic principles: church and secular investments." In *Hammering swords into ploughshares: essays in honour of Archbishop Mpilo Desmond Tutu*, edited by B. Tlhagale and I. J. Mosala. (Johannesburg: Skotaville, 1986), 119.
57.   Mosala, "The Ethics of Economic Principles," 120.
58.   Mosala, *Biblical Hermeneutics*, 4.
59.   The question of whether texts can have ideologies, while not directly relevant to this discussion, is an important one and properly nuances discussions of textual ideology see Fowl 1995; West 2000b. Fowl's careful analysis charts the terrain of such discussions, and is particularly illuminating for this tangential discussion because he deals directly with Mosala's claim above.   My essay joins the discussion by accepting Fowl's analysis, but then goes on to show what is at stake in Mosala's position.
60.   *Biblical Hermeneutics*, 28.
61.   *Biblical Hermeneutics*, 34.
62.   *Biblical Hermeneutics*, 30.
63.   The phrase is Hugo Assmann's [Assmann, 1976 #3053:104].
64.   Gottwald, cited in Mosala *Biblical Hermeneutics,* 31-32.
65.   Norman K.Gottwald, *The tribes of Yahweh: a sociology of the religion of liberated Israel, 1250-1050 B.C.* Maryknoll, New York: Orbis, 1979.
      Gottwald gives considerable space to developing this point (703-706).
66.   Gottwald, 706.
67.   Mosala, *Biblical Hermeneutics*, 31.
68.   Gottwald, 9.
69.   Mosala *Biblical Hermeneutics,* 32.
70.   Mosala, Biblical Hermeneutics, 41
71.   I bid, Biblical Hermeneutics, 28.
72.   Mosala, Biblical Hermeneutics, 3.
73.   *Biblical Hermeneutics*, 41-42.

74. Mosala, "Black Theology," 4; Elisabeth Schüssler Fiorenza makes a similar point when she argues that "The failure to bring a critical evaluation to bear upon the biblical texts and upon the process of interpretation within Scripture and tradition is one of the reasons why the use of the Bible by liberation theologians often comes close to 'prooftexting." Later she adds, "a critical hermeneutic must be applied to *all* biblical texts and their historical contexts" [Fiorenza, 1981 #3204:101-102, 108].

75. Mosala, *Biblical Hermeneutics,* 32); David Tracy notes that "the particular form of 'correlation' [between the tradition and contemporary situation] that liberation and political theologies take will ordinarily prove to be a form not of liberal identity nor one of the several forms of analogy or similarity but rather one of sheer confrontation." "The confrontations will be demanded by both the retrieval of the prophetic tradition's stand for the oppressed and by the suspicions released by the prophetic ideology-critique embedded in that retrieval" David Tracy, Introduction. In *The challenge of liberation theology: a First World response,* edited by B. Mahan and L. D. Richesin (Maryknoll, NY: Orbis, 1981), 2-3.

76. *Biblical Hermeneutics,* 193.

77. *Biblical Hermeneutics,* 41.

78. Ibid, 190-192).

79. Mosala, "Biblical Hermeneutics and Black Theology," 194.

80. My use of the word 'ordinary' as a technical term (West 1999:10) has been questioned by Tinyiko Maluleke [Maluleke, 2000 #3507:93-94]. I value such critique, and as my essay progresses, my debt to the sustained engagement of Maluleke with my work becomes clear.

81. West, Gerald O. *The academy of the poor: towards a dialogical reading of the Bible* (Sheffield: Sheffield Academic Press, 1999), 55-62.

82. West, Gerald O. *Biblical hermeneutics of liberation: modes of reading the Bible in the South African context.* Second Edition ed. (Maryknoll, NY and Pietermaritzburg: Orbis Books and Cluster Publications, 1995).

83. Mofokeng, 40.

84. Mosala, "The Use of the Bible," 184.

85. Mosala, "Race, class, and gender as hermeneutical factors in the African Independent Churches' appropriation of the Bible." *Semeia, 1996,* 73:43-57.

86. Mosala, "Race, Class, Gender," 57.

87. Gerald West, *Contextual Bible Study in South Africa: a resource for* reclaiming and regaining land, dignity and identity. In *The Bible in Africa: transactions, trends, and trajectories,* edited by G. O. West and M. W. Dube. Leiden: Brill 2000; West, *The Academy of the Poor,* 1999. Sibeko, Malika, and Beverley G. Haddad. 1997. Reading the Bible 'with' women in poor and marginalized communities in South Africa (Mark 5:21-6:1). *Semeia* 78:83-92. Speckman, McGlory T. 1993a. For Nolan's sake, let's move on: a plea for a developmental dimension in Contextual Theology. In *Towards an agenda for Contextual*

Theology: essays in honour of Albert Nolan, edited by M. T. Speckman and L. T. Kaufmann. Pietermaritzburg: Cluster Publications. Speckman, McGlory T. 1993b. The Kairos Document and the development of a kairos theology in Luke-Acts, with particular reference to Luke 19:41-44. PhD, School of Theology, University of Natal, Pietermaritzburg.Speckman, McGlory T., and Larry T. Kaufmann, Introduction. In *Towards an agenda for Contextual Theology: essays in honour of Albert Nolan*, edited by M. T. Speckman and L. T. Kaufmann. Pietermaritzburg: Cluster Publications. Speckman, McGlory T., and Larry T. Kaufmann, eds. *Towards an agenda for Contextual Theology: essays in honour of Albert Nolan*. Pietermaritzburg: Cluster Publications. Masoga, Mogomme Alpheus. Re-defining power: reading the Bible in Africa from the peripheral and central positions. In *Towards an agenda for Contextual Theology: essays in honour of Albert Nolan*, edited by M. T. Speckman and L. T. Kaufmann (Pietermaritzburg: Cluster Publications, 2001).

88.   In his retelling of the anecdote Maluleke uses inclusive language, referring to "White people," thereby implicitly capturing the role white women (madams) played in missionary and colonial enterprises [see for example \Comaroff, 1991 #3276:67-70,135-138,144-146; Comaroff, 1997 #3449:236-239,276-277,292-293,299-300,320-322,374]. For a detailed exegesis from the perspective of an African woman biblical scholar and theologian, Musa Dube, 2000. *Postcolonial feminist interpretation of the Bible*. St. Louis: Chalice Press, 2000), #3559:3, 16-21].

89.   Tinyiko S. Maluleke, Black theology as public discourse. In *Constructing a language of religion in public life: Multi-Event 1999 Academic Workshop papers*, edited by J. R. Cochrane. (Cape Town: University of Cape Town, 1998), 61; For a more detailed discussion of notions of 'blackness' in South African Black Theology see [Frostin, and Kritzinger: Frostin, Per. *Liberation theology in Tanzania and South Africa: a First World interpretation*. (Lund: Lund University Press, 1988), #2977:86-103; Kritzinger, J.N.J. Black Theology: challenge to mission, (University of South Africa, Pretoria, 1988), #3542:91-95. West, *Biblical Hermeneutics of Liberation*, #1286: chapter 4]. The predominant biblical hermeneutics of phase one is a hermeneutics of trust, while the predominant hermeneutics of phase two is a hermeneutics of suspicion West, Gerald O. "White men, Bibles, and land: ingredients in biblical interpretation in South African Black theology." *Scriptura* (2000), 73:141-152.

90.   The paper of Maluleke I am referring to here is a brief 'concept paper,' and so I am sometimes making fairly bold inferences from the available clues. Wherever possible, I have used Maluleke's other published work to enhance my understanding of the moves he makes in the concept paper.

91.   Talk of the 'post-colonial' has been slow to find a foothold in the fields of theology and biblical studies in South Africa (and indeed to the north of us); the

reasons for this deserve some attention [see \West, 1997 #3476; Dube, 1996 #3475; Dube, 1997 #3463; Dube, 1999 #3491; Dube, 2000 #3559].

92. Implicit in this formulation is my tentative analysis which locates ATRs and AICs along a continuum. At one end of the continuum would be ATR as a distinct 'faith.' I am not sure what would stand at the other end of the continuum, but along the way would be various manifestations of what we call AICs, gradually becoming less and less (primally) African. My play on 'primal' here is deliberate, alluding to the 'translation' [see \Maluleke, 1996 #3457] trajectory in African theology articulated by Lamin Sanneh [Sanneh, 1989 #3434] and Kwame Bediako [Bediako, 1995 #3451] and the high place it accords ATR as primal religion.

93. Tinyiko Maluleke, "African Traditional Religions in Christian mission and Christian scholarship: re-opening a debate that never started, *Religion and Theology* 5 (1998):121-137.

94. Implicit here is a period of emergence of phases three Black Theology which includes the context of a post-apartheid state; Maluleke would not use this formulation to address the relationship between Black Theology and the apartheid state.

95. Tinyiko Maluleke, Black theology as public discourse. In *Constructing a language of religion in public life: Multi-Event 1999 Academic Workshop papers*, edited by J. R. Cochrane (Cape Town: University of Cape Town, 1998).

96. Maluke, "Black Theology as a public discourse."

97. "Malueke, ATR in Mission," 133.

98. I. Mosala, "The relevance of African Traditional Religions and their challenge to Black Theology." In *The unquestionable right to be free: essays in Black Theology*, edited by I. J. Mosala and B. Tlhagale. (Johannesburg: Skotaville, 1986), 100? (135).

99. I .Mosala, "Biblical hermeneutics and black theology in South Africa" PhD, (University of Cape Town, Cape Town), 194.

100. Malueke, "ATR in Mission," 134.

101. Malueke, "ATR in Mission," 134.

102. Each of Maluleke's publications cited articulates forms of a dialogue between Black Theology and its three related interlocutors: ATRs, AICs, and African Theologies.

103. T. Mofokeng, "Black Christians, the Bible and liberation. *Journal of Black Theology* 2 (1988):34-42.

104. Gabriel Setiloane, Gabriel, Where are we in African Theology? In *African Theology en route: papers from the Pan-African Conference of Third World Theologians, Accra, December 17-23, 1977*, edited by K. Appiah-Kubi and S. Torres. Maryknoll, NY: Orbis, 1977), 64; Maluleke, Tinyiko S. 1997. "Half a century of African Christian theologies: elements of the emerging agenda for the twenty-first century." *Journal of Theology for Southern Africa* 99 (1997):4-23.

105. Malueke, "Half a Century of African Christian Theology, 13.

106. Randall Bailey puts the question slightly differently, but in a closely related sense,

when he argues "that unless one is aware of one's own cultural biases and interests in reading the text and appropriating the tradition, one may be seduced into adopting another culture, one which is diametrically apposed to one's own health and well-being" (Bailey 1998).

107. L.E Cady, "Hermeneutics and tradition: the role of the past in jurisprudence and theology," *Harvard Theological Journal* 79(1986):439-463; West, *Biblical Hermeneutics of Liberation*, 1-3-130.

108. Allan Boesak, *Black and Reformed: apartheid, liberation, and the Calvinist tradition*. (Johannesburg: Skotaville, 1984); Maimela, Simon. Black Theology and the quest for a God of liberation. In *Theology at the end of modernity: essays in honor of Gordon D. Kaufman*, edited by S. G. Devaney. (Philadelphia: Trinity Press, 1991).

109. T. Maluleke, "Black and African theologies in the New World Order: a time to drink from our own wells" *Journal of Theology for Southern Africa* 96 (1996):14.

110. Malueke, "Half a Century of Christian Theologies," 14-16.

111. See for example (Dube 1997; Masenya 1997; Mbuwayesango 1997; Sibeko and Haddad 1997).

112. Cited in Malueke, "Half a Century of Christian Theologies," 15.

113. Malueke, "Half a Century of Christians Theology,

114. Malueke, "Black and African Theologies," 13.

115. Mofokeng, 40.

116. Mofokeng, 41; Mosala, "The Use of the Bible," 184.

117. West, The *Academy of the Poor.*

118. West, The *Academy of the Poor, 89-107.*

119. Gerald O West. 2000c. Mapping African biblical interpretation: a tentative sketch. In *The Bible in Africa: transactions, trends and trajectories*, edited by G. O. West and M. W. Dube. Leiden: E.J. Brill, 2000), 47-49.

120. Tinyiko S. Malueke, "The Bible among African Christians: a missiological perspective." In *To cast fire upon the earth: Bible and mission collaborating in today's multicultural global context*, edited by T. Okure. Pietermaritzburg: Cluster Publications, 2000), 94-95; West, Gerald O. 1997b. On the eve of African biblical studies: trajectories and trends. *Journal of Theology for Southern Africa* 99 (1997):99-115.

121. Malueke, "The Bible among African Christians," 94-95.

122. Malueke, "The Bible among African Christians," 95.

123. West, Gerald O. and Musa W. Dube. *The Bible in Africa: transactions, trajectories and trends* (Leiden: E.J. Brill, 2000).

124. D. Tutu, *Hope and suffering: sermons and speeches.* (Johannesburg: Skotaville, 1983); Mbiti, African *Theology En route.*

125. Malueke, "The Bible among African Christians," 91-92.

126. In my opinion, there is much work still to be done by South African Black Theology; the foundations laid by the past thirty years of Black Theology are deep and fertile, and we ignore them at our peril. We certainly have to go

forward, but we are foolish if we imagine that we can do this without constantly returning to these important fonts. We may move beyond them, but they must remain to shape where and how we go forward.

127. I use inverted commas as a reminder that my problematising of the place of the Bible in Africans' appropriation of the missionary package may turn out to pose important questions about any unitary understanding of Christianity.

CHAPTER IV

SIBLINGS OR ANTAGONISTS? THE ETHOS OF BIBLICAL SCHOLARSHIP FROM THE NORTH ATLANTIC AND AFRICAN WORLDS

Grant LeMarquand[1]

Introduction

In the latter half of the twentieth century a new situation has emerged in the history of biblical scholarship. The existence of scholarly communities in Africa, Asia, and Latin America has made possible a truly international discussion. This paper will provide a brief overview to the ethos of biblical scholarship in both the North Atlantic and African contexts and then examine a proposal of one African biblical scholar, Justin Ukpong, whose advocacy of 'Inculturation Hermeneutics" provides useful avenues of discussion between scholars from differing contexts.

North Atlantic[2] Biblical scholarship

A common characteristic throughout the North Atlantic post-Enlightenment scholarly community, in all of its various disciplines, has been the desire or attempt to learn, describe or study the truth or reality as we experience it in a manner free from subjective bias. Such study was to be done in a way that one independent observer could verify the findings or conclusions of another scholar based upon his or her own observations. The reliability of a scholarly observation or conclusion was judged according to the reproducibility of the findings or evidence upon which the scholarly conclusion was based. Thus evidence-based, reproducible observations and assertions became the standard of North Atlantic scholarship. This was most clearly seen in the empirical method of scientific research,[3] in which this distancing from subjectivity was seen as a move towards gaining clear, objective and reliable insight into the object of study.

Concurrent with this general tendency within the North Atlantic scholarly world, biblical scholarship underwent a shift away from the individual and communal 'knowing' of the Bible as the word of God within the context of the church. In the 18th, 19th and into the 20th centuries, the scholarly biblical guild became more and more distant from ecclesiastical constraints. Study and critique were seen to have little to do with sacrament, worship, or prayer.

As North Atlantic biblical scholars came to see their task as separate from that of speaking for the churches, they have come to see their scholarly activity as related more to the secular academy.[4] The purpose of most of their writing is to contribute to the ongoing scholarly discussion of the ancient texts in the Bible or other texts and artifacts related to the 'biblical world.' Less attention is given to the more 'theological' task of clarifying 'the meaning of the word of God in scripture' or to the 'pastoral' task of 'encouraging the faithful.'

These North Atlantic universities and college-based biblical scholars have opted for a mode of 'knowing' the Bible primarily through the power of reason.[5] Biblical exegesis sought to adhere to a methodology that was neutral. Bias became synonymous with error. A shift from theocentric to anthropocentric dialogue and study became the inevitable correlate. For some this was simply either a limitation of what it meant to know and study the truth, or a liberation from the constraints of the church as an organization imposing its own objectives and its possible 'superstitious' embellishments. For others 'the inevitable march of progress.'[6] Modernity as the study of the objective world by a neutral observer became a guiding principle of research in the North Atlantic context.

One of the clearest expositions of this secular basis of biblical exegesis comes from the nineteenth- century German scholar William Wrede (1859-1906) for whom 'history' is the discipline which rules over the study of the 'New Testament':

> I do not intend to dwell on this question of principle for long, but I must state from the outset that my comments presuppose the strictly historical character of New Testament theology. The old doctrine of inspiration is recognized by academic theology, including very largely the conservative wing, to be untenable. For logical thinking there can be no middle position between inspired writings and

historical documents...How the systematic theologian gets on with
... [the] results [of Biblical theology] and deals with them – that is
his own affair. Like every other real science, New Testament
theology has its goal simply in itself, and is totally indifferent to all
dogma and systematic theology. What could dogmatics offer it?
Could dogmatics teach New Testament theology to see the facts
correctly? At most it could colour them. Could it correct the facts that
were found? To correct facts is absurd. Could it legitimize them?
Facts need no legitimation.[7]

Wrede goes on to argue that the language of 'New Testament theology'
itself is highly problematic: the New Testament documents are simply one
collection of some early Christian writings. The idea that they would be
canonical, that is, normative in some sense, is anachronistic. The idea that they
are any more 'apostolic' than other early Christian writings is untenable.
According to Wrede, the serious researcher, that is the scholar who is interested
in the history of early Christian texts, will recognize that there is no one unified
New Testament theology, but rather a variety of theologies (or, actually,
'religions'). Rather than find *a* New Testament theology, the researcher will
describe the history of early Christian religions and religious ideas, an
essentially anthropocentric task.

For many in the North Atlantic world, the position articulated by Wrede
won the day. In the secular world of biblical exegesis, faith, dogma and church
tradition had no power over the interpreter. Biblical interpretation became
historical-critical investigation as this was pursued by autonomous, reasonable,
individual (usually male) scholars of European universities. Interpretation of
texts that was not based on the canons of historical-critical research was often
denigrated as 'pre-critical' and 'unscientific': more in the realm of speculation,
devotion and the history of dogma than of textual study.[8]

In effect, the biblical guild edited out how other interests could be involved
in the task of interpreting the Bible. Its view of history necessarily became
narrowed. Historical study came to mean only the history of the text in its
ancient setting as this was understood according to the canons of modern critical
research. The scholarly task became confined to uncovering the past. It became
enough for scholars to attempt to describe the meaning of the text to its assumed
original authors and readers. Historical research came to be considered an
objective description of past events and ideas.

It is now more widely acknowledged that the reader of a text will bring his
or her own social location to the interpretative task. For many North Atlantic
scholars one's social location has been a cause of concern only in so far as it is
acknowledged that everyone who reads will necessarily have a bias. This bias is
usually considered a problematic reality and so many North Atlantic scholars
will, therefore, counsel that caution be taken not to read one's own bias into the
text. It is usually argued that the best way to avoid a biased reading is to pay
careful attention to the proper use of critical tools in exegesis. This is certainly
to be considered sage advice. However, the use of critical tools in historical

research is not a complete answer. First of all, the critical tools must still be employed by a particular reader who comes from a particular location. Tools do not necessarily guarantee objectivity. But secondly, and of more importance for our purposes, is the question of whether the discovery of an objective reading is a sufficient goal of biblical research. Often excluded in the traditional historical-critical paradigm is an analysis of the continuing history of the text in the lives of its varied contemporary readers. Readings which purport to be purely historical analyses often bracket the pragmatic implications of historical research. These implications are always present, of course, but they are often considered to be outside of the realm of the biblical scholar.

There are signs, however, that any broadly held consensus about historical-critical exegesis appears to be breaking down. There is presently a growing suspicion that the approach of scholars like Wrede was not entirely value-free, objective, and scientific. Wrede believed in the rather optimistic view that 'facts' are directly accessible if the serious scholar uses the right tools and approaches the text unencumbered by theological concerns. But according to some historical-critical exegesis of the type advocated by Wrede has resulted in a contraction of exegesis. Walter Wink points out that in contrast to the authors of biblical texts "bore witness to events which led them to faith," biblical critics have fostered an attitude of "detached neutrality [which] in matters of faith is not neutrality at all, but already a decision against responding."[9] The scholar who believes in 'the myth of detached neutrality,' which Wink refers to as "objectivism," can only pretend to be neutral since "the scholar, like everyone else, has racial, sexual, and class interests to which he is largely blind and which are unconsciously reflected in his work."[10] In its struggle to be free of theological and ecclesial constraints, historical biblical criticism has in fact cut itself off "from any community for whose life its results might be significant," by which Wink appears to mean the church and its members.[11] Clearly, Wink wants the biblical text and its interpretation to make a practical difference in peoples' lives.[12]

For many like Wink, although certainly not for all, the historical-critical approach which has characterized much of the history of North Atlantic historical-critical exegesis has been weighed in the balance and found wanting. The recognition that what a text is allowed to mean has been restricted by the methods employed in its investigation, has opened the doors to the present situation in biblical studies in which a bewildering variety of methodological approaches to biblical texts is practiced. For example, in recent years the investigation of the Bible as literature has received widespread attention. As Robert Alter and Frank Kermode wrote in 1987, "Over the past couple of decades...there has been a revival of interest in the literary qualities of these texts, in the virtues by which they continue to live as something other than archaeology."[13] The revival in "interest in the literary qualities" of biblical texts has been followed quickly by the emergence of canonical criticism, rhetorical criticism, and sociological and anthropological criticisms.

Even the meetings of academic biblical guilds show signs that questions of theology, of ideology and of culture are now issues that deserve to be (re)considered. No longer are meetings dominated exclusively by historical concerns. Discussions of the present meaning of texts are a regular part of every programme, for example, of the Society of Biblical Literature. The *1998 AAR/SBL Annual Meeting Program* listed (in addition to more traditional program units such as "Aramaic Studies," "Biblical Lexicography," "Greco-Roman Religions," and "Pauline Epistles") units that reflect in their very name a broadening of scholarly interest beyond philological and historical concerns: "Bible and Cultural Studies," "Ideological Criticism," "Women in the Biblical World," "African-American Theology and Biblical Interpretation," "Christian Theology and the Bible," "Character Ethics and Biblical Interpretation" and the "Bible in Africa, Asia, Latin America, and the Caribbean."[14] Although historical-critical study is still the dominant mode of biblical interpretation in the North Atlantic biblical guild, signs are beginning to emerge that point to the growing importance of questions other than the traditional historical-critical ones. Indeed, even within any group of scholars interested in the historical study of 'Q' or 'Paul' there will be a wide variety of interests, approaches and commitments. A cursory investigation of a sample of the plethora of recent studies of the 'historical Jesus,' for example, will uncover not only a variety of historical assessments, but also a wide difference in the political, theological and ideological commitments underlying the different academic investigations.

In other words, the multiplicity of methods being used by scholars may point to some dissatisfaction with the constraints of the dominant paradigm. For many this appears to have opened fresh questions related to epistemology and hermeneutics. What does it mean to say that we understand a text? What does 'knowing' a text mean? Is knowledge simply a matter of having power over a text? That is, is knowledge a matter of mastery, a matter of conquering a passage, so that we can now say that we have subdued it and now have dominion over it?[15] Or is knowing a text also a matter of gaining wisdom for life, a matter of being fed and strengthened by a text

After centuries in which religious hierarchies claimed exclusive rights to the interpretation of the Bible, and after the modern period in which the historical critic was the authority, the issue of whose text this is has come to the surface. It has become clear that biblical scholars have a variety of commitments which they bring to the text. The postmodern situation denies that there is any neutral, god's-eye view from which a scholar can have a clear perspective on the true meaning of a text. As the centrality of historical-critical scholarship has been questioned, a variety of new 'voices' have emerged seeking to bring their own perspectives to the text and claiming that their ways of 'knowing' deserve a hearing. The guild is beginning to listen to the voices of those who speak of the text from perspectives that deeply question what had been the modernist consensus in biblical scholarship. The voices of feminist readers, North Atlantic racial minority readers and liberationist readers, especially from Latin America, are already well known in the North Atlantic scholarly world.

Readers from sub-Saharan Africa, however, are less well known in the North Atlantic world. Although the voices of African scholars have not as yet received much attention outside of Africa, their contributions have the potential to contribute to the emerging global scholarly discussion by putting the question of the practical relevance of biblical interpretation squarely on the table. For African scholars investigation of an ancient biblical text must make a difference in peoples' lives; the text must be read with a view to its implications for living.

African Biblical Scholarship

Current academic African exegesis[16] has emerged in contexts in which the questions of North Atlantic culture, questions of modernity and postmodernity, are discussed not by those who consider themselves to have benefited from the modern world but by those who perceive themselves to be modernity's victims. Modernity, seen from the vantage point of one of its most noted landmarks, the 'discovery' of the Americas by Columbus in 1492, has for Africa, as for the rest of the 'third world,'[17] not been a time of discovering and conquering, but a time of being conquered and dominated.[18]

For Africa in particular, the emergence of a well-defined North Atlantic worldview known as 'modernity' coincided with its invasion by slavers,[19] explorers and colonizers,[20] and missionaries.[21] Africa was dragged into a modern age which was not of its own making and which appears to have been little to its benefit. In most parts of the continent the postcolonial aftermath of Africa's complicated modern history has been a perceived loss of African identity, almost constant political upheaval, continuous economic chaos, wars, political assassinations, widespread malnutrition, lack of education and woefully inadequate health care. According to John Pobee, a New Testament scholar from Ghana,

> Of course there are pockets of poverty in the so-called affluent Northern hemisphere. But poverty in Africa is pervasive and acute. Although there is a small rich elite in every African country, the general run of the people are poor. Everywhere there are signs of the unfulfilled if exaggerated aspirations of the people at independence vis-à-vis decent living standards and security for the future. Large-scale poverty, suffering and degradation mark the continent.
>
> These indices of poverty are as much the result of Africa being assimilated to the North, being treated as the 'backyard' of the nations of the North, as self-inflicted through bad planning and ruthless power-drunk African leaders who have no qualms in 'raping' their own people. Abuses of human dignity are much in evidence everywhere in Africa. Poverty and marginalization then are experienced at the gut level.[22]

The emergence of postcolonial African states has not meant the emergence of African peoples who feel at home with modernity. Even if they do not always function well, African nations do have many of the trappings of the modern North Atlantic world, modern modes of transportation and communication, political, military and legal systems, schools, newspapers and hospitals. Africa has benefited (and suffered) from some of the products of the modern world. Although there have been many changes in Africa in the past century, not all of them could be considered 'progress'. And in many ways Africa has resisted modernity-especially in its religious sensibilities. The North Atlantic perception of the world has little room for God. This is not so in Africa. For most Africans, religion was and still is central to life in all of its dimensions. The universe is not a system closed to the supernatural or the sacred, but is a well-populated place in which ancestors, divinities, and spirits play important roles in day to day living.

The recent history of Africa includes a thriving Christianity.[23] Mission-founded churches, Protestant, Roman Catholic, and Orthodox are found in virtually every city, town and village south of the Sahara. Even more prolific has been the growth of African instituted churches.[24] Some of these churches are groups that have broken away from or have been expelled from mission-founded churches. Many have grown up entirely independent of any other denomination, often called into being by a prophetic leader. These groups are attractive because they are perceived as more authentically African, especially as they incorporate or allow such elements into church life as African music and dancing and tolerance of African forms of family life, and encourage religious practices such as exorcism, healing rituals, divination, prophecy and vision. After many years of discouraging such practices, the mission-founded churches have now begun to learn from African instituted churches and to include some of these same emphases in their own life.

As we saw above in our discussion of the North Atlantic context of exegesis, biblical exegesis does not take place in a vacuum. The social, political, religious and cultural location of the scholar will inevitably have an impact on the shape of the scholarship produced. In particular, the life of the African churches has a strong pull on the African biblical scholar.

But the African scholar is pulled in more than one direction. On the one hand, biblical exegetes in Africa feel the compulsion to interpret the biblical text in the light of the present realities of the African situation. On the other hand, most professional scholarly African biblical interpreters received much of their graduate training in the North Atlantic world, training which focused on the methods and concerns of North Atlantic historical-critical scholarship. Most African exegetes are grateful for their training in the North Atlantic historical critical tradition. Emmanuel Obeng has even argued that if African scholars are to be taken seriously at home and across the world they will need to pay more attention to the precise use of critical tools.[25]

This does not mean, however, that Africans are willing simply to mimic the academic traditions of the North. In the preface to her doctoral thesis, Teresa Okure makes clear reference to the North Atlantic world's lack of openness to new methods of reading biblical texts.[26] In particular the tendency of the North Atlantic tradition to treat the Bible more as a book rooted in the past than as a book which speaks to the present comes under scrutiny from most African scholars.

Samuel Abogunrin's assessment of the North Atlantic critical scholarship in which he was trained is that it lacks power. "Genuine biblical criticism helps us to appreciate the works of the Bible writers better," he says.[27] He argues, however, that there is a danger that the modern views of North Atlantic scholarship may blur the vision of African scholars. African scholars need something that the North Atlantic world could not provide.

> The [African] Biblical scholar requires a spiritual perception that will allow him to translate the Bible in such a way that the Word will become incarnate once again in the language and life of the peoples of Africa. O. Imasogie correctly remarks that by the time Christianity was introduced into Black Africa, the worldview of Western Christian theologians only retained a veneer of Biblical worldview. The missionary worldview had by then become what he called quasi-scientific. Consequently, although the missionaries still talked about God, heaven, angels, Satan, Holy Spirit and evil forces, they were no more than cultural crutches that lacked the existential dynamism they once had before and during the medieval period. Under this type of influence, the theologian thinks it necessary to re-interpret Biblical references to angels, demon possession and spiritual forces. As a result, Christian missionaries emphasized the power of Jesus to save from the power of sin but Christ's power which destroys the power of the devil was not enthusiastically preached.[28]

African biblical scholars must not repeat the mistakes of the West, he says, in emptying Jesus of his power.

There are some North Atlantic scholars who have shown an interest in what Africa can contribute to the scholarly investigation of the Bible. Knut Holter, for example, notes that "In contact with African Old Testament scholars and scholarship I have met new and intriguing questions and approaches to the Old Testament, questions and approaches that have enriched my own understanding of the Old Testament as such, but also of what Old Testament scholarship is all about."[29] Speaking of the Old Testament in particular, Holter notes that the translation of the Bible into African languages has "coincided with what we would call the aspect of recognition. African readers have in the poetry, laws, and narratives of the Old Testament, recognized aspects of their own tradition and situation."[30] This dimension of African research – that African perspectives may open North Atlantic scholars to aspects of the Bible that have been missed - could prove fruitful. Of more importance perhaps is that African readings point to practical implications of the biblical text that North Atlantic scholars often bracket out.

According to Gerald West, the readings of 'ordinary' Africans, by which he means readers who are not biblical scholars and, in particular, readers who are from poor and marginalized communities, can be of help to scholars. 'Ordinary' readers, he says, "read for purposes other than the production of academic papers – they read for survival, liberation, and life."[31] Speaking largely to a North Atlantic audience, West says that scholarship should learn from this kind of reading and develop an ethos of reading which is open to the problems of those who suffer. This has not always or often been central to the scholarly pursuits of academic biblical exegetes.

> Usually the connection between our work as scholars and our life commitments is covert, and if our work is to be used by others we want to remain in control. But clearly the interface [of scholars and readers from poor and marginalized communities] ...demands an overt connection between our biblical research and our social commitments. This requires something of a conversion 'from below'. Biblical scholars must be born 'from below'.[32]

African scholars themselves have had to experience this kind of rebirth. Justin Ukpong sums up the situation well.

> Trained as they have been in the tradition of western biblical scholarship, [African biblical scholars] read the Bible through an interpretive grid developed in the western culture, and then seek to apply the result in their own contexts. One outcome of this has been a visible gap between this academic reading of the Bible and the needs of ordinary African Christians. Another outcome has been the fact that in many ways African social and cultural concerns are not reflected in such reading. All this has happened in spite of the fact that African scholars do bring their own cultural perspectives to bear on the text. The fact is that so long as the grid through which they read the text is foreign, their own cultural input is bound to have a highly limited impact. Not a few African biblical scholars, in recent times, have been exercised by this situation. Many indeed have begun to view critically, against their own background and life experience of African people, the tradition of biblical scholarship in which they were trained. This has resulted in a call for a new mode of reading the Bible that would engage the African social and cultural contexts in the process.[33]

West argues that the resources are already present for African scholars to take up the task of a contextualized reading of the Bible that will be of relevance to Africa. Unfortunately some in Africa have relied too exclusively on North Atlantic traditions and methods.

> How can we 'drink from our own wells' when we denigrate them or deny their very existence and rely on imported, bottled water (or

worse Coca Cola)? Perhaps ordinary African 'readers' can help us to
recover readings of the Bible that our training blinds us to.[34]

The conditions in which most African scholars must work are frustrating
and demanding.[35] It is a great temptation for many of these scholars to move to
Europe or North America where their scholarly contributions are welcomed as
interesting and exotic, and where they are able to find more time, more money,
and more resources for producing their scholarly work. For the many scholars
who remain in Africa, the production of scholarly work has been concomitant
with unwillingness to bracket out the suffering that is a daily part of their own
lives and the lives of those around them. Scholarly work must maintain a
pragmatic dimension.

Inculturation Hermeneutics

An excellent example of an approach to interpretation which attempts to
integrate historical insights into African contexts is laid out by Justin Ukpong[36]
in his 1995 article entitled "Rereading the Bible with African Eyes: Inculturation
and Hermeneutics." According to Ukpong, this method of reading the Bible "is
not a return to a literal reading of the Bible, but a reading that … [is] critical in
its own paying attention to the African socio-cultural context and the questions
that arise therefrom."[37] Ukpong argues that this method does not need to be a
specifically "African" method: "any socio-cultural context can become the
subject of interpretation."[38] Indeed, the contemporary discourse of African
exegesis, of which Ukpong will serve as our example, has never been entirely
separate from the North Atlantic conversation. However, it can be argued that
the African conception of life as a unity actually enables African scholars to
hold together the various dimensions of interpretation – historical, theological,
and practical – in a way that is distinct from the North Atlantic view of life as
compartmentalized and scholarship as specialized.

Ukpong's method contains five distinct features: "an *interpreter* in a certain
context making meaning of a *text* using a specific *conceptual framework* and its
procedure."[39] We will examine each of these features in turn.

The first element of Ukpong's 'inculturation hermeneutic' is the *interpreter*.
In focusing on the reader, Ukpong agrees that his way of reading has much in
common with that group of reading theories which is not only concerned about
the literary qualities of the text itself, or the history behind the text (the historical
event recorded, the author's intentions), but also about the reader of the text as a
dynamic part of the reading process.[40] According to Ukpong, however, the
interpreter should not be understood as an isolated reader, but as a "reader-in-
context," that is as someone who is or has become an insider to the culture for
whom the interpretation is being given.[41] This insider reader should be both
sympathetic to the culture and able to be critical of it at the same time. The
insider knowledge of the culture that the reader possesses should give rise to

certain "biases in the interpreter's mind as he/she approaches the biblical text." These biases are acknowledged and capable of being used positively.[42]

Ukpong's view of the interpreter's role in the hermeneutical process is reminiscent of Michael Polanyi's idea of "personal knowledge." In his critique of scientific detachment as an ideal, Polanyi argues that the subject is always involved in the process of knowing, even in a scientific context.[43] Speaking of Einstein's theory of relativity Polanyi notes,

> We cannot truly account for our acceptance of such theories without endorsing our acknowledgement of a beauty that exhilarates and a profundity that entrances us. Yet the prevailing conception of science, based on the disjunction of subjectivity and objectivity, seeks – and must seek at all costs – to eliminate from science such passionate, personal, human appraisals of theories, or at least to minimize their function to that of a negligible by-play. For modern man has set up as the ideal of knowledge the conception of natural science as a set of statements which is 'objective' in the sense that its substance is entirely determined by observation, even while its presentation may be shaped by convention.[44]

This detached 'modern' view of knowledge assumes that all truth is observable, which is, ironically, a non-observable assumption. Contrary to this, Polanyi speaks of knowledge as 'personal knowledge.' All factual knowledge, he says, is "shaped" by the knower: "the act of knowing includes an appraisal; and this personal co-efficient, which shapes all factual knowledge, bridges in doing so the disjunction between subjectivity and objectivity."[45] Tools, which are an aid to scientific investigation, do not negate the subject who uses the tools, since tools are simply an extension of the investigator. "While we rely on a tool or a probe, these are not handled as external objects...We pour ourselves into them and assimilate them as parts of our own existence."[46]

By implication, then, biblical scholars cannot simply detach themselves from their investigation any more than the scientist can. The tools of biblical critical methodology do not provide the scholar with an objectivity that gives him or her uncommitted detachment. The scholar is still personally responsible for the exegetical decisions made using those tools. The tools of biblical criticism are, rather, an extension of the critic. Nor are the tools themselves above criticism. A scientist or a biblical scholar may engage in a perfectly legitimate task, but come to an erroneous decision by using the wrong tool.[47]

For Ukpong, the interpreter is a participant in the process of interpretation. There is no neutral detachment. Personal and social factors such as the reader's race, gender, status in society, all give an interpreter an angle of vision that can be used in the process of understanding a biblical text.

The second feature of Ukpong's theory highlights another facet of African exegesis: the *context*. By 'context' Ukpong here refers to the context of the reader, rather than the original context of the text being read. In using the term 'context,' Ukpong is pointing to the reality of the African reader as part of a community. Indeed, African personal identity is often described in specifically communitarian terms. For example, the expression, coined by John Mbiti, I am because we are,"[48] stands in contradistinction to the post-Enlightenment (Cartesian) individualistic worldview. A specifically African understanding of personal identity in terms of community identifies the reader of the text as the community. The North Atlantic reader tends to be identified as an individual. For Ukpong, context "refers to an existing human community (a country, local church, ethnic group) designated as the subject of the interpretation" which is informed by "the people's worldview, and historical, social, economic, political and religious life experiences."[49] As human communities "perceive reality from particular, not from universal perspectives,"[50] the inculturation hermeneutic is always contextual in that it is always "*consciously* done from the perspective of a particular context."[51] Ukpong appeals to David Tracy who says "There is no innocent interpretation, no innocent interpreter, no innocent text."[52] The interpreter can only be honest, therefore, if the concerns of his or her context are consciously brought into the hermeneutical dialogue.

This means that one aspect of the scholarly task is to ask how a particular text or a particular reading of a text interacts with, responds to, and is reflective of the lives of those who read or hear that text. African biblical exegetes must ask 'so what?' The question of the practical meaning of a piece of research for the community from which the interpreter comes cannot ultimately be avoided. Contemporary concerns of many North Atlantic scholars are often left unstated, inchoate, and may sometimes be unknown even to the scholar herself or himself. Some scholars, no doubt, are hesitant to state their concerns because the explicit revelation of personal commitment to a particular community may appear to relativize the objective appearance of the academic project. And so this aspect of exegesis, the contextual dimension of research, is often neglected or suppressed in North Atlantic scholarship. This does not mean that the contextual dimensions of a particular reading of a text are not present. But they may be unrecognized. They do, however, constitute the substructure on which the exegetical edifice is built. According to Ukpong, scholars cannot and should not avoid the contextual implications of exegesis.

The third feature of Ukpong's method is *text*. This text has at least three dimensions: it is an ancient text, it is a literary text, and it is a transformative text.

The Bible is a book of the past. "Because the Bible as an ancient document, attention to the historical context of the text being interpreted is demanded of the exegete. This requires the use of historical critical tools."[53] An ancient text arose from a particular socio-cultural context. Therefore, any analysis must include a historical investigation in order to determine "the specific orientation of the text…without which it is not possible to make a clear assessment of the biblical 'world' that made the text meaningful in the first instance."[54]

As well as the historical axis, the African exegete must also be aware of the literary context of a passage. The structures, rhetoric, narrative features and inner logic are necessary components in understanding a text.

The Bible is also a text which has the potential to transform the lives of its readers. Therefore, as well as elucidating the meaning of the text in its original setting, the scholar must also discuss the text's contemporary meaning. In other words, whereas most North Atlantic scholars consider the historical task to be primary, African and other third world scholars engage in history as a means to an end. They use the study of the past as a tool for the transformation of the present. The Bible is not of interest only because it is an ancient document, but because this ancient document is perceived to have the potential to transform the world for the better.[55]

For Ukpong, who is a Roman Catholic Priest, the contemporary relevance of the biblical text is found precisely in its theological meaning. "[B]ecause it is the theological meaning of the text that is sought and not its historical context, historical critical tools are used precisely as servant and not as master."[56] The goal of the interpretation of a text is to discover what Ukpong calls the "gospel message." By "gospel message" Ukpong means that particular word from God for the community of readers, as it emerges in the dialogue between the reader, his or her context and the particular text under discussion. As this message emerges, it may serve as a critique of the culture or the culture may throw light on the text.[57] According to Ukpong, this is not something which can or should be done only by Africans. African scholars who engage in this task, however, will find the 'gospel message' to be of relevance to Africa because that message emerges from a dialogue between the text and the (African) reader. For Ukpong, then, the practical implications of a particular passage of the Bible only emerge for the scholar who is in relationship – in relationship with the community which needs to hear the message, and in relationship with the God of the community who is also the God who speaks through the Bible.[58]

In Africa, practical issues and the personal involvement of the scholar in the production of meaning cannot be bracketed out of the exegetical process. Exegeses produced in situations which are often desperate consider the cultivation of an ethos of detached objectivity to be a luxury. Already in 1976, at the first meeting of the Ecumenical Association of Third World Theologians (EATWOT), scholars from Africa, Asia and Latin America joined in speaking against a form of theological (including biblical) scholarship that did not take seriously the realities of life in the Third World:

> [Theologies from Europe and North America] must be understood to have arisen out of situations related to those countries, and therefore must not be uncritically adopted without our raising the question of their relevance in the context of our countries. Indeed, we must, in order to be faithful to the gospel and to our peoples, reflect on the realities of our own situations and interpret the word of God in relation to these realities. We reject as irrelevant an academic type of theology that is divorced from action. We are prepared for a radical break in epistemology which makes commitment the first act of theology and engages in critical reflection on the praxis of the reality of the Third World.[59]

In Africa, the scholar considers himself or herself to be engaged not only with the text, but also with the people who, in their struggle to attain justice, peace, prosperity, and health, see biblical insight as a necessary component in their transformation. As in the biblical story of the people of Israel at Mt. Horeb, the 'word of God' is not addressed to their ancestors only, but to them directly (Deut 5:1-4). As we shall see, one reason that the pragmatics of interpretation will not be buried is that African exegesis must be seen to serve immediate needs. African biblical scholarship is not neutral. It has as its goal the emergence and enhancement of "survival, liberation and life."[60] According to Ukpong, African scholars neither can nor should avoid the contextual implications of exegesis, because the purpose of investigating a text is to allow the 'gospel message' "to transform and forge history."[61]

The fourth feature of Ukpong's 'inculturation hermeneutic' is what he calls the *exegetical conceptual framework*. The exegetical framework, says Ukpong, is that "mental construct within which exegetes are trained. It is basically an orientation in biblical interpretation geared towards certain areas of concern about the biblical text."[62] Ukpong gives historical criticism, literary criticism and liberation hermeneutics as examples of possible conceptual frameworks. According to Ukpong, current frameworks have not proved satisfactory in Africa. Alluding to Thomas S. Kuhn's theory of paradigm shifts in science,[63] Ukpong argues that Africa needed a conceptual framework different from those usually practiced in the North Atlantic world, because of "questions and issues arising from the African Christian experience with the Bible which our current exegetical frameworks are unable to satisfactorily handle."[64] Ukpong himself argues that the historical critical method is found wanting in an African context because this method, is "derived from the basic assumptions of a particular culture."[65]

> Thus, for example, one cannot think of the emergence of the historical critical method without thinking of Deism, Rationalism and the Enlightenment as its cultural (intellectual culture) context, and the History of Religions movement as its methodological mentor. Nor can one think of the allegorical framework of biblical interpretation of the early church Fathers without reference to the ancient Greek literary culture of the times in which these Fathers were trained.[66]

Ukpong does not condemn either historical criticism or allegory. His linking of these methods with their cultural contexts, however, does relativize any method. Ukpong thus finds historical criticism, as the dominant mode of exegesis in this era, problematic because the assumptions which underlie this method are not commonly received assumptions in Africa. An African inculturation hermeneutic, therefore, must be aware of the basic assumptions of African peoples. This leads Ukpong to attempt a brief enumeration of African assumptions.

This is no simple task. Ukpong is aware that any description of "Africa" will be defective. Africa contains a "multiplicity" of cultures and worldviews. Ukpong does think it possible, however, to name certain features which appear to be common across the board in Africa and to argue that these common features point to the "root paradigm" of African cultures.[67] Ukpong names four aspects of African life that he believes belong to the root paradigm of African cultures.

The first aspect has to do with the nature of the world, the question of "where are we?" Ukpong says that Africans do not make a distinction between matter and spirit, secular and religious. Rather, life is viewed as a unity. There is a distinction, however, between the visible world and the invisible world. Every person has a visible and an invisible dimension. The dead do not cease to be, they have moved into a different sphere of existence whence they impact our visible dimension of reality. Spirits, both good and evil, also interact with the visible world.

The second feature of African life is that this two-dimensional universe has a divine origin. God is the Creator of the world and God continues to be involved in the creation. Because there is a network of relationships between God, humanity and the rest of the cosmos, human actions are not isolated events. Rather, every human action is a social event, affecting relationships not only with one another, but with God and with the rest of nature.

Related to this is the third feature: the African answer to the question "who are we?" The answer is, "we are a community." Since the creation is a network of interrelations, "African authors see the Cartesian dictum *cogito ergo sum* (I think therefore I exist) replaced in the African thought system by *cognato ergo sum* (I am related by blood/I belong to a family, therefore I exist.)" This communal view of humanity has a multitude of implications. There is no such thing as a 'private' matter in Africa.

> Problems and issues in the community are seen and treated not as a function of the actions of and dispositions of the individuals concerned, but primarily as a function of the relationships within the community. Thus, for example, a person is not considered rich through his/her ingenuity and industry alone but through sharing in the blessings of the community. Death and illness are explained not in terms of natural causes but in terms of negative forces, like witchcraft, in the community.[68]

The final African assumption noted by Ukpong is that Africa has an emphasis "on the concrete rather than the abstract, on the practical rather than theoretical."[69] Although Ukpong leaves this point without explanation, this pragmatic dimension of African life has obvious implications for African exegesis: the relevance of scholarship must be made obvious for the task to be considered worthwhile.

Having elucidated what he takes to be the basic cultural assumptions of Africa, Ukpong moves on to explain how these assumptions will operate in his understanding of the process of inculturation hermeneutics. His explanation appears to focus especially on two interrelated issues: the tension between the Bible as an ancient book and the need to find a present meaning; and the tension between historical critical tools and the Bible as a sacred religious book. For Ukpong the goal of exegesis is "to actualize the theological meaning of the text in a contemporary context."[70] Since the Bible is an ancient text, historical tools must be used. However, the task is not completed when the historical meaning is discovered. Since the goal is finding the contemporary theological meaning, the historical tools must always be seen "as servant not as master."[71] The present meaning of the text will emerge in the interaction between the ancient text and the contemporary context. This discovery of the present meaning, however, must be done from a perspective of faith. "Inculturation hermeneutics sees the Bible as a document of faith and therefore demands entry into and sharing the faith of the biblical community expressed in the text." Part of the 'faith of the biblical community' appears to be that the presence in the text "of the supernatural and the miraculous is taken for granted."[72]

Ukpong acknowledges that the text is "plurivalent." This does not mean, however, that the text can mean whatever the reader wishes it to mean. Two limits are put on 'plurivalency'. The first is the canon: "any meaning must be judged in the light of the meaning of the entire Bible." The second is something like the rule of faith: "the theology of any text must be judged against the basic biblical affirmations and principles" such as "the existence of God as creator and sustainer of the universe, love of God and neighbour, etc."[73] Ukpong's language seems to imply that the reading of a particular text is to be judged by its conformity to, or tension with the overall thrust of the biblical message seen as an entirety. Just as an African individual is known in relation to his community, so a biblical passage is only truly 'known' in relation to the whole 'book'. Ukpong further attempts to define "basic biblical affirmations" by which to judge a particular reading in a manner similar to Jesus' use of Torah in his critique of the Pharisees in Matthew's gospel. In Mt 23:23-24, Jesus judges the Pharisees' reading of scripture by appealing to the spirit of the whole of the Torah, as opposed to an atomistic exegesis which neglects the "weightier matters" of Torah.

It is not entirely clear how the limits of 'canon' and 'rule of faith' function for Ukpong. In Ukpong's use of these two limits as a 'standard' by which the validity of a particular reading of the text can be judged, it is not clear, at times, whether it is the interpretation or the text itself which is being judged. What is clear is that Ukpong believes that there are theological limits to exegesis.

The fifth and final element of Ukpong's inculturation hermeneutics is his procedure. According to Ukpong there must be "a preliminary condition and a series of four steps of analysis."[74] The preliminary condition is commitment to the Christian faith and to the process of "actualizing the Christian message with the context" of people's lives, in this case, in Africa. In other words, who does the exegesis is as important as the steps of analysis that the exegete will use. For Ukpong, inculturation hermeneutics is not a neutral enterprise. Inculturation hermeneutics excludes those who are not engaged with the faith of the church and committed to the task of incarnating that faith in a particular place. Ukpong does not make class, gender or racial exclusions here.[75] These distinctions are not critical. Commitment, however, is critical.

The first step in the actual exegetical process is to identify a dynamic correspondence between the reader's current context and the historical context of a biblical passage.[76] This, of course, implies that the exegete has some knowledge both of the contemporary context and of the text. Given this, the scholar engaging in inculturation hermeneutics must seek to find the common ground between the two. In a study of Lk 16:1-13, for example, Ukpong finds that Luke's gospel speaks of the "rich" in largely negative terms. In Ukpong's reading, the rich man in this parable has no doubt become rich because of an exploitative economic system which gave him the advantages he needed to acquire wealth. Seeing a similar disparity of wealth in the exploitative economic system at work in Africa, he brings the text and the context together.

> The cultural context informing this biblical interpretation is primarily that of exploited peasant farmers of West Africa as well as the concerns of the international debt burden of the Two-Thirds World. While most interpretations have read the parable from the perspective of the rich man's economic system, this article reads the story from the perspective of the peasant farmers in the story.[77]

Ukpong does not limit his work to the socio-economic, however. Any text whose historical context appears analogous to an African idea or situation would be considered appropriate material for the inculturation hermeneutics project.[78]

Step two in Ukpong's procedure is analysis of the context of interpretation. The (contemporary) background against which the text will be read must be analyzed from as many different perspectives as necessary: socio-anthropologically, historically, socially and religiously. For a reading of Lk 16:1-13, for example, the African exegete must acquire some knowledge of peasant conditions in West Africa. To do an African reading of Leviticus, one should undertake an investigation of African sacrificial rituals and ideas and so on.

The third step is an historical analysis of the biblical text. Ukpong does not often differ from the majority of North Atlantic scholars in his use of specific historical-critical tools. The difference is that many North Atlantic scholars would consider exegesis complete after just this one step – an end in and of itself. For Ukpong historical analysis is important, but in his method it is relativized by being only a part of a larger process.

Ukpong's fourth step is "analysis of the text in the light of the already analyzed contemporary context."[79] If the goal of exegesis is "to actualize the theological meaning of the text in a contemporary context" then this step moves the reader toward that goal by putting questions to the text "arising from insights gained from the analysis of the context of interpretation in order to gain insight into the nature of the text in relation to the context."[80] For example, if Nigeria's ecological system is threatened by an inefficient political system which allows an oil pipe line to leak unchecked, one of the things the biblical scholar must do is bring the question of the care of the creation to the biblical text to see if there is insight to be gained for that current Nigerian situation.[81]

The final step of the procedure is not only to draw together the fruits of this analysis in a coherent fashion, but also to express "a commitment to actualizing the message of the text in concrete life situation."[82] In other words, engagement with the text alone is insufficient. The scholar must also be engaged with the community. Because "the Bible is life-oriented" exegesis must lead to the transformation of the scholar into an activist and to the transformation of the community in the light of scripture.[83]

Ukpong is not doctrinaire about the order of his procedures and steps. However, his method clearly exemplifies the African demand that biblical scholarship intrude into areas of research that, in the North Atlantic world, are often left to scholars of other fields. For Ukpong, however, the integrity of the discipline of biblical studies demands more than the single focus of a narrow specialization. The scholar must become involved in whatever area is demanded by the material of the text, precisely because the material he or she studies is 'life-oriented.' Neither the text nor the context leaves the scholar with the option of delegation, compartmentalization or narrow specialization. This would be an abdication of responsibility.

For many years the dominant model of biblical scholarship in the North Atlantic world has been historical-critical. In this model the text is studied as one part of the evidence to be used in the reconstruction of a world of the past. The emergence of African biblical studies with its much more pragmatic concern for the present world appears to be at odds with North Atlantic scholarship. Justin Ukpong's 'inculturation hermeneutic' provides a model that may help North Atlantic and African scholars to begin a conversation about ways the Bible can and should be read in and for the 21st century world.

Endnotes

1.　This article was originally published in an abridged form in African Journal of Biblical Studies XIX (Nov. 2003) 2: 23-29.

2.　For the purposes of this essay 'North Atlantic' refers to Europe and North America, that part of the world which produced and experienced the intellectual impact of the Enlightenment, and which was transformed by the Industrial Revolution. Because they tend to approach research in the same way as Europe and North America, Australia, New Zealand and to some extent Japan, may be added to this group. In many works this world is referred to as the 'West'. Designations such as 'Western' or 'North Atlantic' are, of course, inaccurate generalizations.

3.　See, for example, the opinion of John Dewey (*Reconstruction in Philosophy* [New York: Henry Holt, 1929], 48): "there is a growing belief in the power of individual minds, guided by methods of observation, experience and reflection, to attain the truths needed for the guidance of life."

4.　The churches themselves have also undergone a shift in focus. From at least the time of Schleiermacher theology itself has moved towards being anthropocentric. It has become a discipline which investigates the religious experience of believers rather than the self-revelation of God. The shift to a more anthropocentric emphasis within the churches is related to the fact that much North Atlantic training of clergy now takes place in academic institutions in one way or another related to the secular university.

5.　See, for example, the essays in Hans Dieter Betz, ed. *The Bible as a Document of the University* (Chico, CA: Scholars Press, 1981).

6.　Dewey (Reconstruction, 49): "The patient and experimental study of nature, bearing fruit in inventions which control nature and subdue her forces to social use, is the method by which progress is made."

7.　Quoted from William Wrede, "The Task and Methods of 'New Testament Theology" in Robert Morgan, ed. and trans. *The Nature of New Testament Theology: The Contribution of William Wrede and Adolf Schlatter* SBT (second series), 25 (London: SCM, 1973), 69.

8.　This is the reason most histories of interpretation focus almost exclusively on the modern period. See, for example, William Baird, *History of New Testament Research. Volume One: From Deism to Tübingen* (Minneapolis: Fortress, 1992); Werner Georg Kümmel, *The New Testament: The History of the Investigation of its Problems* S. McLean Gilmour and Howard C. Kee, trans. (Nashville / New York: Abingdon Press, 1970); Stephen Neill and Tom Wright, *The Interpretation of the New Testament 1861-1986* (Oxford / New York: Oxford University Press, 1988); John K. Riches, *A Century of New Testament Study* (Valley Forge, PA: Trinity Press International, 1993.

9.　Walter Wink, *The Bible in Human Transformation: Toward a New Paradigm for Biblical Study* (Philadelphia: Fortress, 1973).

10.　Ibid, 7.

11.　Ibid, 10.

12. Whether Wink's particular interest in Jungian interpretation is helpful is not our primary concern here.

13. "General Introduction" pp.1-35 in *The Literary Guide to the Bible* (Cambridge, MA: The Belknap Press of Harvard University Press, 1987), 1-2.

14. For a discussion of the first four years of this group (1990-1993, then known as "Bible in Africa, Asia, and Latin America Group"), see Phyllis Bird, "Authority and Context in the Interpretation of Biblical Texts" Neotestamentica 28/2 (1994): 323-37; recent papers presented at the SBL group have been published in R.S. Sugirtharaja, ed. *The Postcolonial Bible* (Sheffield: Sheffield Academic Press, 1998).

15. "Knowledge is power' was the famous axiom expressed by Francis Bacon, the formulator of the 'scientific method' of inductive experimentation still used in research today. René Descartes wrote in 1637 (*Discourse on Method,* chapter 6, in *Essential Works of Descartes*, trans. Lowell Bair [New York: Bantam, 1961], 37) of the need for a 'practical' philosophy as opposed to the merely speculative, enabling humanity to become "the masters and possessors of nature." This view of the relationship between knowledge and praxis was and is widespread in the post-Enlightenment, scientific and philosophical communities. Knowledge was translated into action and action was oriented to control and dominion. The post-Enlightenment world has applied this understanding of knowledge to every area of life – including viewing knowledge of texts as having a 'mastery' over them.

16. There was, of course, a long and influential tradition of biblical interpretation on the continent of Africa dating back to ancient times. Exegetes like Origen and Augustine continue to influence the world's churches even today. This work will focus on biblical interpretation as it has emerged in sub-Saharan Africa in the modern, largely postcolonial, period.

17. There are no satisfactory designations for that large part of the world, mostly in the Southern Hemisphere, that is characterized as the 'third world.' The term arose during the so-called 'Cold War' in which "newly independent countries refused to line up behind the communist East or the capitalist West. In 1955 representatives from twenty-nine of these countries met at the famous Bandung Conference, the first of many conferences of 'nonaligned' nations. It was there that the term 'Third World' was born, as a description of this newly politically independent section of the world." (William A. Dyrness, *Learning about Theology from the Third World* [Grand Rapids: Zondervan, 1990], 12-13). In spite of this history it is still difficult for many to hear the term 'third world' without hearing connotations of 'third rate.' The term 'developing world' may be even worse, assuming that the North Atlantic context sets the pattern towards which all other nations should aspire. In recent years some 'third world' scholars have begun using the term 'Two-Thirds World,' and defining that term as that region of the world which is characterized largely by "poverty, powerlessness and religious pluralism." (See Vinay Samuel and Chris Sugden, eds. *Sharing Jesus in the Two Thirds World: Evangelical Christologies from the contexts of poverty, powerlessness and religious pluralism. The Papers of the First Conference of Evangelical Mission Theologians from the Two Thirds World. Bangkok, Thailand, March 22-25, 1982* [Bangalore: Partners in Mission-Asia, 1983]).

18. Brian Walsh and Richard Middleton, *Truth is Stranger Than It Used to Be: Biblical Faith in a Postmodern Age* (Downers Grove: Intervarsity Press, 1995) 9-10.

19. See William Phillips Jr., *Slavery from Roman Times to the Early Transatlantic Trade* (Minneapolis: University of Minnesota Press, 1985); James Walvin, *Black Ivory: A History of British Slavery* (London: Fontana, 1993). For a first hand account, see Bernard Martin and Mark Spurrell, eds., *The Journal of a Slave Trader (John Newton) 1750-1754* (London: Epworth Press, 1962).

20. Ronald Robinson and John Gallagher with Alice Denny, *Africa and the Victorians: The Official Mind of Imperialism* (London: Macmillan, 1967).

21. C.P. Groves, *The Planting of Christianity in Africa* 4 vols. (London: Lutterworth, 1948-58); Adrian Hastings, *The Church in Africa 1450-1950* (Oxford: Clarendon Press, 1994).

22. *Who are the Poor? The Beatitudes as a Call to Community* (Geneva: WCC Publications, 1987).

23. For statistics on the growth of Christianity in Africa, see Mbiti, *Bible and Theology in African Christianity* (Nairobi: Oxford, 1986) and David Barrett, et al, eds. *World Christian Encyclopedia: A comparative survey of churches and religions in the modern world* (second ed.; Oxford, N.Y.: Oxford, 2001).

24. The bibliography on these churches is now quite immense. For an overview, see especially F.B. Welbourne and B.A. Ogot, *A Place to Feel at Home* (London: Oxford University Press, 1966); David Barrett, *Schism and Renewal in Africa: An Analysis of Six Thousand Contemporary Religious Movements* (Nairobi: Oxford University Press, 1968); M.L. Daneel, *Quest for Belonging: Introduction to the Study of African Independent Churches* (Gweru: Mambo Press, 1987); David Barrett and John Padwick, *Rise and Walk! Conciliarism and the African Independent Churches, 1815-1987* (Nairobi: Oxford University Press, 1989).

25. "The Use of Biblical Critical Methods in Rooting the Scriptures in Africa" in Hannah W. Kinoti and John M. Waliggo, eds., *The Bible in African Christianity: Essays in Biblical Theology* (Nairobi: Acton Publishers, 1997), 8-24.

26. *The Johannine Approach to Mission: A Contextual Study of John 4:1-42* (Tübingen: J.C.B. Mohr [Paul Siebeck], 1988).

27. "Biblical Research in Africa: The Task Ahead" *African Journal of Biblical Studies* 1/1 (1986): 11.

28. Abogunrin, 14. Cf. Osadolor Imasogie: "[W]e conclude that by the time Christianity was introduced into Black Africa in the fourth decade of the nineteenth century the world view of the Christian theologian retained only a veneer of the biblical world view... [T]he theologian found it necessary to reinterpret [spiritual forces] at best as symbols without ontic content or, at worst, as figments of the imagination of a primitive age under the influence of an ancient world view. By virtue of such a reinterpretation of the Bible, Christians could talk of Christ's power to save from sin but not enthusiastically of his power to destroy the works of the Devil and to save, to the utmost, those who are committed to him." (*Guidelines for Christian Theology in Africa* (Ibadan: University Press, 1986), 52.)

29. "Editorial: not another journal?!" *Newsletter on African Old Testament Scholarship* 1 (1996): 1 [now renamed *Bulletin for Old Testament Studies in Africa)*.

30. *Tropical Africa and the Old Testament*, 12.

31. *The Academy of the Poor: Towards a Dialogical Reading of the Bible.* Interventions, 2 (Sheffield: Sheffield Academic Press, 1999) 114.

32. West, 55. In addition to West's "social commitments" I would add 'religious and theological commitments.'

33. "Rereading the Bible with African Eyes: Inculturation and Hermeneutics," *Journal of Theology for Southern Africa* 91 (1995): 4.

34. West, *The Academy of the Poor*, 93.

35. African scholars do not often have the same kind of resources that are found in Europe and North America. Many biblical scholars in Africa have at least the same kinds of administrative and teaching loads as their counterparts in the North Atlantic world. But their workload does not end here. Faculty members at the Lutheran Theological College in Makumira, Tanzania need to spend several hours a day working in the garden in order to help to feed their families. In 1998 only one African member of the faculty of St. Paul's United Theological College, Limuru, Kenya, had a computer, and he did not have Internet access. Teachers at the Nile Theological College in Khartoum, Sudan, cannot display any public sign for fear that the government will bulldoze their facility. Bishop Gwynne College, an Anglican theological college in Juba, Sudan, rarely has enough food to feed the students, faculty and their families more than one meal a day. The Religious Studies Department at the University of Ibadan, Nigeria, a department with a long and illustrious history, has had frequent interruptions to its operations because of military coups and student strikes. Bishop Tucker Theological College in Uganda (now Uganda Christian University) has gone through many years of having no electricity after sunset. Needless to say, the libraries in Africa are rarely well stocked with the latest books. Few colleges or even universities have much access to the World Wide Web. On a recent visit to the Catholic Institute of West Africa in Port Harcourt, Nigeria, it was discovered that communications within the country were so difficult that the library and most of the faculty there were unaware of many of the theological journals published in other parts of their own country. Producing scholarly works in such an environment has meant that Africans have been unwilling to bracket out the suffering that is a daily part of their own lives and the lives of those around them. Scholarly work must maintain a pragmatic dimension.

36. Justin Ukpong was educated in Nigeria, Canada and Rome. He is a Roman Catholic priest and he teaches New Testament at the Catholic Institute of West Africa in Port Harcourt, Nigeria. For full bibliography of Ukpong's biblical studies publications up the year 2000 see the relevant sections of Grant LeMarquand "A Bibliography of the Bible in Africa." in *The Bible in Africa: Transactions, Trajectories and Trends*, Gerald O. West and Musa W. Dube, eds. (Leiden: Brill, 2000), 633-800.

37. Ukpong, "Rereading the Bible," 4.

38. Ibid, 5. [italics his]

39. Ibid. [italics his]

40. See John Barton, "Classifying Biblical Criticism," *Journal for the Study of the Old Testament* 29 (1984): 19-35.

41. Ukpong, "Rereading the Bible," 5.

42. A similar positive use of the idea of bias as an aid to biblical interpretation has been articulated by Daniel L. Smith-Christopher in "Gandhi on Daniel 6: Some Thoughts on a 'Cultural Exegesis' of the Bible" (*Biblical Interpretation* 1/3 [1993]: 321-39).

43. *Personal Knowledge: Towards a Post-Critical Philosophy* (Chicago: University of Chicago Press, 1958).

44. Ibid, 15-16.

45. Ibid, 17.
46. Ibid, 59.
47. Morna D. Hooker, "On Using the Wrong Tool," *Theology* 75/629 (1972): 570-81.
48. *African Religions and Philosophy* (Nairobi, Ibadan, London: Heinemann, 1969), 108.
49. Ukpong, "Reading the Bible," 6.
50. Ibid.
51. Ibid.
52. *Plurality and Ambiguity: Hermeneutics, Religion, Hope* (San Francisco: Harper and Row, 1987), 79.
53. Ibid, 9.
54. Ibid, 7.
55. For third world scholars "interpretation is undertaken not primarily to solve intellectual queries: the paramount concern of hermeneutics is to transform society." (R.S. Sugirtharajah "Postscript: Achievements and Items for a Future Agenda," *Voices from the Margin: Interpreting the Bible in the Third World* 1st ed. (London: SPCK, 1991), 438.)
56. Ibid, 10.
57. Ibid, 6.
58. For Ukpong, then the Bible is in some sense the book of the Church, although he understands the 'Church' as the people of God rather than as an institution. The case could certainly be made that, in Latin American liberation theology and in 'popular' theology from so-called Christian Base Communities, the Bible is not so much the book of the Church as the book of the people, although most of the people involved with the Bible are in some sense members of the Christian community. But the Bible is not seen as the property of the Church as an institution that has the final authoritative word on the meaning of the text. See Leif Vaage, ed. *Subversive Scriptures: Revolutionary Readings of the Christian Bible in Latin America* (Valley Forge, PA: Trinity Press International, 1997) for examples of Latin American scholarship done "as a part of a particular people's ongoing effort to have as satisfying a life together as possible." (p. viii). Cf. Carlos Mesters who says that in Latin America "The Bible was taken out of the people's hands. Now they are taking it back. They are expropriating the expropriators: 'It is our book! It was written for us...The Bible has moved to the side of the poor. One could almost say it has changed its class status." ["The Use of the Bible in Christian Communities of the Common People," 119-33 in Norman Gottwald, ed. *The Bible and Liberation: Political and Social Hermeneutics* (Maryknoll: Orbis, 1983). In Africa it is true that scholars generally read the Bible within a confessional or ecclesial context. However, popular reading of the Bible is sometimes more broadly 'religious' than specifically 'Christian.' Some Africans who may or may not profess to be Christians nevertheless have a profound respect for the Bible as religious literature or as a religious object. Ukpong has documented how the Bible is often used as an amulet, placed under a pillow before sleep, carried in a purse to ward off evil, verses written on the sides of buses for protection. See "Inculturation Biblical Hermeneutic: Reading the Bible with African Eyes," (unpublished paper presented to the Bible in Africa Project Consultation held in Glasgow, Scotland 13th-17th August 1994). Cf. Wynnand Amewowo, "Experiences and Discoveries with the Bible in West Africa,"

Mission Studies 3/1 (1986): 12-24; S.A. Adewale, "The Magical Use of the Bible Among the Yoruba Christians of Nigeria," *Biblical-Pastoral Bulletin* 1[sic] (1989): 48-55; David Tuesday Adamo, "Distinctive Use of Psalms in Africa," *Melanesian Journal of Theology* 9/2 (1993): 94-111.

59. Sergio Torres and Virginia Fabella, eds. *The Emergent Gospel: Theology from the Underside of History* (Maryknoll: Orbis, 1978), 269.

60. West, *The Academy of the Poor,* 114 and passim.

61. Ukpong, "Rereading the Bible," 7.

62. Ibid.

63. *The Structure of Scientific Revolutions* 2nd ed. (Chicago: University of Chicago Press, 1970 [1962]).

64. Ukpong, "Rereading the Bible," 7-8.

65. Ibid, 8.

66. Ibid.

67. According to Victor Turner a root paradigm is a pattern of assumptions about the fundamental nature of the universe. These assumptions are usually unconscious but become visible especially in times of crisis. (*Dramas, Fields and Metaphors: Symbolic Actions in Human Society* [Ithaca: Cornell University Press, 1974], 34-44; cited in Ukpong "Rereading the Bible," 8).

68. Ibid, 9. The citing of witchcraft as an example is a good illustration of the importance and place given to the interaction of the 'spiritual realm' with the physical realm in African thought. A myriad of illustrations could elucidate this point. Concerning illness it is readily accepted by African people that malaria is caused by an infection passed by mosquitoes. This does not answer the question which for them is more basic: "who sent the mosquito?" On the question of 'riches,' an African Anglican bishop was recently giving a presentation to a North American funding agency, an agency associated with the church. He was asked, "Why should we give you our money?" The bishop expressed surprise at the question and said that he had been under the impression that God as the Creator was the owner of all things. It was not 'their money'.

69. Ibid.

70. Ibid.

71. Ibid, 10.

72. Ibid.

73. Ibid.

74. Ibid.

75. One might have thought that only Africans should undertake a specifically African inculturation hermeneutic. Ukpong does not say this. He does add that anyone engaged in this task must have made a "critical review of his/her own conditioning and biases for the purposes of utilizing them critically and creatively." (Ibid, 10). It is noteworthy that Ukpong has included female and even white scholars in the task of African hermeneutics in his editorial work. See Justin Ukpong, ed. *Gospel Parables in African Context* (Port Harcourt: CIWA Press, 1988).

76. Ukpong, "Rereading the Bible through African Eyes," 10.

77. Justin Ukpong, "The Parable of the Shrewd Manager (Luke 16:1-13): An Essay in Inculturation Biblical Hermeneutic," *Semeia* 73 (1996): 189.

78. Among his many works, Ukpong has written on biblical texts dealing with sacrifice, prayer, Christology, mission, cultural pluralism, all from the perspective of an African context.

Chapter V

'A Small Herb Increases Itself (makes impact) by a Strong Odour': Re-imagining Vashti in an African South African Context

Madipoane Masenya (ngwana' Mphahlele) (Unisa)

Introduction[1]

Though the proponents of the historical-critical methodologies would let us believe otherwise, it is currently an indisputable fact that the different social locations of readers consciously or unconsciously shape their way of reading (biblical texts). Though the narrators present a story in a certain way to influence their readers to interpret it in a particular way and present characters in certain ways to achieve particular aims, they do not always succeed in persuading the readers to accept their opinions.

When reading about the character of Vashti in Esther 1, being informed by my South African social location, I was reminded of the Northern Sotho proverb: *Serokolo se sennyane se ikoketša ka go nkga*: "A small herb increases itself / makes impact by a strong odour." If applied literally, the proverb shows that though the herb in question is small (compared to its human users), once it is applied for use, it releases a strong (therapeutic) odour. One of the tenors of this proverb is as follows: those who are deemed small or insignificant may have a way of making their influence felt by those who are bigger/stronger than they are. This small herb is important since it is believed that just chewing a small part of it will make the patient feel a difference. The significance of such a small herb in the African South African context, should remind all of us, particularly those members of Earth who have always deemed themselves more important than others, and frequently impose themselves on the 'smaller' others, that all members of the created order/family are worthy and thus deserve fair treatment.

I hail from an oral African context, a context replete with folklore; proverbs, idioms and riddles used in our daily conversations in our attempt to come to terms with life. In a traditional African setting, it will be enough for the preacher, particularly one of my kind, who deliberately re-reads biblical texts to retrieve, re-imagine, and resuscitate suppressed female voices in the Christian Bible, to read the text of Esther 1, particularly verses 10 to 12 in the Northern Sotho language and cite the above-named proverb. The use of the proverb will be sufficient to summarise the views of the preacher about Vashti. To those listeners initiated into Northern Sotho lore, the proverb will give opportunity to rethink and re-imagine Vashti who, especially despite her volatile situation, managed to make her influence felt. To those who are not conversant with the lore, particularly the younger generation, like most of my audience here, saying the proverb would not mean anything as most of these listeners are not conversant with this rich heritage of their traditional culture.

One must, however, hasten to observe that the story of Vashti appears in the Judeo-Christian canon (though the Scroll itself was not easily included in this canon), a canon which still enjoys a vast amount of authority in my ecclesiastical context.[2] Thus citing this proverb as a core of what is supposed to be an inspiring message/sermon will not make sense even to listeners initiated in the African lore. It may not make sense for the following reasons:

1   As a result of our colonial past, some members may wonder why a preacher can use proverbs / traditional 'uninspired' sayings to deliver the word of God. However, when the prophets in the Hebrew Bible delivered the word of YHWH by using proverbs, it is acceptable. The proverbs in the Book of Proverbs in the Hebrew canon also inspire them in their daily devotions.

2   The second and related reason is that sermons preached on the character of Vashti in my context would normally demonise her. Unlike Esther, Vashti is an example of a woman whom African Christian women should resist. As I stated earlier:

> One afternoon I attended a woman's session at a church. The preacher was one of the pastor's wives. Her sermon was based on Esther 1 and Esther 5. Vashti (cf Esther 1) was cited as an example of a foolish woman whose example women should challenge and resist. On the other hand, women were encouraged to follow the example of Esther (cf Esther 5) who humbled herself

before her husband, the king; a wise woman who ultimately got
what she wanted.[3]

For fear of being misunderstood by both my church audience and my
present audience, let me in the following lines describe what I mean by a re-
imagination of the character of Vashti informed basically by this proverb from
my African South African social situation.

I first want to justify my choice of Vashti among all the characters in the
Book of Esther.

1. I was attracted by the space given to Vashti by the narrator in the book
of Esther. In my view, though she plays a minor role despite her royal position
(cf the prominence given to her male counterpart), she remains one of the most
important characters in the book. Though I agree with those commentators who
argue that Vashti's episode is a ploy used by the narrator so that Esther can
appear. I also agree with those commentators who argue that Vashti cannot be
erased from the whole story,[4] and as such plays or remains an integral part of the
story as Beal remarks:

> One may find traces of Vashti in the one who replaces her. Most
> obviously Esther is the queen and Vashti is the queen. And
> although Vashti was banished into oblivion, the king does not
> forget her. Indeed, it is actually the memory of Vashti and not
> lack of a queen that motivates the pageant-search for a
> replacement.[5]

In my view, though the Jewish narrator attempts to erase her from our
memories in favour of a 'worthy'/better Jewish queen, Vashti manages to
survive, though only to an extent.

I attribute the small space given to Vashti by the narrator of the book to the
patriarchal orientation not only of the narrator of this story, but also as this same
narrator has clearly portrayed, of the world which produced this story, the world
of the Persian exile in the Achemenaid period. In a heavily androcentric canon,
the space occupied by women is limited not only in terms of quantity, but also in
terms of the quality of what is presented. In most cases, female voices are
filtered through male voices. It thus remains the task of concerned
female/women readers to retrieve these voices and try to imagine what they
could/should have said had they been given the opportunity to do so.

2. Vashti's boldness to defy the command of the king, given the
precariousness of her position in a patriarchal context boggles my mind. When
the latter happens, however, I am consoled by the following Northern Sotho
proverb: *Mmago ngwana o swara thipa ka bogaleng* (the mother of a child holds
the sharp part of the knife). As a woman, one can better understand the local
situation/household, particularly as it affected the children of the empire
(particularly given the folly of the husband she was coupled with). An African
South African woman reader could/can therefore identify with her refusal to
appear before the king under those circumstances /before drunken men. As such,

the tenor of the proverb is that in tough circumstances, it is the mother who will stand firm or will be tough for the safety/welfare of the children, and is usually rewarded positively for that.

Vashti, however, does not reap the benefits of her holding the sharp part of the knife by refusing to appear before the king when she felt it was not necessary. This action has serious repercussions for her royal status and the fruits thereof are reaped but by yet another woman! Though a woman is despised and denied legitimate space as an equal human being in a patriarchal context, the latter cannot exist without her! The main difference in this context is the ethnicity of the substitute woman; a non-Jewish disobedient woman/queen must disappear in favour of an obedient (yet manipulative) Jewish woman/queen.

My re-imagination of the character of Vashti will make more sense if one tries to imagine the world in which Vashti lived, through the help of the narrator and some of the commentators.

VASHTI'S SOCIAL LOCATION/WORLD

In the Book of Esther we are confronted with the story of how a foreign woman, a member of the Jewish exiles, ultimately found favour in the eyes of a Persian king and without much trouble, made her way into the Persian court.

The author/narrator narrates this story, of which the main aim is to account for the origins of the Purim feast, as though it is history. In the very first chapter of the Scroll/Book of Esther, the story is set within the known geographical setting: The name of the king whose kingdom is presented here is well known in Persian history. That some Persian kings had a craving to show their honour by displaying their wealth is attested to in other sources. The description of the situation of the royal court/palace in Susa tempts the reader to assume that the narrator is portraying a situation which indeed happened in history.[6]

There are, however, many elements in the story that make the world presented by the narrator unrealistic, elements that cause us to read this Scroll as a story, such as:

1.   The observation that a king, irrespective of his wealth and his class-consciousness could determine to spend 180 days displaying his honour and feasting with his officials does not sound realistic. If that actually happened, one fails to imagine the damage such a move could have made to the economy of the country. One cannot imagine a community of the nobility spending almost half of the year in a drunken revelry!

From South African Northern Sotho context, for example, a portrayal such as this would also be unthinkable. Though African peoples attach great significance to feasts, the duration of the feast presented here would not make sense in this context. Even if a *kgoshi*/traditional leader organised a feast for the people, he would be in the background because in this context, a *kgoshi* does not easily rub shoulders with ordinary people.

2.   That a king, while in a drunken state, could summon his wife to come and appear before his drunken friends is also not realistic. However, if we read the episode within the context of the whole Book of Esther and are willing to understand and accept the character of Xerxes as the narrator intends us to understand it, namely as that of a leader who neither has backbone nor the capacity to think for himself, we may believe that such summons could have been made. This might have been possible particularly given the male-orientedness of the world presented by the narrator in Esther 1. Male royalty is so obsessed with the *baalship* /mastership /lordship of men in the patriarchal household that one 'deviant' act by one woman, necessitate that a royal decree reinforcing the patriarchal status quo be written, 'declaring that every man should be master in his own house'. What is ironic in this case is that the very proclaimer of this command, king Xerxes, fails to be master in his own house; a private family matter is resolved by another male since Memuchan actually 'beats the drum' in the king's household. As the one who is now playing the role of *baal* in the king's house, he has also decided that the king's wife is no longer fit to appear before the king.

In my context, it would be unthinkable for *kgoshi* to summon a queen, a married woman, to appear before the public, particularly for parading in order to display her beauty. As a matter of fact, in this context, the queen mother is not supposed to be seen by everybody. If needs be, she might even be advised by *kgoshi* to go into hiding for safety. As the bearer of the future leader of the people, great efforts are taken to ensure her safety.

If Vashti were unmarried, for example, that would make sense in being more akin to what happens to Esther and the maidens in chapter 2. The aim here would be for the *kgoshi* to be able to choose a wife for himself or for his counsellors to be able to choose wives for themselves. We are here reminded of the present case of the Swazi monarch, king Twala 111 who, in the name of African culture, got himself and royalty into a mess by abducting the eighteen-year- old Zena Mahlangu, as one of his wives, against the will of her mother. The latter has opened a court case against the monarch.

3.   In my view, given the patriarchal orientation of the world as presented in the text, it is also unthinkable that a queen, a woman, when summoned by the king, particularly the one who had such immense power to have any one who appeared before him without having been summoned, killed, could flatly and unapologetically refuse to appear before him. If that could happen, one would think that the punishment would probably have been much more severe than deposition. Even in the African South African traditional context, it would be impossible for anyone, let alone a woman, to refuse to appear before *kgoshi*. A Northern Sotho proverb says: *Lentšu la kgoshi le agelwa lešaka*, which literally means that the voice of *kgoshi* has a fence built around it. The proverb means that a subject cannot dare to transgress the word of a traditional leader, let alone a female subject.

Whatever the situation might have been, the narrator has managed to give the readers his 'realistic' imagination of Persian life in the Diaspora. In this world, it was a matter of the survival of the fittest as it portrays a social location in which power resided in few individuals who through shrewd means could abuse it for their own ends.

It is a context in which the have's had the guts to display their possessions to the have-nots, where to those who have, even more was given: a longer banquet was hosted 'for all his officials and ministers. The army of Persia and Media and the nobles and governors of the provinces were present, while he displayed the great wealth of his kingdom and the splendour and pomp of his majesty for many days, one hundred and eighty days in all' (vv 3-4). In this social location, the have's, as symbolised by the king, do not seem to delight in sharing the wealth with the have-nots, giving them hand-outs for a period of seven days seemed enough to clear the conscience(s) of the have(s). What must happen to the poor after these seven days is not the concern of our story, yet some of us who live in contexts in which people struggle to survive in the midst of poverty, will find it difficult to read a text like this and not ask this and related questions. According to Mosala, the text of Esther 1 depicts the surplus of the economy squandered on non-productive goods and a luxury lifestyle among the ruling class but remains silent on the conditions and struggles of the non-rulers: peasants, serfs and the underclasses.[7]

This is indeed a world which foregrounds the haves. Most characters foregrounded in this chapter belong to this category. Even Vashti is not an ordinary woman – she is a member of the royal family, a Persian queen. One may speculate that her socio-economic status probably gave her the guts to refuse to appear before the king. Fox argues that 'Vashti's indignation is probably motivated by sense of rank rather than any protofeminist ideals. She is after all a queen, not a mere concubine to be toyed with. ... By appearing before males, including commoners – especially when the king himself "was lightheaded with wine" – Vashti would be behaving like a mere concubine'.[8] If her class had a say in her refusal to appear before the king, Vashti cannot be a model for many African South African women of whom the majority remain at the bottom of the country and/or the continent's economic ladder.

This is a world in which, as we have previously noted, power still lies with men as well. Female characters are erased and/or survive in the story in terms of the rules of the game of patriarchy. Women who like Vashti are bold enough to defy the rules of the game, are confronted with narrators and/or characters who are quick to remove them.

Though Esther 1 does not mention any of the Jewish main characters of the story, it has prepared fertile ground for the drama of the exiled Jews to unfold. In the next chapters, we will be presented with tactics which the exiles had to use to survive in a foreign and hostile environment.

Alice Bach correctly argues that a reader reads her own experience into the text when she constructs a character out of a text.[9] In re-imagining the Vashti character from the point of view of my social location, I will not necessarily be presenting the agenda which the author/narrator had in mind when he presented the character. My presentation will hopefully reveal that I am definitely not the type of narratee whom the narrator had in mind.

How may we read Vashti informed by an African context in South Africa? This is the subject of debate in the following lines / part of the paper. For this purpose, the character of Vashti is discussed under the following sub-headings:

In exile at home
Her gender speaks louder than all the other factors (ethnicity and class)
A fighter who gets what she wants
Vashti's model: instilling hope for women?

In exile at 'home'

The Book of Esther reveals the situation of Jewish exiles in a foreign country. This was a context characterised by oppression and assimilation. The latter entailed many compromises on the part of the exiles (cf Esther breaking the rules of sexuality in chap 2; and Esther hiding her identity). The Jews had to learn survival tactics in order to survive under those circumstances. An exile is one who lives under the shadow as well as the mercy of those who exiled him/her.

In Vashti, however, we see an example of an exile in her country. This situation reminds us of South Africans in the apartheid era. We lived under suppression and repression in our own country. One had to be assimilated into the culture of the powerful White minority in order to survive.

It may be argued that even the narrator in Esther 1 treats Vashti like a stranger to the Persian community. In the narrative, Vashti, the woman, is presented in relation to her husband, the king. The banquet organised is not her own initiative one would argue. She is presented as an uncooperative woman who flatly refuses to honour her husband's appreciation of her beauty. As a matter of fact, Vashti never really stands as a character in her own right except when she breaks the code of conduct according to the standards of the time: refusing to appear before the king, an act which culminated in her removal from the scene. Like an exile in a foreign land, she cannot be allowed to have her own will. She can only survive through being assimilated by patriarchy. A refusal of the demands imposed on her by patriarchy can only be disastrous not only to her but also to all the women in the Persian Empire. The latter will sooner or later be reminded by a written decree that their husbands must lord it over them in the household exile. Vashti is a stranger in what is supposed to be her own territory. Her situation is very similar to what is still obtaining in post-apartheid South Africa. In this context, there is an apparent understanding that the equality clause pertaining to the equality between men and women applies in the work-place. In many family contexts (not excluding church contexts), African women are still regarded and treated as exiles. It is in these settings, that one's sex determines the extent of one's assimilation. It is thus the women's duty to invent strategies of how to determine, when and to which extent they can release their useful odours.

One important question which we ask as we conclude this aspect of Vashti's character is to imagine what would have happened if Vashti were a Jewish woman. Would she have received such treatment in the hands of a Jewish narrator? Would her exile be less severe than it is now portrayed in the present text?

As could have been noted in the preceding lines, what actually makes Vashti an exile in her own country is her sex. In the following section we thus demonstrate that her sex speaks louder than her ethnicity and her class.

The Odour of Vashti's Sex is stronger than that of Other Factors

The negative portrayal of the Vashti character by the narrator tempts one to speculate that she receives such a harsh treatment because she is a woman in a world which did not legitimate the power of women. She is an example of one who, though socio-economically strong (cf her class as a queen married to a wealthy king), and ethnically legitimate and powerful, continues to be haunted by her problematic sex. The latter will determine the violation she will receive not only from the male narrator who presents her story, but also from fellow Persian characters who, though being socio-economically not as powerful as she is, belong to the sex that legitimates the power which they can exercise over her.

There are commentators who argue that the narrator is neutral or sympathetic towards the Vashti character, leading the readers to sympathise with her unfair deposition particularly given the nature of the king's summons. Fox argues that the author's sympathy toward her comes from the way Vashti is made the victim of the instability of Xerxes and the insecurity of the princes. Though I agree with Fox that the narrator in the Book of Esther chooses to reserve his judgement about the book's characters, including Vashti, I doubt if the narrator has any sympathy towards Vashti. If that were the case, why did he choose to argue his point / introduce the story by presenting an episode in which a defiant non-Jewish woman is deposed? Was there no way of introducing the story rather than presenting a story of a defiant woman whom patriarchy rewards through humiliation? If these characters – a king who is insecure and too status conscious, drunken officials and a defiant woman – belonged to his ethnicity, would they have received the same treatment? Or, put in other words, if this story were presented by a Persian of the time, would it have followed the same pattern?

Though when rated with the male characters around her in this chapter, her sex speaks louder than her class, it might be argued that compared to other female characters who are mentioned and not named or not mentioned at all, her class as a matter of fact advantages her over other females in her context. This situation reminds us that women of all ages have never experienced patriarchy in the same way. We therefore agree with Kwok Pui lan that there is no universal women's experience. This situation is typical of a multi-racial, multi-cultural post-apartheid South Africa.

Vashti is a Fighter who gets what she Wants

If one looks at the Vashti character, one is tempted to classify her with bold people. She seems to know what she wants and she will do all it costs to get what she wants irrespective of what the repercussions might be. Her fight is rewarded in that she actually gets what she wanted: not to appear before the king.

Though the narrator presents her as a fighter, one who does not care to upset the ruler of the empire as well as the patriarchal status quo, one would hesitate to classify Vashti as a liberated woman and/or a feminist.[10] That would in my view be reading too much of what is happening in our twenty-first century contexts into this fourth century context.

The challenge that we face as female readers of female characters such as Vashti as they appear in the Hebrew canon, is the scant information provided about them. For example, in the present episode the narrator does not give us any reasons why Vashti dared to do what she did. Given the patriarchal orientation of the context of the world which produced this text (as already noted) and the observation that women (cf Esther and other 'tricksters' in the Hebrew Bible) acquired certain survival tactics in such contexts as well as the observation that issues around the liberation of women are fairly recent compared to this context, one would hesitate to call her a fighter for the rights of women. Fox's argument that Vashti's indignation was probably motivated by a sense of rank rather than any protofeminist ideals thus makes sense. In this instance, Vashti as a queen and not a concubine, would have wanted to protect her rank.

Any reasons we may forward for Vashti's refusal to appear before the king will remain mere speculation. In my view, the omission of such an important information, given the consequences that this character is made to suffer because of this act, is another proof that the character of Vashti in this book, particularly here in the beginning of the story, is not important in its own right according to the narrator, she is merely used as a ploy for the 'proper' queen, the Jewish queen to appear on the scene. When she comes into the picture, one of the main characters of this story, even queen Esther, her reasons for refusing to appear before the king are made clear by the narrator (Es 4:11).

Vashti's boldness though, especially in her volatile situation as a woman, of being an exile in her own home, is worth writing home about. She can thus serve as model for women who have been socialised to agree with everything said by their husbands/men.

An important question to be addressed towards the end of this paper is whether such boldness is good for the survival of those people for whom life is a continuous struggle to survive. Is releasing a strong therapeutic odour in a context where many patients are still suspicious about the significance or the worth of the odour an exercise in wisdom or folly? Is Vashti's model instilling hope for marginalised women of Africa in South Africa?

Vashti's model: Instilling Hope for marginalised Women in African South Africa?

To conclude: Can the character of Vashti as presented in Esther 1 serve as a model of hope for women of Africa living in South Africa? Is the odour she releases in her context strong enough to dismantle all forces which deny life to women in our day?

The answer to this question can be neither a simple yes nor a simple no. I prefer to attempt an answer by asking yet another question: If it were possible for us to trace the female audience of this story in its setting and hear the views of the women about the character of Vashti and what it means for them, one could speculate that the answer they would give would not differ (much) from the answer one can expect from many South African women readers of this story (cf traditional anti-Vashti interpretations still rife in our settings). Vashti's defiance of her husband cannot be appropriated as a quality of a God-fearing woman in these contexts. What feminists have called boldness, independence or courage on the part of Vashti might be interpreted as folly, carelessness and defiance by many Christian women who continue to yearn for a God-fearing kind of relationship with their husbands. Obviously, for such women, Vashti cannot serve as a model for survival in an environment which continues to exile them through factors such as patriarchy, poverty, ethnicity and race amongst others.

Despite all arguments to the contrary, Vashti has in my view, succeeded in showing the people and particularly the men of her time, that women also have a will and can exercise that will whenever they want to, irrespective of what the consequences may be. In that sense, she has really shown us that the mother of the child is indeed the one who holds the sharp part of the knife. Vashti, symbolising a small herb, has succeeded in releasing an appropriate odour: the one that for a moment challenged even the main upholder of the patriarchal status quo – the king. An important question, however, is: Was Vashti strategic when she released the odour? Did she keep in mind her exiled position when she released this odour? It does not seem to me that that was the case. We may speculate that though she was a small herb in the midst of big hostile ones, she released the odour as though she was one of their kind. Hence the strong opposition she got, a response which not only did harm to the noble women of the time, but has continued to harm even the twenty-first century female readers of her story. Her strategy, manifested in her refusal to appear before the king, led to her removal from the story. The latter, one would argue, is one of the factors which has contributed to a lack of interest in her story. It is no wonder that very few commentaries, even by women liberation scholars, dedicate more space to this character (unlike the character of Esther, for instance). In this way, the narrator has thus succeeded in partially erasing her from the memories of the hearers of the story through all ages.

In a hostile environment, a context which has not yet fully come to grips with the humanness of women, the latter will do well to learn and master ways in which they can be like royal cows as the Northern Sotho proverb says: *Swana ya moshate e fenya e sa rage* (A royal cow conquers without kicking). In some instances, even as women struggle to survive in these hostile contexts, we might be forced to strategise to shoot at the enemy one shot at a time lest we miss this enemy completely!

Endnotes

1. This article was originally published in *Old Testament Essay* Volume 16 /2 (2003), 332-342. This editor is grateful to the Old Testament Society of South Africa for the permission to republish it in this book.
2. S. Nadir, Gender, power,Sexuality and Suffering Bodies in the Book of Esther: reading the Charactyers of Esther and Vashti for the Purpose of Social Transformation," *Old Testament Essay* 15/1 (2002), 114-115.
3. Madiapone Masenya, Liberation in Africanization, Liberatin & Transformation in theological Education, *NICTE* (2000), 20-26.
4. T.K Beal, Tracing Esther's beginnings, in Brenner, A (ed), *A Feminist Companion to Esther, Judith and Susana*, 1995, 87-110. Sheffield: Sheffield Academic Press, 1995), 2:1-2, cf 2.17.
5. Beal, 1995, 2.1-2; cf 2.17.
6. Cf. Fox, M V 1991. *Character and ideology in the Book of Esther.* Columbia: University of South Carolina. S A White, Esther: A feminine model for Jewish Diaspora, in Day, P (ed), *Gender and difference in Ancient Israel*, (Minneapolis: Augsburg Fortress, 1989), 161-177.
7. I.J.Mosala, *(??? See p 6).* Implications for the text of Esther for African women's struggle for liberation in South Africa. *JBTSA*, 1992)2, 134.
8. Fox, 1999, 168.
9. A. Bach, "Signs of the flesh: Observations on characterization in the Bible," in Bach, A (ed), *Women in the Hebrew Bible*, (New York/London: Routledge, 1999), 351-365.
10. (cf Fox [quoting others] and J.M Cohen, 1996. Vashti an unsung heroine. *Jewish Bible Quarterly* 24 (1996), 103-106.

CHAPTER VI

SUB-SAHARAN AFRICAN DOCTORAL DISSERTATIONS IN OLD TESTAMENT STUDIES, 1967-2000: SOME REMARKS TO THEIR CHRONOLOGY AND GEOGRAPHY

Knut Holter

The twentieth century made the Old Testament an African book, in the sense that the ancient texts were translated into hundreds of African languages, and subsequently interpreted in homes, schools, churches and universities throughout the continent. The major enterprise of these various interpretations—those of the grass-roots as well as those of the university—was to express an *interpretatio africana* of the Old Testament, that is an interpretation capable of building bridges between the ancient texts and the traditional and modern contexts of their contemporary African readers.

The present paper is part of a research project on academic interpretation of the Old Testament in Sub-Saharan Africa.[1] Doctoral dissertations in Old Testament studies, written by scholars from this part of Africa,[2] in Africa or abroad,[3] play an important role in this project, and the paper will go into some aspects of the institutional context of these dissertations, or, to be more precise, it will make some remarks to their chronology and geography. The institutional context of doctoral dissertations is indeed a very narrow segment of African interpretation of the Old Testament, as it excludes not only popular approaches on verbal (for example sermon, testimony, song, prayer, conversation) or non-verbal (for example through the visible arts, drama, dance, rituals) levels, but also academic approaches of other genres than the doctoral dissertation (for example journal articles, monographs, textbooks), and even more thematically oriented analyses of the same dissertation material.[4] However, taking into account, positively, the hermeneutical presuppositions and research political priorities that are always reflected in the relationship between a dissertation and its institutional context, but also, negatively, the general lack of interest for this material in current bibliographies[5] and other analyses of African biblical interpretation,[6] I would say that this narrow segment deserves some attention, also from perspectives such as the chronology and geography of the dissertations.

In my work with this material, I have till now been able to identify 85 dissertations;[7] the first one was completed in 1967, and for pragmatic reasons I have decided to end with those completed in 2000. A preliminary version of the bibliographical data of the dissertation material has been published elsewhere,[8] and a more detailed analysis of the material will hopefully be completed in a not too distant future.

The following table presents some institutional aspects of this material: the vertical axis presents the nationality of the researchers,[9] the horizontal axis presents the nationality of the degree-giving institution,[10] and where the two axes meet is a figure telling the number of dissertations and the time-span between the first and the last of these particular dissertations.[11] Finally there is a column noticing whether the dissertations are written in English or French.

	Belgium	Cameroun	France	Germany	Italy	Netherlands	Nigeria	Sweden	S. Africa	Switz	U.K.	U.S.A.	Total	English	French
Burkina Faso					1:83								1		1
Burundi			1:83										1		1
Cameroon			4:68-88										4		4
Cent. Afr. Rep.						1:00							1		1
Chad					1:84							1:95	2	1	1
DR Congo	4:88-89			1:91	3:72-97								8		8
Eritrea												2:75-93	2	2	
Garbon			1:88										1		1
Ghana				1:84	1:83								4	4	
Kenya													3	3	
Madagascar			3:84-99										3		3
Malawi									2:98		1:91		3	3	
Namibia									1:94				1	1	
Nigeria	1:85			2:94-99	11:67-98		10:83-00				3:80-85	7:80-99	3-4	3-4	
Rwanda		1:92			1:69					1:98			3		3
Sieria Leone												1:98	1	1	
Tanzania					2:83-96			1:80					4	4	
Togo					1:78							1:00	1		1
Uganda											1:87		1	1	
Zambia									1:99				1	1	
Zimbabwe											1:89	3:79-98	4	4	
Unknown					2:83-95								2		2
Total	5	1	9	4	23	1	10	1	4	1	6	20	8-5	8-5	2-6

drawing detailed statistical conclusions. It is, for example, just accidental that Tanzania has four dissertations, whereas Kenya has only three. However, it is probably not accidental that Nigeria has a high number, 34, all written in English, whereas another West African country, Burkina Faso, has a very small number, only one, written in French. I will therefore argue that it is possible, to a certain extent, to draw some conclusions from this table. And I will use it, carefully, to make some remarks to the chronology and geography of the dissertation material.

Chronology

The first institutional aspect of the dissertation material concerns its chronology. Of the total number of 85 dissertations, three were completed in the 1960s (1967–1970), 13 in the 1970s (1971–1980; of these four in 1980), 29 in the 1980s (1981–1990), and 40 in the 1990s (1991–2000).

Let me make two remarks to these chronological figures. First, the figures should be related to the almost explosive growth in the number of academic institutions in Africa in the same period. Africa had in 1960, at the dawn of independence, only six universities, whereas the number now, four decades later, has passed 150; incidentally, Nigeria alone has approximately 40 universities. As for church-related theological institutions, there is a parallel growth; the total number has actually passed one thousand. Most of these are of the bible school type; however, an increasing number of theological seminaries, graduate schools of theology, and theological faculties in church-related universities manage to keep a relatively high academic standard. Most of these institutions have a strong need for formalized competence, and competence in biblical studies has often been prioritized. Accordingly, the successive growth in number of Old Testament dissertations from the late 1960s throughout the 1990s reflects the same period's successive growth in number of academic institutions.[12]

Secondly, the chronological figures should be related to the more general development of Old Testament scholarship in Africa in the same period. I have elsewhere argued that the 1960s and 70s can be characterized as the "background" of an independent Old Testament scholarship in Africa, and that its "breakthrough" came in the 1980s and 90s.[13] The 1960s and 70s, on the one hand, deserve the label "background", because the various attempts at establishing Old Testament scholarship in Africa in this period, and this includes the institutional contexts of the doctoral dissertations, were quite sporadically.[14] The 1980s and 90s, on the other hand, deserve the label "breakthrough", because this period more systematically developed infrastructural and hermeneutical contexts for an Africanization of Old Testament scholarship. First, as far as infrastructure is concerned, an increasing number of institutions established post-graduate programs in the Old Testament, and this development created a strong need for scholars holding a Doctor's degree. In most cases these programs offered Master's studies, but a few state universities in Nigeria established programs for doctoral studies, too, the first one already in the early 1980s. Another aspect of the development of an infrastructure was the launching of journals for dissemination of research, and research based on doctoral dissertations played an important role here. Of particular significance was that the Nigerian Association for Biblical Studies in 1986 launched their *African Journal of Biblical Studies*. Secondly, as far as hermeneutics is concerned, the 1980s and 90s saw a significant development with regard to the understanding of the *raison d'être* of an Africanized Old Testament scholarship. In particular in journal articles,[15] but eventually also in doctoral dissertations,[16] it was argued that the task is not to develop a parallel to western scholarship, but to develop a scholarship which reflects the concerns of Africa, and which lets these concerns be the interpretive subjects of the Old Testament.

Geography

The second institutional aspect of the dissertation material concerns its geography. Three points should here be noticed. First, the nationality of the researchers, where one notices that more than one third of the dissertations, 34 out of a total number of 85, are written by Nigerians. The second largest group of researchers, eight in number, comes from The Democratic Republic of the Congo. Then follow smaller groups of four and three. There is, in other words, a clear Nigerian dominance in the material. Secondly, the nationality of the degree-giving institution, where one notices that almost one third of the dissertations, 23 of 82, are related to Italian institutions. Then comes USA with 20, and then Nigeria with ten. And thirdly, the languages in which the dissertations are written, where one notices that more than two thirds, 59 of 85, are written in English, and that the remaining ones, 26 in number, are written in French; consequently, none are written in German. However, one should also notice that the imbalance between English and French is strongly affected by the fact that all the Nigerian dissertations are written in English; it should therefore, be acknowledged that although researchers from 12 countries write in English, there are still researchers from ten countries who write in French.

Let me make two remarks to these figures related to the geography of the dissertation material. First, I would like to point out that the relationship between the nationality of the researcher and that of the degree-granting institution in most cases follow well established connections. Research is very much a question of funding, and funding agencies for this kind of research are very often located in ecclesiastical or political structures. On the ecclesiastical level this explains, for example, why two out of four researchers from Tanzania, both being Lutherans, did their research in Lutheran institutions in Scandinavia and USA, whereas the two others, both being Roman Catholics, did their research in pontifical institutions in Rome.[17] The major producers of dissertations are Italian and American institutions, and a few words should be said about them. First, it probably comes as no surprise that the 23 Italian dissertations all are related to pontifical institutions in Rome. However, it should be noticed that only two of these are issued at the Biblical Institute, the most prestigious pontifical institution with regard to biblical studies,[18] whereas no less than 14 are issued at the Urbanian University, with its particular focus on contextual theology.[19] Secondly, as far as the 20 American dissertations are concerned, one can also see many examples of ecclesiastical structures. Approximately half of the dissertations come from typical evangelical institutions,[20] some from other denominational institutions,[21] and a few from non-denominational institutions.[22]

As for the political level, a corresponding pattern can be seen. On the one hand, structures from the colonial past are still reflected, as various forms of political and economic agreements on culture, education and research cooperation tend to bind former colonizers and colonies together. In the present dissertation material this explains, to some extent, why students from Cameroon and Madagascar tend to do their research in France, or why students from The Democratic Republic of the Congo tend to do their research in Belgium. On the other hand, however, also neo-colonial developments are reflected in the material. The American dominance is one obvious example; the growing influence of post-apartheid South Africa is another.

As a second remark to the geography of the dissertation material, I would like to point out that the significant Nigerian dominance has a rather complex background. Of course it reflects the fact that Nigeria has a large population, with a strong Christian presence. Of approximately 111 million inhabitants, 51 million belong to a Christian church. However, this strong Christian presence in Nigeria does not fully explain the Nigerian dominance in the dissertation material. Other countries, too, have a strong Christian presence, without such an accumulation of Old Testament dissertations. The Democratic Republic of the Congo, for example, has a population of approximately 51 million, of which 49 million belong to a Christian church, that is more or less the same as in Nigeria, but the number of Old Testament dissertations is considerably lower.[23]

Therefore, it should be acknowledged that the Nigerian dominance in the dissertation material also reflects university political differences between Anglophone and francophone Africa. Generally speaking, francophone Africa follows the French tradition of not allowing departments of religious studies or theology in universities controlled by the state, whereas anglophone Africa follows the more open tradition of British universities, including departments of religious studies,[24] and, in some cases, even faculties of theology in state universities.[25] Consequently, there are few, if any, structural possibilities in the state universities in francophone Africa for Old Testament scholarship, whereas the opposite is the case in anglophone Africa. A comparison of Nigeria and The Democratic Republic of the Congo will then show that whereas Congo has no structural possibilities in state universities for Old Testament scholarship, the opposite is the case in Nigeria. Many of its approximately 40 universities have departments of religious studies, and at least nine of the 32 researchers whose dissertations are presented in this paper are at the time being working as lecturers or professors in departments of religious studies in state universities in Nigeria.[26]

Concluding remark

In this paper I have made some remarks to the chronology and geography of African doctoral dissertations in Old Testament studies. My purpose has been to point out some aspects of the relationship between the dissertations and their institutional contexts.

The first generation of African Old Testament scholars—that is more or less the generation whose dissertations are presented in this paper—had for various reasons to go through training and do their doctoral research in contexts where the discussion partners were mainly western scholars. Although this situation can be regretted, it is nevertheless understandable. However, it would not be understandable, but most unfortunate, if the second generation of Old Testament scholars, too, would have to do their research in a context where the discussion partners for all practical purposes are still western scholars. Not only would this continue the current tendency of marginalizing African Old Testament scholarship, but it would also prevent the second generation from relating their research to the interpretive experiences of the first generation. On this background I will argue that it is of major importance for African Old Testament scholarship to let the interpretive experiences of the first generation is voiced and analyzed. In other words, there is a need for further work with African Old Testament doctoral dissertations, and this includes critical analysis of the hermeneutical presuppositions and research political priorities of their institutional contexts.

Appendix: List of African Old Testament doctoral Dissertations

Abe, Gabriel Oyedele (Nigeria), "Covenant in the Old Testament", Ph.D., University of Ibadan, Ibadan, Nigeria, 1983.

Abegunde, Solomon O. (Nigeria), "A philosophy and method of translating the Old Testament into Yoruba", Ph.D., The Southern Baptist Theological Seminary, Louisville, Kentucky, USA, 1985.

Adamo, David Tuesday (Nigeria), "The place of Africa and Africans in the Old Testament and its environment", Ph.D., Baylor University, Waco, Texas, USA, 1986: Publ.: *Africa and Africans in the Old Testament.* San Francisco: Christian University Press, 1998.

Ademiluka, S. Sola (Nigeria), "The Genesis accounts of creation and fall in an African setting", Ph.D, University of Ilorin, Ilorin, Nigeria, 1998.

Adeogun, Ebenezer Olutosin (Nigeria), "Biblical apocalyptic literature and its relevance to the church in Africa, with particular reference to the book of Daniel", Ph.D., University of Ibadan, Ibadan, Nigeria, 1988.

Adutwum, Ofosu (Ghana), "The root *batach* in the Old Testament", Th.D., University of Hamburg, Germany, 1984.

Ajayi, Joel Aderoju Adedokun (Nigeria), "Wisdom and old age in ancient Israel: A critical study of the correlation of wisdom with advanced years in the Hebrew sapiential tradition", Ph.D., Baylor University, Waco, Texas, USA, 1997.

Akaenyi, Chudi-Peter (Nigeria), "Judah's definitive infidelity and the divine response in Jer. 7:1–8:3: An exegetico-theological study in the nature and implications of false religion in Israel", Th.D., Pontifical Urban University, Rome, Italy, 1989.

Akao, John Osemeikhian (Nigeria), "The burning bush: An investigation of form and meaning in Exodus 3 and 4", Ph.D., Glasgow University, Glasgow, United Kingdom, 1985.

Akpunonu, Peter (Nigeria), "Salvation in Deutero-Isaiah: A philological-exegetical study", Th.D., Pontifical Urban University, Rome, Italy, 1971.

Apuri, Joseph W. (Ghana), "Human sacrifice, Isaac and Jesus: A study of human sacrifice in the Ancient Near East and Ashante and related tribes, in the light of the blood of Jesus in the Epistle to the Hebrews", Th.D., Pontifical Urban University, Rome, Italy, 1983.

Ariri-Chidomere, Ahamdi Cyriacus (Nigeria), "The background to the accession of Solomon to the throne of David: An exegetical and historical study of 1 Kg 1–2 within the context of the Succession Narrative (2 Sam 9–20, 1 Kg 1–2)", Ph.D., Katholieke Universiteit Leuven, Leuven, Belgium, 1985.

Arulefela, Joseph Oluwafemi (Nigeria), "An analysis of the biblical and Yoruba concepts of covenant with implications for the Christian education of Yoruba Christians", Ph.D., New York University, New York, USA, 1980. Publ.:

Covenant in the Old Testament and in Yoruba land. Ibadan: Daystar Press, 1988.

Aworinde, John Ademola (Nigeria), "A comparative analysis of destiny in the Old Testament and in Yoruba philosophy of life", Ph.D., University of Jos, Jos, Nigeria, 1997.

Bediaku, Buame Yawo J. Baptiste (Togo), "Etude comparée de la célébration pénitentielle dans l'ancien testament et chez le peuple Ewe du Togo: Pour une catéchèse de la célébration pénitentielle en Afrique noire", Th.D., Pontifical Lateran University: Academia Alfonsiana, Rome, Italy, 1978.

Bessole, Paul Mba (Gabon), "La traduction du prophète Osée de l'hébreu en fang: Les problèmes de linguistique et d'exégèse", Th.D., Institut catholique de Paris, Paris, France, 1988.

Boniface-Malle, Anastasia (Tanzania), "Interpreting the Lament Psalms from the Tanzanian Context: Problems and prospects", Ph.D., Luther Seminary, St. Paul, Minnesota, USA, 2000

Byamungo, Gosbert T.M. (Tanzania), "Stronger than death: David's winning story in an intertextual perspective of 1 Sam 13 – 2 Sam 5", Th.D., Pontifical Gregorian University, Rome, Italy, 1996. Publ.: *Stronger than Death: Reading David's Rise for Third Millennium.* Rome: Urbaniana University Press, 1996 (Pontificia Universitas Urbaniana: Varia; 59).

Carew, M. Douglas (Sierra Leone), "To know and not to know: Hosea's knowledge in discourse perspective", Ph.D., Trinity Evangelical Divinity School, Deerfield, Illinois, USA, 1998.

Chingota, Felix L.B. (Malawi), "The use of the concept 'fear' in Deuteronomy to denote the relationship between God and Israel", Ph.D., University of Aberdeen, Aberdeen, United Kingdom, 1991.

Dinzolele Nzambi, Philippe (The Democratic Republic of the Congo), "Proverbes bibliques et proverbes kongo: Étude comparative de Proverbia 25–29 et de quelques proverbes kongo", Th.D., University of Tübingen, Tübingen, Germany, 1991. Publ.: *Proverbes bibliques et proverbes kongo: Étude comparative de Proverbia 25–29 et de quelques proverbes kongo.* Frankfurt A.M.: Peter Lang, 1992 (Religionswissenschaft; 5).

Ebo, D.J.I. (Nigeria), "'O that Jacob would survive': A study on hope in the Book of Amos", Ph.D., University of Nigeria, Nsukka, Nigeria, 1985.

Gakindi, Gédéon (Rwanda), "La bénédiction aaronique et la *berakah* de l'ancien testament", Ph.D., Yaoundé Faculty of Protestant Theology, Yaoundé, Cameroon, 1992.

Gitau, Samson Njuguna (Kenya), "A comparative study of the transmission, actualization and stabilization of oral traditions: An examination of traditions of circumcision in Africa and ancient Israel", Ph.D., Boston University, Boston, Massachusetts, USA, 1994.

Grantson, Emmanuel Francis Yankum (Ghana), "Death in the individual psalms of lament: An exegetical study with implications for theology and mission", Th.D., Lutheran School of Theology, Chicago, Illinois, USA, 1991.

Habberstad, Rakotondrazaka (Madagascar), "Le fin d'Israël selon la prophétie d'Amos: Nature et fonction des récits de vision", Th.D., Université de Sciences Humaines de Strasbourg, Strasbourg, France, 1999.

Habtu, Tewoldemedhin (Eritrea), "A taxonomy of approaches of five representative scholars to the nature of wisdom in the Old Testament, in the light of Proverbs 1–9", Ph.D., Trinity Evangelical Divinity School, Deerfield, Illinois, USA, 1993.

Himbaza, Innocent (Rwanda), "Transmettre la Bible: Une critique exégétique de la traduction de l'Ancien Testament. Le cas du Rwanda", Th.D., Université Catholique de Fribourg, Fribourg, Switzerland, 1998.

Ilonu, Anthony E. (Nigeria), "The New Testament common priesthood and the Hebrew passover: A comparative study", Th.D., Pontifical Urban University, Rome, Italy, 1971.

Kabasele Mukenge, André (The Democratic Republic of the Congo), "La supplique collective de Ba 1,15–3,8: Traditions et réécriture", Th.D., University of Louvain, Louvain, Belgium, 1992.

Kafang, Zamani B. (Nigeria), "A semantic and theological investifation of the concept of 'poor' in the Psalms", Ph.D., Trinity Evangelical Divinity School, Deerfield, Illinois, USA, 1993.

Kalugila, Leonidas (Tanzania), "The wise king: Studies in royal wisdom as divine revelation in the Old Testament and its environment", Th.D., University of Uppsala, Uppsala, Sweden, 1980. Publ.: *The Wise King: Studies in Royal Wisdom as Divine Revelation in the Old Testament and its Environment.* Lund: CWK Gleerup, 1980 (Coniectanea Biblica. Old Testament Series; 15).

Kawale, Winston Raphael (Malawi), "God and nature in Genesis 1:1–2:4a and Chewa cosmogony", Th.D., University of Stellenbosch, Stellenbosch, South Africa, 1998

Koudouguéret, David (Central African Republic), "Poétique et traduction biblique: Les récits de la Genèse dans le système littéraire Sango", Ph.D., University of Leiden, Leiden, The Netherlands, 2000. Publ.: *Poétique et traduction biblique: Les récits de la Genèse dans le système littéraire Sango.* Leiden: University of Leiden, 2000 (CNWS Publications; 92).

Kubulana Matendo, Siméon (The Democratic Republic of the Congo), "Justice et royaume messianiques: Essai de relecture exégètique de la prophétie de Michée. Eléments d'une théologie de l'espérance pour une église en crise", Th.D., Faculté Universitaire de Théologie Protestante, Bruxelles, Belgium, 1998.

Kwasi, Ugira (The Democratic Republic of the Congo), "La problématique de la mort dans les écrits sapientiaux postexiliques: Une contribution à la relecture du Yahviste", Th.D., Faculté universitaire de théologie protestante, Bruxelles, Belgium, 1988.

Lasebikan, George Latunji (Nigeria), "Prophecy or schizophrenia? A study of prophecy in the Old Testament and in selected Aladura churches", Ph.D., University of Ibadan, Ibadan, Nigeria, 1983.

Lezoutie, Jean Salomon, "Relations entre les vivants et les morts en 2 M 12,38–45; Mt 5,23–26; Lc 16,1–13; Ap 7,9–17", Th.D., Pontifical Urban University, Rome, Italy, 1995.

Mafico, Temba Levi Jackson (Zimbabwe), "A study of the Hebrew root *shafat* with reference to Yahweh", Ph.D., Harvard University, Cambridge, Massachusetts, USA, 1979.

Manda, Joel William (Malawi), "Battling with words only: A rhetorical interpretation of the function of proverbs within Old Testament kingship narratives", Th.D., University of Stellenbosch, Stellenbosch, South Africa, 1998.

Mbele, Philémon (Cameroon), "La justice sociale ou l'ultime possibilité de salut pour Israël selon le prophète Amos", Th.D., Faculté de théologie protestante de Montpellier, Montpellier, France, 1988.

Mbuwayesango, Dora Rudo (Zimbabwe), "The defense of Zion and the House of David: Isaiah 36–39 in the context of Isaiah 1–39", Ph.D., Emory University, Atlanta, Georgia, USA, 1998.

Mebi-Obam, René (Cameroon), "Le Dieu qui repond: Essai d'analyse d'un thème biblique", D. Rel., Faculté de theol. prot., Univ. des sciences humaines, Strasbourg, France, 1982.

Meluma, Buse, "Pactes de sang africains et alliances bibliques par le sang: Etude comparative des significations et des fonctions du sang de l'alliance", Th.D., Pontifical Urban University, Rome, Italy, 1983.

Mianbé Bétoudji, Denis (Chad), "El, le Dieu suprême et le Dieu des patriarches (Gen 14:18–20)", Th.D., Pontifical Urban University, Rome, Italy, 1984. Publ.: *El, le Dieu suprême et le Dieu des patriarches (Genesis 14,18–20)*. Hildesheim: Georg Olms Verlag, 1986 (Religionswissenschaftliche Texte und Studien; 1).

Monsengwo Pasinya, Laurent (The Democratic Republic of the Congo), "La notion de *nomos* dans le Pentateuque grec", Th.D., Pontifical Biblical Institute, Rome, Italy, 1972. Publ.: *La notion de* nomos *dans le Pentateuque grec*. Rome: Biblical Institute Press, 1973 (Analecta Biblica; 52 / Recherches Africaines de Théologie; 5).

Muthengi, Julius, K. (Kenya), "Missiological implications of the book of Jonah: An African perspective", D.Miss., Trinity Evangelical Divinity School, Deerfield, Illinois, USA, 1992.

Naré, Laurent (Burkina Faso), "Proverbes salomoniens et proverbes mossi: Étude comparative à partir d'une nouvelle analyse de Pr 25–29", Th.D., Pontifical Biblical Institute, Rome, Italy, 1983. Publ.: *Proverbes Salomoniens et Proverbes Mossi: Étude Comparative à Partir d'une Nouvelle Analyse de Pr 25–29*. Frankfurt a.M.: Peter Lang, 1986 (Publications Universitaires Européennes; xxiii/283).

Ndiokwere, Nathanael I. (Nigeria), "Prophetic movements in the independent African churches in confrontation with Old Testament prophetism: A comparative study", Th.D., Pontifical Urban University, Rome, Italy, 1977.

Publ.: *Prophecy and Revolution: The role of Prophets in the Independent African Churches and in Biblical Tradition.* London: SPCK, 1981.

Ndjerareou, Abel Laondoye (Chad), "The theological basis for the prohibition of idolatry: An exegetical and theological study of the Second commandment", Ph.D., Dallas Theological Seminary, Dallas, Texas, USA, 1995.

Nelumbu, Martin (Namibia), "Analytical study of the theme of liberation in the Psalms", Ph.D., University of Natal, Pietermaritzburg, South Africa, 1994.

Ngally, Jacques (Cameroon), "Jérémie 28 & le problème des faux prophètes", Th.D., Faculté libre de théologie protestante, Montpellier, France, 1968.

Ngewa, Samuel M. (Kenya), "The biblical idea of substitution versus the idea of substitution in African traditional sacrifices: A case study of hermeneutics for African Christian theology", Ph.D., Westminster Theological Seminary, Philadelphia, Pennsylvania, USA, 1987.

Niyibizi, Francois (Rwanda), "L'analyse des énoncés de péché chez le prophète Jérémie et les péripéties de conversion", Th.D., Pontifical Gregorian University, Rome, Italy, 1969. Publ.: *L'analyse des énoncés de péché chez le prophète Jérémie et les péripéties de conversion.* Rome: Pontifical Gregorian University, 1977.

Njoku, Mark Chiaka (Nigeria), "The image of the prophet Jeremiah in the 'so-called Baruch biography' and cognate texts: A theological consideration of the canonical text", Th.D., Universität Freiburg, Freiburg, Germany, 1994. Publ.: *The Image of the Prophet Jeremiah in the So-Called Baruch Biography and Cognate Texts: A Theological Consideration.* Owerri: Assumpta Press, 1994.

Ntagwarara, Jean (Burundi), "Alliance d'Israël au pays de Moab (Dt 28,69–30,20): Analyse exégétique, histoire rédactionelle et théologie", Th.D., Université des sciences humaines de Strasbourg, Strasbourg, France, 1983.

Ntreh, Benjamin Abotchie (Ghana), "Transmission of political authority in ancient Israel: A tradition historical study of the demise and succession of kings in the Deuteronomistic history and in the Chronicler's history", Th.D., Lutheran School of Theology, Chicago, Illinois, USA, 1989.

Nwaoru, Emmanuel (Nigeria), "The imagery of the prophecy of Hosea: A literary and exegetical survey of Hosea's metaphores and similes", Th.D., Katholisch-theologisches Fakultät, Universität München, München, Germany, 1997. Publ.: *Imagery in the Prophecy of Hosea.* Wiesbaden: Harrassowitz, 1999 (Ägypten und Altes Testament; 41).

Obeta, Julius Sunday (Nigeria), "Eschatological concepts in Job", Ph.D., University of Nigeria, Nsukka, Nigeria, 2000.

Obiajunwa, Chukwudi J. (Nigeria), "Semitic interference in Theodotion-Daniel", Ph.D., The Catholic University of America, Washington D.C., USA, 1999.

Ogunkunle, Caleb Oladokun (Nigeria), "Imprecatory psalms: Their forms and uses in ancient Israel and some selected churches in Nigeria", Ph.D., University of Ibadan, Ibadan, Nigeria, 2000.

Ojo, Adewale Anthony (Nigeria), "'Honur your father and mother' (Ex 20,12): The dignity of parents and the duties of children in the Pentateuch", Th.D., Pontifical Urban University, Rome, Italy, 1996.

Okoye, James C. (Nigeria), "An examination of the non-literal exegesis in Targum Pseudo-Jonathan to Gen 1–11", Ph.D., University of Oxford, Oxford, United Kingdom, 1980.

Okoye, John Ifeanyichukwu (Nigeria), "Speech in Ben Sira, with special reference to 5,9–6,1", Th.D., Pontifical University of S. Thomae in Urbe, Rome, Italy, 1994. Publ.: *Speech in Ben Sira, with special reference to 5,9–6,1*. Frankfurt a.M.: Peter Lang, 1995 (European University Studies, xxiii/535).

Okwueze, Malachy Ikechukwu (Nigeria), "Myth: The Old Testament experience", Ph.D., University of Nigeria, Nsukka, Nigeria, 1995.

Onaiyekan, John (Nigeria), "The priesthood among the Owe-Yoruba of Nigeria and in pre-monarchical ancient Israel: A comparative study", Th.D., Pontifical Urban University, Rome, Italy, 1976.

Orji, Chukwuemeka (Nigeria), "And Yahweh delivered David wherever he went (2 Sam 8:6b.14b): Composition and redaction criticism of 2 Sam 1–8", Th.D., Pontifical Gregorian University, Rome, Italy, 1998.

Osuji, Boniface Anthony (Nigeria), "The Hebrew and Igbo concept of religion and sin compared in the light of biblical and rabbinic literature: Anthropo-ethnological study – partially explanatory", Th.D., Pontifical Urban University, Rome, Italy, 1967.

Osume, Charles Ereraina (Nigeria), "A study of the Okpe theophanises and their correspondences in the Old Testament", Ph.D., University of Aberdeen, Aberdeen, United Kingdom, 1984.

Pungumbu Shaondo, Lody (The Democratic Republic of the Congo), "L'intervention sociale d'Amos: Une contribution à l'étude de la mission prophétique en Afrique aujourd'hui", Th.D., Faculté universitaire de théologie protestante, Bruxelles, Belgium, 1991.

Ramarosata, Aline Raholisoa (Madagascar), "La notion du Dieu de l'alliance dans la tradition 'D' avec ses incidences sur le Nouveau Testament et sa portée oecuménique", Th.D., Faculté libre de théologie protestante, Paris, France, 1984.

Ravalomanana, Charlotte (Madagascar), "Création et providence: Étude exégétique du Psaume 104", Th.D., Faculté libre de théologie protestante, Montpellier, France, 1997.

Rwehumbiza, Rulange K. Phil. (Tanzania), "A comparative study between the development of Yahwistic monotheism and the concept of God among the Bantu people of Africa south of the Sahara: A biblico-theological evaluation", Th.D., Pontifical Lateran University, Rome, Italy, 1983. Publ.: *A Comparative Study Between the Development of Yahwistic Monotheism and the Concept of God Among the Bantu People of Africa South of the Sahara: A Biblico-Theological Evaluation*. Rome: Pontifical Lateran University, 1983.

Simbandumwe, Samuel S. (Zimbabwe), "Israel in two African prophet movements", Ph.D., University of Edinburgh, Edinburgh, United Kingdom, 1989. Publ.: *A Socio-Religious and Political Analysis of the Judeo-Christian Concept of Prophetism and Modern Bakongo and Zulu African Prophet Movements*. Lewiston: Edwin Mellen Press, 1992 (African Studies; 28).

Tchape, Jean-Bosco (Cameroon), "La terre promise dans le Deutéronome: Signification juridique et religieuse", Th.D., Université des sciences humaines de Strasbourg, Strasbourg, France, 1987.

Tesfai, Yacob (Eritrea), "This is my resting place: An inquiry into the role of time and space in the Old Testament", Th.D., Lutheran School of Theology, Chicago, Illinois, USA, 1975.

Tshidibi Bambila, Donatien Aimé (The Democratic Republic of the Congo), "La rétribution négative dans l'histoire monarchique d'Israël", Th.D., Pontifical University of S. Thomae in Urbe, Rome, Italy, 1997. Publ.: *La rétribution négative dans l'histoire monarchique d'Israël*. Rome: Pontifical University S. Thomae in Urbe, 1997.

Udofia, Sylvester Dan (Nigeria), "Documents from Old Testament times: Their implications for African Christians", Ph.D., University of Nigeria, Nsukka, Nigeria, 2000.

Ugwueze, Francis Oko (Nigeria), "Igbo proverbs and biblical proverbs: Comparative & thematic research", Th.D., Pontifical Urban University, Rome, Italy, 1976.

Ukpong, Justin S. (Nigeria), "Ibibo sacrifice and levitical sacrifice: A comparative study of the sacrificial systems of the Ibibio people of Nigeria and of ancient Israel as recorded in the book of Leviticus", Th.D., Pontifical Urban University, Rome, Italy, 1980. Publ.: *Sacrifice – African and Biblical: A Comparative Study of Ibibio and Levitical Sacrifices*. Rome: Urbaniana University Press, 1987.

Uzele, Kasamba Michel (The Democratic Republic of the Congo), "Proverbes 10,1–22,16: Essai de regroupment et d'interprétation des 'Meshalim'", Th.D., Pontifical Urban University, Rome, Italy, 1982.

Wafawanaka, Robert (Zimbabwe), "Perspectives on the problem of poverty in traditional Africa and in ancient Israel", Th.D., Boston University, Boston, Massachusetts, USA, 1997.

Yilpet, Yoiliah K. (Nigeria), "A rhetorical/intra-textual study of Isaiah's use of sedeq/sedaqa: 'righteousness' as order", Ph.D., Trinity Evangelical Divinity School, Deerfield, Illinois, USA, 1997.

Zinkuratire, Victor (Uganda), "The kingship of Yahweh in Israel's history, cult and eschatology: A study of Psalm 47", Ph.D., University of Cambridge, Cambridge, United Kingdom, 1987.

Zulu, Edwin (Zambia), "A Ngoni assessment of the role of ancestors within Israelite world-views and religion in Genesis 11:28–50:26", Th.D., University of Stellenbosch, Stellenbosch, South Africa, 1999.

Endnotes

1. For earlier examples of my research on academic interpretation of the Old Testament in Africa, cf. K. Holter, *Tropical Africa and the Old Testament: A Select and Annotated Bibliography*. Oslo: University of Oslo, 1996 (Faculty of Theology: Bibliography Series; 6), and *idem, Yahweh in Africa: Essays on Africa and the Old Testament*. New York: Peter Lang, 2000 (Bible and Theology in Africa; 1). For a presentation of the institutional context of this research, cf. the web-page of the "Africa & Old Testament Program" of the School of Mission and
    Theology, Stravanger , Norway:
    http://www.misjonshs.no/res/ot_africa/africa.html.

2. Let me make one remark to my use of the term "African" in this context: Generally speaking, I very much subscribe to a geographical and not for example a racial or cultural definition of "Africa." From this follows that the Arab north and the white south, in my view, are just as much "African" as anything else throughout the continent. Nevertheless, in the present paper I will for pragmatic reasons concentrate on Sub-Saharan Africa, and I will exclude dissertations written by South African scholars and also by scholars from the Maghribian countries.

3. The Association of African Universities has recently launched a project entitled *Database of African Theses and Dissertations*, and in this (forthcoming) database only dissertations written in and accepted by African universities will be included; for further information about this project, cf. its web-page (2001.04.22): http://www.aau.org/datad/. I think that is a correct decision for such a wide project. However, when it comes to the present project, the situation is very different. Here dissertations in one particular subject are focused, and then even a subject where only a few African universities and research institutions have established programs for post-graduate studies. I have therefore decided to include dissertations written by African scholars in non-African and South African universities and research institutions.

4. Three recent essay collections can exemplify the broad variety of African approaches to the Old Testament: M. Getui, K. Holter & V. Zinkuratire (eds.), *Interpreting the Old Testament in Africa: Papers from the International Symposium on Africa and the Old Testament in Nairobi, October 1999*. New York: Peter Lang, 2001 (Bible and Theology in Africa; 2); G.O. West & M.W. Dube (eds.), *The Bible in Africa: Transactions, Trajectories and Trends*. Leiden: Brill, 2000; H.W. Kinoti

& J.M. Waliggo (eds.), *The Bible in African Christianity: Essays in Biblical Theology.* Nairobi: Acton Publishers, 1997 (African Christianity Series).

5. The most recent and comprehensive bibliography in this area is G. LeMarquand, "A bibliography of the Bible in Africa", G.O. West & M.W. Dube (eds.), *The Bible in Africa: Transactions, Trajectories and Trends.* Leiden: Brill (2000) 633–800; for preliminary versions, cf. his "A bibliography of the Bible in Africa", *Bulletin for Contextual Theology* 2/II (1995) 6–40, and "Bibliography of the Bible in Africa", *Journal of Inculturation Theology* 2 (1995) 39–139. An online bibliography on "Africa and the Bible" has been compiled at the University of Stellenbosch, South Africa; its web-address (2001.04.22) is: telnet://oldlib.sun.ac.za. However, only a minority of the doctoral dissertations presented in the present project are listed in LeMarquand's bibliographies or in the Stellenbosch bibliography.

6. The closest is probably K. Holter, "The institutional context of Old Testament scholarship in Africa", *Old Testament Essays* 11 (1998) 452–461. For more general research surveys, cf. G.O. West, "On the eve of an African biblical studies", *Journal of Theology for Southern Africa* 99 (1997) 99–115; *idem*, "Mapping African biblical interpretation", G.O. West & M.W. Dube (eds.), *The Bible in Africa: Transactions, Trajectories and Trends.* Leiden: Brill (2000) 29–53; J. Punt, "Reading the Bible in Africa I", *Scriptura* 68 (1999) 1–11; *idem*, "Reading the Bible in Africa II", *Scriptura* 71 (1999) 313–329; K. Holter, "It's not only a question of money", *Old Testament Essays* 11 (1998) 240–254; *idem, Yahweh in Africa: Essays on Africa and the Old Testament.* New York: Peter Lang (2000) 9–25 (Bible and Theology in Africa; 1); J.S. Ukpong, "Developments in biblical interpretation in modern Africa", *Missionalia* 27 (1999) 313–329.

7. A remark to the question of sources: Basically the collection of this dissertation material reflects my own journey into African Old Testament scholarship. As a result of a number of visits to universities, theological seminaries, and theological and biblical conferences in various parts of Africa, I have had the priviledge of making personal acquaintance with many of the researchers whose dissertations are presented in this project. Many of them have provided me with information which else would have escaped my attention. In addition to these personal contacts, some written sources have been used: For a few of the Nigerian dissertations: *African Journal of Biblical Studies* 1/II (1986) 177–189; for some of the European dissertations: *Revue Théologique de Louvain*'s annual "Index international des dissertations doctorales en théologie et en droit canonique"; for most of the US dissertations: *Dissertation Abstracts.* As far as the Rome dissertations are concerned, I had the privilege to do research in all the Pontifical universities in Rome during a sabbatical in the spring term 2000, and all dissertations were made accessible to me.

8. In order to secure the findings a xeroxed version of my bibliography was distributed amongst approximately one hundred Old Testament scholars in 25 countries

throughout Africa in July 2000; a second version was published in November 2000 as K. Holter, "Old Testament researchers north of the Limpopo", *Bulletin for Old Testament Studies in Africa* 9 (2000) 6–21. These preliminary versions included general bibliographical information, but they had no abstracts of the dissertations. In both cases I received very valuable response.

9. Burkina Faso, Burundi, Cameroon, Central African Republic, Chad, Democratic Republic of the Congo, Eritrea, Gabon, Ghana, Kenya, Madagascar, Malawi, Namibia, Nigeria, Rwanda, Sierra Leone, Tanzania, Togo, Uganda, Zambia, Zimbabwe. Then follows a line with references to two dissertations where I have not been able to ascertain the nationality of the researcher.

10. Belgium, Cameroon, France, Germany, Italy, The Netherlands, Nigeria, Sweden, South Africa, Switzerland, United Kingdom, United States.

11. One example to demonstrate how the table goes: four researchers from Cameroon have completed their doctoral studies in France; the first one in 1968, the last one in 1988, and they all wrote their dissertations in French.

12. Cf. K. Holter, "The institutional context of Old Testament scholarship in Africa", *Old Testament Essays* 11 (1998) 452–461.

13. Cf. K. Holter, *Yahweh in Africa: Essays on Africa and the Old Testament.* New York: Peter Lang (2000) 9–25 (Bible and Theology in Africa; 1).

14. For a glimpse into the role of Old Testament studies in some African academic institutions in this period, cf. E.G. Newing, "A study of Old Testament curricula in Eastern and Central Africa", *Africa Theological Journal* 3 (1970) 80–98.

15. Cf. for example S.O. Abogunrin, "Biblical research in Africa", *African Journal of Biblical Studies* 1/1 (1986) 7–24; N. Onwu, "The current state of biblical studies in Africa", *Journal of Religious Thought* 41 (1985) 35–46; B.A. Ntreh, "Toward an African biblical hermeneutics", *Africa Theological Journal* 19 (1990) 247–254; J. Ukpong, "Reading the Bible with African eyes", *Journal of Theology for Southern Africa* 91 (1995) 3–14; *idem*, "Developments in biblical interpretation in modern Africa", *Missionalia* 27 (1999) 313–329.

16. Cf. for example Grantson: 1991; Wafawanaka: 1997; Zulu: 1999.

17. The two Lutherans are Kalugila: 1980 (University of Uppsala, Sweden) and Boniface-Malle: 2000 (Luther Seminary, St. Paul, USA). The two Roman Catholics are Rwehumbiza: 1983 (Pontifical Lateran University, Rome) and Byamungo: 1996 (Pontifical Gregorian University, Rome).

18. Monsengwo Pasinya: 1972; Naré: 1983.

19. Akaenyi: 1989; Akpunonu: 1971; Apuri: 1983; Ilonu: 1971; Lezoutie: 1995; Meluma: 1983; Mianbé Bétoudji: 1984; Ndiokwere: 1977; Ojo: 1996; Onaiyekan: 1976; Osuji: 1967; Ugwueze: 1976; Ukpong: 1980; Uzele: 1982.

20. Such as for example Trinity Evangelical Divinity School: Carew: 1998; Habtu: 1993; Kafang: 1993; Muthengi: 1992; Yilpet: 1997.

21. Such as for example Lutheran School of Theology, Chicago: Grantson: 1991; Ntreh: 1989; Tesfai: 1975.

22. Such as for example Harvard University: Mafico: 1979; and New York University: Arulefela: 1980.

23. The figures of population and Christian presence are taken from D.B. Barrett & al. (eds.), *World Christian Encyclopedia*. Oxford: Oxford University Press (2001) 211, 549.

24. For a survey that emphasizes this point, cf. J. Platvoet, "The institutional environment of the study of religions in Africa south of the Sahara", M. Pye (ed.), *Marburg revisited: Institutions and Strategies in the Study of Religion*. Marburg: Diagonal-Verlag (1989) 107–126.

25. An illustrating example could here be the situation in the University of Malawi; cf. K.R. Ross, "What has Jerusalem to do with Athens?", *Ministerial Formation* 56 (1992) 3–6; K. Fiedler & K.R. Ross, "Postgraduate theology degrees at the University of Malawi", *Ministerial Formation* 72 (1996) 15–19.

26. Cf. Prof. G.O. Abe (Ondo State University), Prof. D.T. Adamo (Delta State University), Dr S. Ademiluka (University of Ilorin), Prof. J.O. Akao (University of Ibadan), Dr A.C. Ariri-Chidomere (Lagos State University), Dr D.J.I. Ebo (University of Nigeria), Dr G.L. Lasebikan (University of Ibadan), Dr M.I. Okwueze (University of Nigeria), Dr Y.K. Yilpet (University of Jos).

CHAPTER VII

AFRICA AND AFRICANS IN THE ACTS OF APOSTLES

Joseph Enuwosa and Friday Udoisang

Introduction

The Acts of Apostles, while presenting the post ascension activities of the apostles especially Peter, Paul, Barnabas and a few others, can also be described as the record of the Acts of the Holy Spirit in the believers and church. Guy describes it as a history book of the spread of Christianity in the first century AD. It shows how the faith spread to the end of the earth and the Spirit's incorporation of the gentiles into the church. The apostolic epistles can likewise be described as correspondences reflecting the interaction of the early Apostles with certain persons and group of persons within the body of Christ, which carried divine authority and imparts grace to its readers.

The focus of this study is how the Africans participated in the early church in Acts. It reveals the extent to which Africans were involved in the Church of the Apostles. The research shows how Africans were used by the Holy Spirit in the spread and growth of the church. It answers the basic questions on, 'what were Africa and Africans' contributions to the growth and the spread of the church? The study, therefore, is an interesting research on the role of Africa and Africans in the Acts of the Apostle.

The hermeneutical approach of this study is critical exegesis and historical method. The text of Acts is critically interpreted in the light of classical and recent writings on ancient history. The combination of rational and historical interpretation helps to establish a definite and objective meaning of a biblical passage. The Methods includes Africa and Africans in the Bible Approach. This is Africentric method of biblical interpretation. The idea behind this approach, according to B.E Klem is retrieval of lost meaning from a text that once disclosed the core of a community's self —understanding.[2] This can save the passage in the Bible from meaningless interpretation. In this sense, meaning is not the subjective construction of the interpreter[3] as in historico—form criticism of the West. Here the real meaning to recover from the biblical text is the author's intention.

There are reasons to believe that Africa and Africans did not only participate in the Acts of the Holy Spirit and gospel of grace, but were active members of the church and participated in the spread of Christianity. They also interacted with the early Apostles and distinguished themselves among the brethren. African presence can be seen where Luke mentioned the names of African proselytes in Acts 2:5-13, who got converted on Pentecost day. (Acts 2:37-41), the mention of the Ethiopian Eunuch (Acts 8:26-39), African preachers and teachers in Acts 13:1, Lydia in Acts 16:14-15, 40 and Rufus (Rom. 13)

Defining Africa and Africans in the Acts of the Apostles

The word Africa is not mentioned in the New Testament as such. Its wide usage is recent. According to D.T. Adamo, the colonial masters, applied this to the continent during the scramble for Africa. In antiquity, the Greeks used Libya to refer to a limited part of North Africa, the portion opposite the coast of Greece and west of Egypt. The Greeks refer to the entire continent of Africa as Ethiopia and the Romans Africa[4] Africa is derived from the Latin root Aprica meaning sunny or the Greek Aphrika meaning without cold[5].. It was mainly applied to the Northern coast of African continent which was regarded as the Southern extension of Europe.

Africa is also the English translation of the Arabic wordIfriqiyah.[6] Old Testament Hebrews were very familiar with Egypt in Africa and referred to Libya with the name Lehabim (Gen. 10:13) and Lubim (2 Chron. 12:3). Other parts of Africa known to the Hebrews were Cush, Wawat, Nehesi, Magan, Meluha, Ethiopia and Put[7] whose inhabitants were regarded as the Hamitic stock. In this way, we use the term Africa as the land of the blacks and Africans for the citizens of the black continents as it was known to the ancient Greeks, Hebrews and the Romans. Thus, at the time of the New Testament, the term, Africa was well known to the Jews, Greeks and Romans. The Hebrews sometimes used various names of tribal groups for Africa. These names as found in the New Testament are *Aiguptos/Aiguptios* (Egypt/Egyptians, Matt 2:13-19, Acts 2:10); Libues (Libya, Acts 2:10);Aithiops (Ethiopians, Acts 8:27); Niger (Niger, Acts 13:1).

Aiguptos (Egypt)

Aiguptos is the Greek word for Egypt. It is one of the terms used in the New Testament for Africa and Africans. (Matt. 2:13-19; Acts 2:10; 7:9-10; 21:38; Heb. 3:16; 8:9; 11:26-29; Jude 5; Rev.11:8). The Hebrews called Egypt *Mitzrayim*[8] While Egypt appeared twenty four times in the New Testament, Egyptians surfaced five times. According to C. Brown, the Greek word *Aiguptos* is derived from the Egyptian *hwt — k²— pth* which is pronounced *ha — ku — ptah*. It was the name of the ancient capital of Egypt opposite modern Cairo. The term was later used for both the country as well as its capital[9].

Some scholars agreed that Ham was the ancestor of the Egyptians and Egypt was the land of Ham. Walter Arthur McCray said that the name Ham means hot, heat and by implication black[10]. This implies that the Cushites, Egyptians, Putites and Cananites were Africans because they were sons of Ham. C.A. Diop believes that ancient Egyptian civilisation was a Negro Civilisation. They are people of the same race with Egyptians. Diop did not dispute the popular tradition that Ethiopia was the ancestral home of the Egyptians. He asserts that the assimilation of the white race into the black populace over the years did not change the Negro features of the Egyptians[11].

Josephus treats Egypt as the land of Ham (Ant. IV, 1.2; Gen. 10:23; Ps. 78:57; 105:23). He described the Egyptians as follows, ... for the four sons of Ham, time has not hurt the name Chus, ... the memory also of the Mesraities is preserved in their names; for all that inhabit Judea call Egypt/Egyptians — Mastre, Mastrean[12].

David Tuesday Adamo discussing Wallis Budge contended that the testimonies of the Egyptians themselves are clear about their origin. The inscriptions of Hatsheput mentioned several expeditions to a place called Punt. It recorded that during the reign of the Queen, they went as far as Cape Guardefui where plenty of gifts from the Queen were presented to the governor of Punt called Pa-hehu. From the expedition, they brought back ebony, ivory, gold, incense, myrrh and precious stones[13].

The Queen saw the Puntites as their ancestors. In other words, the Egyptians agreed that Punt was their place of origin. Some scholars located Punt in the present Somali land instead of Arabia. The African origin of Egyptian people and civilisation is, therefore, incontestable.[14] All living things considered, it seems tolerably certain that the men of Punt, spice-land who influenced the manners, customs, and belief of the people in the Nile Valley, were of African origin[15]

Libues (Libya)

One of the terms also used in the New Testament for Africa and Africans is the Greek language was *Libues* (Acts 2:10). It is Libya in English language. Libya or Libyans are translated from three distinct Hebrew words as follows:
(i) *Kub:* King James Version Has Chub and LXX translated it *Libues*
(ii)*Lubim*: This is the tranlation in King James Version, AV and RSV (Libues, Plural)
(iii) *Put:* LXX has Phout, KJV Phut and RSV Put.

Put is identified in Genesis 10:6 as one of the Sons of Ham the brother of Cush, Egypt and Cannan. The term Lehabim in Genesis 10:13 is generally regarded by some scholars as an alternative spelling for Lubim. Hence it is a reference to Libyans who inhabit the desert region of North Africa, West of the Nile valley in Egypt[16] J.E. Harris stated that Put was the founder of Libya and regarded the inhabitants as Phutites.[17] Other Old Testament reference to Libya link it with Egypt and Ethiopia (2 Chron. 12:3; 16:8; Ezek. 30:5; Dan 11:13; Nahum 3:9)

The New Testament also links Libya with Egypt. Cyrene was one of the Libyan cities in antiquity with a large Jewish colony almost like that of Alexandria. Greek and Roman historians and poets used the word *Libyes* for the inhabitants of North Africa. David Tuesday Adamo maintained that Herodotus (480 — 425 BC) and Sallust (86-35 B.C) used Libya for the whole continent of Africa.[18] Diodorus employed the term Libya to denote Africa of the Nile as far as Egypt.[19]

The New Testament mentioned some Cyrenians of Libya such as Simon of Cyrene, Alexander and Rufus (Matt. 27:32; Mk 15:21; Lk. 23:26; Acts 13:1). We also have Cyrenius who was the governor of Syria and might have been an African from Cyrene. The city was the capital of the province of Cyrenica. It is also called Pentapolis founded in 630 BC by Dorian Greek from Crete.[20]

Aithiops (Ethiopia)

Ethiopia is another term used in the New Testament to designate Africa and its inhabitants. The word Ethiopia, occurs only in one passage in the New Testament (Acts 8:27). It refers to the black people inhabiting the land south of the Mediterranean coast of Africa. In recent time, the work of D.T. Adamo reveals the various contentions concerning the origins and meanings of the word *Aethiops* (Ethiopia) [21] The derivations of *Aethiops* in his study can be summarised as follows:

1. The 19th century BC inscription in the palace of Nesor at Pyles by ancient Crete used ai-ti-jo-go from where Aethiops is derived.
2. Homer employed *Aethiops* in his Odyssey and Illiad in the 9th century BC and mentioned two Ethiopia.

3. Original name of Zeus in the Island of Chios meaning glowing or black.
4. Pliny, the Elder: *Aetiops* as son of Vulcan, god of mortal and fire.
5. Edward Glasser: *Etiopyawan* derived from the abundance of incense in the region.
6. Environmental theory: Aethiops as burnt-faced persons referring to people of dark skin colour, the result of intense heat of the sun.

Thus, in Hesiod theogony, Ethiopians were black. The consensus that can be inferred from scholars' views is that Aethiops (Ethiopia) is a Greek word used by Greco-Roman poets, historians and geographers to describe African people in terms of skin, wisdom, distance and might. The Greek writers were conscious of an idealised far away land, the end of the earth. The land is mystified. This romantic approach gave Ethiopia a pride of place.

The argument of Homer and Herodotus on two Ethiopians has a strong implication. It raises the question if Jews can be Africans. D.T. Adamo, citing Wallis Budge who interpreted Herodotus said:

> It seems certain that classical historians and geographers called the whole region from India to Egypt, both countries inclusive, by name Ethiopia, and in consequence they regarded all the dark-skinned and black people who inhabited it as Ethiopians. Mention is made of Eastern and Western Ethiopians. I have been driven to the conclusion that the Ethiopians whose manner and customs have been so fully described by Herodotus, Diodorus, Strabo, Pliny and others were not Abyssinians at all, but the natives of Upper Nubia and the Islands of Meroe...[23].

In this way, the black race or Africans were regarded as Ethiopians including those in the Persian Gulf, India and South America. They were, therefore, descendants of Cush. We may deduce from this wide geographical usage of Ethiopia that Ur of Chaldeans (Gen. 11:29) was one of the Ethiopian cities. The reason is that Eastern Ethiopians were the Hamitic race who migrated to Asia with Nimrod. They formed large cities. Nimrod was one of the sons of Cush. (Gen. 10:8). He was a great black ancestor who founded Babylonian and Assyrian Kingdoms (Gen. 8-11). The book of Genesis described him as a mighty hunter before the Lord (Gen. 10:9).

The Bible in Genesis shows the land and cities of Nimrod. Nimrod's Kingdom began in Babylon and expanded into Assyria. He founded Babel, Erech, Accad and Calneh which formed his Babylonian Kingdom. Nineveh, Rehoboth, Calah, and Resen (Gen. 10:9-11), made up his Assyrian Kingdom. [24]. According to G. Eghagha, there were two migratory waves by Hamites. First Mizraites migrated through Malayan region spreading along the South and East coasts of the Mediterranean. Second, some Cushites went through the Persian Gulf spreading Eastward to India.[25]

The Jews, therefore, can be regarded as Africans because the Hebrew great ancestor Abraham came from Ur of Chaldeans (Gen. 11:29) which was part of the Babylonian kingdom founded by Nimrod, the son of Cush. Ur of Chaldeans is forty miles to Erech, the present day Warka.[26] G. Eghagha discovered that the writings and the language of Ur are Hamitic.[27] Hence W.A McCray pointed out that the culture and civilisation spawned by Nimrod from Southern to Northern Mesopotamia.[28] The Jews also became Africans through naturalisation. The long stay of some Jews in Egypt particularly, Alexandria and Cyrene made them African natives. An immigrant becomes a native after ten years of residing in the place. So we have Alexandrian Jews, Ethiopian Jews.

In the New Testament era, Egypt played host to not fewer than a million Jews. They became very prosperous, influential and well-cultured especially in the city of Alexandria where some Jews held important state offices under the Ptolemiac dynasty. This disposition of African Egypt made the holy family to find comfort in Africa when they were in danger (Matt. 2:13). Moreover, the process of intermarriages can make some to become Africans and Africans to be Jews. Africans also were made Jews in the Bible as Proselytes

In this way, there can hardly be any doubt that Ethiopians and Mizraites have common historical link with Israel. Thus a Cushite, a black man in the person of Nimrod founded the first monarch in the world. In further proof of the relation between Ethiopia and Chaldea, said Adamo all the tradition of Babylonians and Assyrians point to a connection in very early time to Ethiopian culture.[29] He agreed with G. Rawlison that all Ethiopians, both in Africa, India, and the Euphrates valley belong to the same race[30].

J.E. Harris cited an inscription discovered by A.H. Sayer and G.C. Griffith in 1914. It contains the way the Ethiopians described their land as the land *Qevs, Kesh.*[31] This is rendered with the Egytian word *Kush* translated in Hebrew as Cush. This was the designation applied to Ethiopians by Egyptians and the Old Testament for thousand of years. While Adamo used Kush, McCray preferred Cush.[32] Cush was one of the sons of Ham. Others are Egypt, Put and Canaan (Gen 10:7). The Cushite Kingdom had its capital at Kerma or Moroa. We have emphasised Ethiopia, it is the name found in Acts of the Apostles (Acts 8:27). Cush is not used in the New Testament.

Ancient Egyptians also, knew Ethiopians and its people with other names. The earliest known record is the inscription on the Palermo stone (3000 BC). In it, the region immediately South of Egypt was designated *Nehsyw* or *Nahasi* which means black or land of the blacks. Other names with which Ethiopia was known in Egypt include the words, *Khent* (borderland), *Ta-Sti* (land of the bow), and *Nub* (gold). These portray Ethiopia as the land of bow men, the land of gold as well as the land of blacks.

Hebrew and Asian sources show that Cush and Cushites were used in ancient time in place of Ethiopia/Ethiopians (1 Chron. 1:8-10; Ps.7). J.E. Harris cited Josephus who said that of the four sons of Ham, time has not at all hurt the name Cush for the Ethiopians over whom he reigned, are even at this day both by themselves and by all men in Asia called Cushites[33]. In antiquity, therefore, Cush and Cushites were used to refer to both Ethiopians and blacks in general. They denote Ethiopia, Africa and Africans.

Νιγερ (Niger)

Νιγερ is the term used in the New Testament for Africans. It is translated Niger. The word is used only once in the New Testament (Acts 13:1). J.H. Thayer said that the word Niger is a Latin name meaning, black. Thayer considers the Niger in Acts 13:1 as the surname of Simon.[34]. it means that Niger was his initial.

Cushite is the most frequently used word with colour significance for the black person (an African) in the Old Testament. The Greek equivalence for an African is *Aethiops*. Whereas the Roman equivalence is Niger. Hence C.B. Copher said that Greek and Latin terms were used to translate the Hebrew word Cush and related terms in the Old Testament for Africa and Africans. [35] In the New Testament, Niger and Ethiopia were used to translate Cush and related Old Testament terms for blacks.

Thus, Niger translates the Old Testament word in the New Testament for the Hebrew term Cush and the Greek word Ethiopia. These terms were used for Africans on account of their black colour, coiled and woolly hair-characteristics. Luke in Acts 13:1 used the word to describe the African prophet who was probably Simon of Cyrene. We would, therefore, agree with D.T. Adamo that the use of the names, *Cush, Aethiops, Libues* and Put by ancient Greek writers is an indication that the name Ethiopia was not only used for the area of Meroe. It included all the modern territory of the continent of Africa.[36]

This appears very probable when one examines the reports of Herodotus. Herodotus reported that the Phoenicians circumnavigated Ethiopia. Eudoxus of Cynicus and Hanno passed by Ethiopia and came to Mauritania and Senegal. They reported that Ethiopia was surrounded by the Ocean.[37] Thus, Ethiopia, Cush, and *Aiguptos* were used in a more general sense by Homer, Hesiod, Herodotus and Diodorus. They were used for all dark-skinned people and the land which they inhabited. So in every passage where the word Ethiopia and Niger occur in the New Testament can be translated Africa, African or Black. This term is the most natural equivalent of the biblical term for Africa today.[38]

Some of these names in the ancient (Cush, Nubia, Put, Nehesi) were no longer in vogue at the time of the New Testament. The geography and names of places and people in this period started to take a definite shape. The vagary that characterized the knowledge of places and people was no more. Places were precisely known by their names. Ethiopia was precisely known as Ethiopia and Egypt. *Aphrike* or *Ifriqiya* was in vogue and used as substitute for Cush as a reference to Africa or Africans. In fact most of the ancient names for cities faded away, some were changed and others were destroyed by wars or natural disasters. The Roman, Barbarian and Arab conquests devastated the ancient world of the Bible.

African Proselytes at Pentecost (Acts 2:5-13, 37-41)

The records in Acts 2:5-13, 37-41 give us an indication that Africans were present on the Pentecost day at Jerusalem and probably among those who responded to Peter's message for repentance and accepted Jesus as their Saviour. According to Guy, Acts 1-12 tells us how Jerusalem was the centre for Jewish Christianity.[39] The passage (Acts 2:5-13, 37-41) is an information to Theophilus about what took place on Pentecost day in Jerusalem and of the audience that witnessed, participated and testified to that incident.

F.J. Jackson and K. Lake consider the narrative in Acts 1:6-2:47 as coming from the Jerusalem source and possibly from Peter.[40] While M. Black said that Luke took over a single Aramaic document which emanated from Jerusalem which translated and expanded the first 15 chapters, [41] F.J. Jackson and K. Lake[42] connect the sources of Acts 1-15 to individuals as Peter, Philip and John Mark. They also admit that traditions may have grown up around places as well as around persons. We can believe that Luke got his information from oral traditions in Jerusalem and from trust- worthy individuals.

Pentecost was the Jewish feast of weeks that was celebrated on the fiftieth day after Passover, Historically, it commemorated the giving of the law at Sinai and completed the in-gathering harvest. In Christianity, Guthrie said that the outpouring of the Spirit on Pentecost concluded the act of ascension which is a direct fulfilment of Old Testament prophecy.

Luke recorded that the Pentecost day was marked by the descent of the Holy Spirit in a spectacular, noisy way that attracted Judaizers from every land who were at Jerusalem for the Pentecost festival. To their amazement, these worshippers heard those who had received the Holy Spirit speaking in languages that were identified to be different from the popular Greek, Aramaic and Hebrew. They were the more surprised when they saw the Galileans speaking in the native languages of their different nations. Such nations included Egypt and parts of Libya near Cyrene (Lk. 2:10). Acts 2:11 adds that the crowd was made up of Jews and converts to Judaism.

R.H. Pfeiffer cited Philo, an Alexandrian Jew who lived between 20 BCE-50 CE. He said that there were not fewer than one million Jews in Alexandria Egypt in his time. He also mentioned that two of the five quarters into which Alexandria was divided were called the Jewish.[43] Apart from Alexandria, the Jews also settled in other parts of the country. Thus, Egypt opened up her learning facilities to the Jews. This made possible the translation of the Hebrew scripture into Greek in Alexandria, the then capital of Egypt in 250 BCE.

Many Jews also settled in Cyrene and other Libyan cities and villages doing various jobs. The Jews in Cyrene, as in Alexandria, enjoyed enormous rights like the Greeks. The Jews also established synagogues where they and their converts (proselytes) met for worship, prayer and reading of the Torah in all places of settlement. Proselytes were attracted to Judaism by the practice of circumcision, Sabbath rest, and avoidance of swine meat, monotheism, imageless worship and high ethical conduct of the Jews in Diaspora. These concepts were not new to Egyptians. They were already taught in their mystery systems. These ideas must have attracted more Africans to the Jewish faith than other nations.

Jesus (Matt. 23:15), and Paul (Rom. 2:9) mentioned the proselytizing zeal of the Jews in the first century A.D. The influx of proselytes into the Jewish communities abroad (outside Palestine) made the Jewish population to increase. These converts were naturalized into the Jewish nations or became citizens of Israel by adopting the tenets of Judaism. Those who would not fully adhere to these demands remained as mere adherents proselytes of the gate or just fearer of God. The semi-proselytes sent contribution to the Temple in Jerusalem from time to time for pilgrimage during festivals. The proselytes from Egypt and Libya must have included Africans and other foreigners dwelling in Egypt and Libya.

The later appearance of persons like Simeon (called Niger) and Lucius of Cyrene who were Africans (Acts 13:1) among the Christians who later left Jerusalem to Antioch due to the persecution proved that the proselytes who were converted on Pentecost day (Acts 2:37-41) included Africans.

Luke reported that after Peter's address, the listening crowd in the day of Pentecost were cut to heart and said to Peter: Brother, what shall we do? After a call for repentance, about three thousand persons accepted Christ that day (Acts 2:38-41). There must have been African natives among the number of the proselytes that witnessed that occasion. Africans, therefore, were among the first converts after Pentecost. They learnt from, and interacted with the Apostles thereafter together with other Jews from Cyrene and Alexandria whom they came with. While some African converts may have returned home after the festivals during persecution that affected Stephen, some went to Antioch with other Christian brethren (Acts 11:20) for preaching.

African Teachers and Preachers (Acts 13:1)

The appearance of Africans in Acts 13:1 confirms the fact that some of those who left Jerusalem to Antioch (whom Luke describes as men from Cyrene, Acts 11:20) were Africans.

Luke records that within the church at Antioch, outstanding Africans named Simon called Niger and Lucius of Cyrene were numbered in the leadership. The clear identification of these men who were among the prophets and teachers brings to rest any doubt about the presence of African proselytes among those who accepted Christ on Pentecost day and who formed the nucleus of the first generation church.

While examining the terms used for Africa and Africans in the synoptic gospels, we discovered that Niger was a Latin name for black. The Greek equivalent of this name was Ethiopia which in the Old Testament is translated as Cush.[44] There is no doubt that this term was used here to describe an African in the light of his colour and Negroid characteristic. We noticed that the name (Σιμον) Simon, is also a Greek name for a flat nosed person.

This Simon was same as the Simon of Cyrene who with his children were well known in early church (Mark 15:21) and who also bore the cross of Jesus. Although Barclay said, Simon was a Jew who moved in Roman circles,[15] it is doubtful if the Romans gave the name Niger to a person who had no African characteristics. There is no reason to doubt if Simeon and Lucius were Africans. If they were diasporas Jews in Cyrene, Luke would have said it.

In this subsection, Africans from Egypt, Cyrene in Libya, and other unnamed Africans were among the proselytes who were converted on Pentecost day. They were affected by the first Christians persecution and began to proclaim the good tidings of Christ like the Jews. Moreover, they were among the distinguishing prophets and teachers of God's word in Antioch in Syria, some of them returned to Africa to evangelize. Thus, Simon and his household became strong believers in Christ. He related his experience to his children, Rufus and Alexander. He migrated to Antioch where they became leaders of the church in Antioch that had a large African population. They might have participated in the laying-on of hands on Paul and Barnabas for the ministry. These Africans were, therefore, among Christians who founded the Church in Antioch (Acts 11:20).

African Education of Moses and Its Effects in the New Testament (Acts 7:20, 37).

Apart from Jesus Christ, it is doubtful if the influence and teachings of any biblical figure surpasses that of Moses. All Old Testament prophets and teachers were appealing to the law of Moses as the most inspiring and authoritative religious code for God's people. Judaizers claimed to be the disciples of Moses (John 9:28). Those who despised the law of Moses were to die (Heb. 10:28). In the dispute between Stephen and members of the oppositions group in Acts 6, the strongest case thought out by the opposition group against Stephen that attracted instant condemnation and death was the charge of blasphemy against Moses and against God in the following words.

> For we have heard him say that this Jesus of Nazareth will destroy
> this place and change the customs handed down to us (Acts 6:14).

The main disagreement between Judaizers and Christians, was the point of changing the laws or custom of Moses which the Judaizers presumed Christians and their masters were against (Matt 5:17, 19-20). His disciples also had this view about him. This shows that the Judaizers and Jesus with His disciples held Moses in high esteem. None of them wanted to be guilty or changing the laws of Moses.

In Stephen's defence of his faith, he recalled the great works of Moses among the Jews and charged them to be breakers of the law of Moses, hence their action of murdering the righteous one (Acts 6:20-52). This shows that both judaizers and Christians of all ages have validly held the law of Moses in their relationship to God and fellowman. It shows that Moses did influence New Testament belief. Who was this Moses that is influencing men up till now? Where was he trained? Stephen informed us as follows about the upbringing of Moses:

> At that time Moses was born, and he was no ordinary child. For three months he was cared for in his father's house; when he was placed outside, Pharaoh's daughter took him and brought him up as her own son. Moses was educated in all the wisdom of the Egyptians and was powerful in speech and action (Acts 7:20-22).

Josephus confirmed the above report about the adoption of Moses by an African Princes and has gained the name of that Princess as Thermuthis. According to Josephus, Moses was named by Thermuthis from the Egyptian words mo meaning water and Uses meaning that saved out of it.[46] Mo plus Uses which equals Moses means one saved out of water in Egyptian language. The name Moses is, therefore, an African name.

One of the things, reported by Josephus about Moses is the foretelling of his birth by an Egyptian sacred scribe. This prophecy scared the King and this caused the destruction of Jewish male infants as reported by Stephen and in Exodus. However, for the beauty of Moses and favour of God, Moses was preserved through Thermuthis who got him educated. In this way Egyptian education was given to Moses. The result was that Moses understanding became superior to those of his age, far beyond their standard. For when he was taught, he discovered greater quickness of apprehension in him than was usual of his age, and his action at that time was promising when he would come to the age of a man.[47]

According to the Pyramid Texts, (PT), the coffin Texts (CT), the Ramesside Stela, the Book of the Dead (BD), the Memphite Theology, the Leiden Papyrus (LP), the Amarna letters and other scrolls contain speculative thoughts of Egyptian cosmology from the first dynasty to the Ptolemaic period. (these have been translated by Egyptians such as James P. Allen, E.A. Wallis Budge),[48] the Egyptians had three religious centres. These centres were manned by priest — scholars who were the intellectual class in Egypt and Kings were subject to them. These priest-castes were living a life of leisure, far from material pre-occupations, and had all the time necessary to deepen theoretical thoughts. All classes of knowledge and philosophy, recently credited to the Greeks, started in these schools and notable Greek scholars had to visit Egypt to complete their education.

Joseph quotes Manetho as saying that Moses was one of the learned Priests of Heliopolis. Manetho is also quoted as saying that the priest who ordained

Jewish policy and their laws was by birth of Heliopolis and his name was Osarsiph from Osiris, who was the god of Heliopolis. But that when he was gone over to his people (the Jews), his name was changed and he was called Moses[17]

There is every likely-hood from the report of Stephen, Josephus and Manetho, in consideration of the special education Pharaoh's daughter gave to Moses, that Moses did not only schooled in the Heliopolitan mystery system school in Egypt, but he must have undertaken studies from the Memphite and Hermopolitan schools. He must have been properly taught about all Egyptian cosmology. Research reveals that such great doctrines as contained in the Old and New Testaments such as monotheism, immortality of soul, circumcision, creation stories, virtues, constitution of man, Trinity and incarnation of God were not only taught in these schools, but were found in Egyptian mythologies even before the time of Moses.

Herodotus said that the Egyptians were the first to have maintained the doctrine that the soul of man is immortal[16]. Pharaoh Akhenaton (1350 BCE) of the 18th dynasty was already reviving and promoting monotheism at the time when Moses was being trained in Egypt. It would not be out of order to state that Moses' theological concepts were highly influenced not only by his education in the African mystery schools, but he was in sympathy with monotheism spearheaded by Akhenaton. If we accept Manetho's statement as reported by Joshepus above, Moses must have been a distinguished priest of the Heliopolitan system before the crisis that made him escape from Egypt into the desert. In writing the law later, Moses must have employed written documents, which had been handed down from early times[17]. Creation stories as reported in Gen. 1 and the God-word discourse in John 1:1-3 show great resemblance with those of the three Egyptian systems blended together.

However, while we will allow that in the light of the special revelation received by Moses at Sinai, Yahweh would have changed and transformed him including most of his theological concepts. He would not have thrown away all that was African which were not in conflict with his new experience. Rather, he might have adapted and modified Yahwism and improved on the foundations laid in his African training to create a new theology with African background. When Jesus came to introduce the new covenant, he claimed to be fulfilling the Laws of Moses. On that premise, he modified some laws, did away with the unnecessary, (Matt. 5: 17, 21-43; Luk. 10: 25-28). Paul with his Damascus-road experience used his background in pharisaic training in Judaism, Hellenistic exposure and his view to work out a new theology with a background that was Hellenistic — Judaism. Both Jesus and Paul had their background in Moses, and Moses had his background in African training in Egypt and especially the Heliopolitan system.

We can, therefore, say that the New Testament theology is African theology modified. In fact, the African theology was what Moses Yahwesized and Christians Jesusized. In the light of these submissions, we can say that all references to the teaching of Moses, and the typologies, and symbolism or prototypes enunciated in the Old and New Testaments, especially the epistles, such as sacrificial systems in the book of Hebrews, have their background in Africa. They are an up-liftment of African theological concepts, which came to the Jews through the African education of Moses. To recognize the contribution of Moses in the New Testament is to recognize African contribution to the New Testament writings.

The Ethiopian Eunuch (Acts 8: 26- 39)

One of the clearest and undeniable presences of an African in the New Testament is the story of conversion of the Ethiopian Eunuch. The Ethiopian Eunuch is said to be the finance minister of Candace, the queen of the Ethiopians. The Ethiopian kingdom of the queen is Meroe. Ethiopia, then, was made up of many kingdoms and Meroe was one of the kingdoms. The New Testament used Ethiopia in the Greco-Roman world to refer to the African race including that part of the continent. Candace was a royal title of the Queen. It was used in the place of the title King. The persecution and the dispersion encouraged the spread of the gospel in which Philip one of the seven deacons was active. The Eunuch was on his way back from pilgrimage to Jerusalem. He was reading the book of Isaiah on his chariot when the Holy Spirit directed Philip to meet him for better explanation. After a careful explanation of the passage by Philip, the Eunuch believed in Christ and demanded to be baptized.

After the baptism, Philip left him and he continued his journey to Ethiopia. The word (*Eunoucho),* Eunuch can mean an emasculated person[18] or a government officer[19]. The Greeks explained Eunuch as a compound of *eune* (bed) and *echo* (hold). Hence it means a holder or a guardian of bed.[20]

In the Old Testament, *Euvouxos* also translate the Hebrew word *saris* which at times used for a court officer without indication of he was castrated or not (Gen. 39: 1; 40:2).[21] It is likely that in Acts 8: 27, its usage is no more than a high court official. According to D.T. Adamo, *eunoukos* means officer rather than a castrated person in this context. The Greek words *Eunoukos* and *saris* mean a very high officer. Both words denote a high political or military officer.[21]. It does not imply castration because the Old Testament shows that a castrated person cannot be a member of the Jewish community (Deut. 23:1). But, the Eunuch was admitted into Judaism as a proselyte. In the New Testament, mention is made of different types of Eunuch's who were not necessarily castrated (Matt. 19: 12).

If the Ethiopian Eunuch was castrated, he would not have been allowed to enter the temple to worship according to Jewish law (Deut. 23:1). For this reason, the phrase is better translated African Officer. Luke specifically referred to him as treasurer. Biblical scholars are still not sure if he was a full proselyte or just a worshipper at the gate. Whatever may be the case, biblical interpreters are not in dispute as to the African origin of the Eunuch in Acts 8:26-40. It is interesting to note how this African searched the scriptures as he took leisure in reading from the prophets. His use of Isaiah indicates that he was literate. It also indicates that Africans were already acquainted with the Old Testament before the birth of Christ. The Bible, therefore, had a place in the lives of Africans since its existence. The Holy Spirit directed Philip to meet him for greater enlightenment. With a ready heart, he received Jesus Christ and requested to be baptised. The baptism of the Ethiopian indicates that membership in the early church actually includes Ethiopians/Africans from the very beginning[22] in fulfilment of the scriptures (Ps. 68:31). Why was the eunuch singled out? This was due to a divine direction (Acts 8:29). It shows that the ministry of Philip to the Ethiopian eunuch was specially arranged by God.

According to Gregory of Nyssa, Christ came to make blacks white and that in the Kingdom of Heaven, Ethiopians became white.[23] A tradition grew that the Eunuch became an apostle not only to Ethiopia, but also to Arabia.[24] By baptism of the Eunuch, Philip proclaimed that consideration of race and external conditions are of no significance in determining membership of the church. Thus, there was no colour prejudice of any kind against Africans in the Old and New Testaments. It is also to prove that God never left out Africa and Africans in whatever he does with mankind. Here again is an instance of an African worshiper whom God reached in the New Testament and who left his country to be a witness for Christ in the first century AD. It is important to know that this narrative is a remarkable lesson on the universality of the church. It was a further step in the history of the gospel from its strictly Jewish enclave to a full-fledged gentile mission. The gospel having conquered Samaria was truly on its way to the end of the earth (Act 18).

Lydia-The African Convert in Asia Minor (Acts 16: 14-15, 40)

During the second Missionary journey of Paul, he spent most of his time evangelizing Europe. At Philipi, he met a purple cloth dealer by name Lydia. She was a native of Thyatira in the then Asia Minor province. Luke reports that she was a worshipper of God, and that after listening to Paul's preaching, God opened her heart to respond to Paul's message and got baptized. She also provided hospitality to Paul and his men.

There is every reason to believe that this woman was an African in Diaspora. The first indication of this is through her name Lydia. Thyatira where she came from was a city under the district known as Lydia during the Persian Empire (500BCE).

This district was known as Lud in the ancient world (2000-1550 BCE). Lydia, therefore, has its root from the word Lud (in singular) and Ludim (in plural). It was common for people to bear ethnic names. Lydia is then a personal name and an ethnic name[25]. In Genesis 10, Lud is a Semite city (v. 22) and Ludim is a city of Hamites (v. 13). In Jeremiah 46:9, Ludim is associated with Ethiopia. In Ezekiel 27:10, it is linked with Put (Libya) and Persia. In Ezekiel 30:5, Lud is connected with Ethiopians and Put (Libya) as allies of Egypt. This shows that the Ludites or Lydians were associated with Africans and may have lived in North Africa. It is possible that the people of Ludim were associated with the Lydians (Lud) in Assyria and in Asia Minor due to intermarriage and migration from the native of North Africa at an early stage of their history. There is an archaeological evidence of their presence in Western Asia Minor before the middle of 2000 BCE.[26]

According to Josephus, the people from Lud are called Ludians.[27] Wenham says they were not Semites but Hamites.[28]. The fact that the Lydians were blacks is reinforced by the consideration that ancient Egyptians and Cushites dominated and colonized the Babylonian, Assyrian and most Asiatic kingdoms in antiquity, such as the exploits of Nimrod, Sesostris, Tithonus, King of Ethiopia, Memnon himself and others.[29] William Hansbery relates a tradition in the Aegean world which says that people of inner Africa were famed as valiant warriors and used to send great forces abroad into other countries where they succeeded in bringing many parts of the world under their dominion. Another account has it that long before the Trojan War, there was a nation situated in Northern Africa on the borders of Ethiopia which was ruled by a long line of powerful female sovereigns. Under the leadership of one of these, an Amazon queen named Merina, there arose a large army which did not only over run vast regions of Northern Africa and Western Asia, but also conquered many island in the Mediterranean Sea.[31]

Herodotus said that Colchians were the descendants of African soldiers left behind by Pharaoh Sesotris on the banks of Phasis River in Asia Minor during his military expedition. They have thick lips, broad noses, and woolly-hair and burnt skin just as the Egyptians and Ethiopians.[32]According to Onyewuenyi, the sketch of the ancient Egyptian empire under Pharaoh Sesotris and Pharaoh Thutmose III makes it clear that Ionia was a colony of Egypt.[35]

In the light of biblical records linking Ludim with Ethiopians and Egyptians, and the proven record from Herodotus, Strabo and other classical writers about the black origin of the Ionians and Colchians and other black peoples of Asia Minor, it is reasonable to conclude that Lydia was an African woman. It becomes an interesting fact that Paul's first convert in Europe was an African. She showed what Africans are noted for — hospitality, which she offered to Paul and his team. This is another instance to show that even in Greco-Roman period, Africa produced successful businessmen and women even in non-African lands.

Rufus — Chosen in the Lord: (Rom. 16:13; Mk. 15:21).

An African, who possibly appears in the Epistles, was Rufus whom Paul described as one chosen in the Lord in Romans 16:13. The possibility that he may have been an African is the appearance of Rufus as Son of Simon of Cyrene in Mark 15:21. Rufus was one among the Christians whom Paul sends greeting to in Rome.

Paul described Rufus' mother as his (Paul's) mother. This indicates that the family was well known to the Christian church of the first century. The same observation related to the way Mark mentioned Rufus and Alexander. Paul's remark about Rufus' mother fits with noble virtues noted in Lydia. They were both hospitable. Scholars, however, have not agreed if this Rufus is the same as the Rufus of Mark 15:21. Also they disagreed whether chapter 16 of the Roman Epistle is for Ephesians or a note for Phoebe that was attached to the Roman letter. Whatever the case, it is not out of order to expect Rufus, the son of Simon of Cyrene, to enjoy wide popularity throughout the early church.

Conclusion

The contribution of Africa and Africans in Acts is outstanding. The Acts is primarily the action of the Spirit and the risen Lord in the spread of the gospel. The study recognizes God's interest of disclosing this revelation to other nations and to make them an active partner in the history of salvation. It shows God's involvement with Africa and Africans. God engaged Africa and Africans in his saving task in Acts. We may, therefore, assert from this study that Africans did not only participate in the Pentecost experience, they were also part of the leadership team of the early Church. They joined hands with Jewish Christians to take the gospel to other lands. They also served as prophets and teachers of the early Church.

Some of these men were Simon, the black (Niger) and Lucius of Cyrene. From all probabilities, Simon of Acts 13:1 is the same person as Simon of Cyrene in the gospels. The African identity of the Ethiopian Eunuch cannot be doubted. He believed in Christ and went back to Ethiopia to evangelize his people. Thus, the work of redemption is not a prerogative of the Jews alone. It is a privileged revelation addressed to all people. This is the theological lesson to learn in African presence in Acts because other nations were saved and also participated in the propagation of the gospel.

The planting of the Church in Acts of the Apostles did not exclude Africa and Africans. In this way Africans have helped to shape the goodnews of Christ in the early Church. They spread and propagated the gospel and were foundational members of the early Church.

Perhaps the best way to appreciate the presence of Africa in the New Testament is to study the teachings of Moses and their effects. The African education of Moses was the background of Judeo-Christian beliefs. Jesus said that he came to fulfil the law of Moses (Matt. 5:17) and Moses' concept of monotheism has its root in Africa. Monotheism was an off-shoot of the Amarna revolution spearheaded by Pharaoh Akhenaton of the 18th dynasty.

Coincidentally Moses was at the court of Pharaoh in Egypt in Africa during Akhenaton revival of monotheistic belief. He seemed to have been in sympathy with this belief. When he led Israel on Exodus, Moses taught that Yahweh is the only God that must be worshipped. So monotheism became one of the strong pillars of Judaism and Christianity. Beside monotheism, many important biblical themes have their origin in African religious cosmology. In this way, the teachings of Moses and Jesus are modified African concepts. Jesus came, therefore, to fulfil not only the Old Testament, but African theological speculations of the distant past.

Moreover, the Acts of the Apostles reveals that Africans have been worshippers of God, the God of Israel. There are some Africans who have had the concept of the biblical God for many centuries before the colonization of Africa by Europe. Some of the proselytes on the Pentecost day were Africans and the Ethiopian Eunuch is a classic example (Acts 2:5-13; 37-41; 8:26-39). This disproves early European writers who argued that Untutored Africans cannot conceive God.[69]

Africa has gone through several traumatic experiences that have produced endurance. In the most crucial time, the God of Israel visits, uses and moves her through history. For this reason, Africa must redefine itself in the context of the Bible in the struggle against prefabricated concepts and globalization. To shape a future that is different from the colonial past, we have to break with Western categories in the way we relate to the Bible. Authentic future for Africa cannot be achieved from foreign interpretation besides our own activity.

Endnotes

1. A. Guy, *The Acts of the Apostles*, (London: Macmillan, 1973), 5.
2. E. Klemm, "Hermeneutical Inquiry," *Journal of the American Academy of Religion*, Vol. 1 (1986), 2, 36.
3. Ibid.
4. D.T. Adamo, *Africa and Africans in the New Testament*, (manuscript to be published), 9.
5. Ibid.
6. Ibid.
7. D.T. Adamo, *Africa and Africans in the Old Testament*, (San Francisco: Christian University Press, 1998), 10.
8. Adamo, *Africa and Africans in the New Testament*, 9.
9. K. Johnson, *Josephus and the History of the Jews*, (Philadelphia: Hodder and Stoughton, 1975), 62.
10. W.A. McCray, *The Black Presence in the Bible and the Table of Nations, Genesis 10:1-32*, (Chicago: Black Light Fellowship, 1990), 70.
11. C.A. Diop, *The African Origin of Civilization*, (Chicago: Lawrence Hill & Co. 1974), 25.
12. Flavius Josephus, *Antiquity*, 1 VI. 2.
13. Adamo, *Africa and Africans in the New Testament*, 12.
14. Ibid.13.
15. Ibid. 14.
16. W.A. McCray, *Black Presence in the Bible and the Table of Nations, Genesis 10:1-32*, 70.
17. J.E. Harris, "*Africa and Africans As Seen by Classical Writers,*" *African History Note* (Washington: Howard University Press, 1981), 123.
18. Adamo, *African and Africans in the New Testament*, 30.   See also C.O.G. Ndubukwu, "Some Concepts of the Africans in Classical Literature," Ph.D. Thesis, University of Ibadan, (Ibadan, 1979), 12-14.
19. Ibid.
20. Ibid.
21. Ibid.
22. Ibid.
23. Ibid, 23.
24. W.A. McCray, *Black Presence in the Bible and the Table of Nations, Genesis 10:1-32*, 90-94.
25. G. Eghagha, *The Races of Mankind*, (Warri: God's Kingdom Society Press, 1993), 30.
26. C.I. Onyewuenyi, *The African Origin of Greek Philosophy: An Exercise in Afrocentricism*, (Nsukka: University of Nigerian Press, 1993), 120.
27. Eghagha, *The Races of Mankind*, Ibid, 95.
28. McCray, *Black Presence in the Bible...*
29. Adamo, *Africa and Africans in the New Testament*, 12.
30. Ibid.
31. Harris, *Africa and Africans as Seen by Classical Writers*, 58.

32. Adamo, *Africa and Africans in the Old Testament*, 11. McCray, *Black Presence in the Bible* ... Ibid, 12f.
33. Harris, *Africa and Africans as Seen by Classical Writers*, 120.
34. J.H. Thayer, "Niger", *The New Thayer's Greek-English Lexicon of the New Testament*, (Lafayette: The Book Factory, 1979), 841.
35. C.B. Copher, *Black Biblical Studies*, (Chicago: Black Light Fellowship, 1993), 90.
36. Adamo, *Africa and Africans in the New Testament*, 26.
37. Ibid.
38. Ibid, 27.
39. Guy, *The Acts of the Apostles*, 5.
40. F.J. Jackson and K. Lake, "Acts of the Apostoles," *The Broadman Bible Commentary*, Vol. II, ed. C.I. Allen, (Nashville: Broadman Press, 1970), 5-6.
41. M. Black, *An Aramaic Approach to the Gospels and Acts*, (Oxford: Clarendon Press, 1946), 1-2.
42. F.J. Jackson and K. Lake, "Acts of the Apostles", 15.
43. R.H. Pfeiffer, *History of New Testament Times with an Introduction to the Apocrypha,* (London: Adam & Charles Black, 1987), 197.
44. H. Louis, *History of Herodotus*, Trans. G.Rawlinson, New York, Tudor Publishing, 1956), 124.
45. W. Barclay, *The Acts of the Apostles*, (Philadelphia: Westminster Press, 1953), 105.
46. F. Josephus, *Against Apion*, 1 Section 31.
47. Johnson, *Josephus and the History of the Jews*, Ibid. 62.
48. Onyewuenyi, *African Origin of Greek Philosophy*, Ibid, 178.
49. Josephus, *Against Apion*, Ibid.
50. Louis, *History of Herodotus*, Ibid.
51. C.F. Pfeiffer (ed.), "Moses," *Wycliffe Bible Encyclopedia*, Vol. 2, (Chicago: Moody Press, 1975), 120.
52. Eghagha, *The Races of Mankind*, Ibid. 96.
53. J.H. Thayers, "Eunouchos," *The New Thayers Greek-English Lexicon of the New Testament*, 85.
54. Pfeiffer (ed.), "Eunouchos", *Wycliffe Bible Encyclopedia*, 9.
55. C. Brown (ed.), "Eunuch," *The New International Dictionary of the New Testament Theology*, Vol. 1, (Grand Rapids: Zondervan, 1967), 45.
56. Adamo, *Africa and Africans in the New Testament*, Ibid, 22.
57. J. Schneider, "eunouchos," *Theological Dictionary of the New Testament*, ed. G. Kittel and G. Friedrich, (Grand Rapids: Eerdmans, 1985), 277.
58. Adamo, *Africa and Africans in the New Testament*, 63.
59. R.J. Dillon, "Acts of the Apostles," *New Jerome Biblical Commentary,* (London: Geoffrey Chapman, 1993), 743.
60. J. D. Douglas (ed.), "Lydia", *New Bible Dictionary*, (Leicester: Intervarsity Press, 1970), 215.
61. Adamo, *Africa and Africans in the Old Testament*, 75.
62. McCray, *The Black Presence in the Bible...*, Ibid, 999.
63. Johnson, *Josephus and the History of the Jews*, 81.
64. G.J. Wenham, *World Biblical Commentary*, (Waco: Word Book Publishers, 1967), 230.
65. Louis, *History of Herodotus*, Ibid. 88.

66. W. Hansberry (ed.), "Preface," *African History Note*, (Washington: Howard University Press, 1977), IV-VI.
67. Harris, *Africa and Africans As Seen by Classical Writers, African History Note,* Ibid. 26.
68. Onyewuenyi, *African Origin of Greek Philosophy*, Ibid, 134.
69. E.B. Idowu, *African Traditional Religion: A Definition*, (London: Fountain Publications, 1991), 88.

PART TWO

CONTEXTUAL INTERPRETATION OF TEXTS

CHAPTER VIII

THE IMPRECATORY PSALMS IN AFRICAN CONTEXT

David Tuesday Adamo

Introduction[1]

Many scholars have testified to the fact that the imprecatory Psalms belong to some of the most troublesome parts of the Bible. Interestingly we have about one hundred verses of this type of Psalms in the Bible. These Psalms express the desire for God's vengeance on their enemies. These involve actual call for vengeance. The following Psalms are widely recognized and classified as imprecatory Psalms: 5:10; 6:10; 7:6,9, 15-16; 9:19-20; 10:15; 17:13; 28:4; 31:17-18; 35, 4-6, 8,19, 24-26; 40:14-15; 52:5; 54:5; 55:9, 15, 15; 56:7; 58:6-10; 59:5, 11-13; 68:1-2, 30; 69:22-25, 27-28; 70:2-3; 71:13; 74:11, 22-23; 79:6, 10, 12; 83:9,11, 13-18; 94:1-2; 104:35; 109:6-15, 17-20, 29; 129:5-8; 137:7-9; 139:19, 21-22; 140: 8-11; 141:10; and 143:12.[2] They are a total of ninety-eight verses in thirty-two chapters.[3] It has been observed that there are about 94 words describing enemies. This emphasis on enemies makes Erick Zenger to observe that hatred enmity, violence, retaliation, and even the word revenge are not by any means a sub-theme in the Psalter.[4]

One notices that although many of the imprecatory Psalms are considered community laments, the majority are Psalms of individual laments (Hicks 1997: 10).[5] Few are hymns (e.g. 68) and thanksgivings (e.g. Psalm 41).[6] Imprecatory

Psalms have been branded different kinds of names such as "cursing Psalms," "Psalms of vengeance," "Psalms of violence,"[7] "Psalms of hate," and others because of the nature of the contents of these Psalms. The fact that this Psalms express the desire for God's vengeance on one's enemies and enemies of God, many Christians, especially Western Christians, have condemned these Psalms as un-Christian, and to be avoided altogether. These group of Psalms are said to be morally consonant with the Old Testament but inconsistent with the New Testament because Christians are to love their enemies (Matt. 5:44), bless, and not curse (Rom. 12:14). Some biblical scholars considered it as mere literary device.

Are the imprecatory Psalms merely a linguistic style or ordinary literary device of which the authors do not really take seriously? Or do they reflect the theology of the Old Testament only and have nothing to do with the New Testament? Are Psalms such as Psalms *137:9* which call for dashing of infants against the rock, or Psalms **58:10** which also call for the washing of one's feet in the blood of the wicked Christians?

Although this paper will make some attempts to mention some of the Western attempts to answer some of these questions, the main purpose of this essay is to discuss the Africentric approach to the imprecatory Psalms. More specifically, I will discuss how the African indigenous churches have interpreted these Psalms in such a way that is different from that of the Western interpretative tradition. Although there will be more emphasis on the indigenous churches in West Africa, these Africentric approach has spread through the African continent and beyond. This Africentric interpretation is a reality among African Diaspora all over the world.

Eurocentric Interpretation of Imprecatory Psalms

As stated above, since the main concern in this paper is not the discussion of the Eurocentric interpretation of the imprecatory Psalms, I will discuss briefly, some
major interpretative opinion of some major representatives of modern scholars who belong to the Western interpretative tradition.

Having regarded the imprecatory Psalms as Psalm of "curse," "violence," "hate," and "vengeance," the obvious conclusion of most Eurocentric scholars who are the leading interpreters of the Psalms is mostly that of condemnation. The Imprecatory Psalms are believed to be example of lack of spiritual insight of what the New Testament stands for by the Old Testament writers. It was further explained that the Old Testament people did not know the full message of grace and forgiveness that Jesus taught in his ministry on earth. In other words, these passages reflect a lower standard of ethics than the one Christ espoused (Jackson 2001: 1-4).[8]

Other Western scholars have argued that the imprecations are product of the Psalmist's own sinful nature. To such scholars, the imprecatory Psalms are records of prayers that came to the heart of the Psalmist and not what he should have prayed. Others argued that they are the Poetic Hyperbole. In other words, they are written with well-crafted picturesque words, for the purpose of achieving beauty and of catching the attention of the readers of these Psalms so as to make the reader see the seriousness of the matter.

Some people regard these imprecatory Psalms to be part of prophecy in the Old Testament. Such interpreters see the Psalms as not belonging to the personal wish of the speakers to see the doom happen to the enemies, but a prophecy of doom that God has promised that will come to his enemies. Others argue that the composers of these Psalms speak in the indicative mood rather than imperative mood. In other words, they are merely stating what would happen to the wicked and that they are not actually asking God to destroy their enemies (Jackson 2001:1-4).[9] Some argue that the idea that it reveals human nature without Christ is untenable because such idea fails to recognize the universal nature of humankind to revenge.

Grenshaw believes that imprecatory Psalms are Psalms of curse. He titles the section on the imprecatory Psalms "The Cursing of Enemies."[10] He maintains that the prayer for vengeance cannot be justified theologically no matter how understandable it is.[11] According to him prayer for vengeance cannot be justified theologically whether in term of an altruistic concern for victims of injustice, or defence of divine honour. He further sees it as arrogance and pride when Christians try to identify their enemies as the enemies of God and that such sin is more grievous than the sin of the so called enemies that earns them death penalty.[12] Such prayers of imprecatory Psalms run the risk of infecting religious people with harmful attitudes.[13]

Brueggemann calls this Psalms, Psalms of "disorientation," and Psalms of "darkness."[14] Although Brueggemann sees these Psalms as Psalms of disorientation and darkness, he believes that the use of such Psalms is not "inappropriate."[15] Although such Psalms may be considered by the world as "an acts of unfaith and failure," its use is "an act of bold faith,"[16] and, in fact, "a transformed faith" because it "insists" that "the world must be experienced as it really is and not in some pretended way." According to him, nothing about the use of these Psalms is out of bounds, nothing precluded or inappropriate."[17]

McCann, Jr. sees imprecatory Psalms as "affirmation of God's compassion for the poor and needy."[18] According to him, these Psalms reveal the vengeful nature of human kind and that anger is a legitimate response to victimization. In fact, he concludes that what others called "un-Christian and violent Psalms" are non-violent Psalms. He says, "This vehement, violent-sounding prayer is, in fact, an act of non-violence[19]. It is an act of non-violence because the Psalmist submits his or her anger to God in prayer and wait for justice.[20]

Zenger interprets imprecatory Psalms as the affirmation of Justice. He sees it as affirmation of justice and God's righteousness on earth.[21] Thus he "understands this prayer for vengeance as an affirmation of divine integrity in the face of strong evidence to the contrary."[22] In other words, the imprecatory Psalms are realized theodocy. The Psalmists who offer this prayer places everything in God's hand and the same time longing for God to say the last word.

Africentric Interpretation of the Imprecatory Psalms[23]

Having discussed very briefly the Eurocentric interpretation of the imprecatory Psalms, I want to discuss in this section the Africenctric approach to the interpretation of the imprecatory Psalms, which closely reflect the cultural background of the African people.

Unlike most Western biblical scholars who labelled imprecatory Psalms as Psalms of violence, hate, darkness, disorientation, and others, Africentric biblical scholars consider them as Psalms of "protection" and "defence" against enemies.[24] Since this Africentric interpretation is closely tied to the understanding of Africentric interpretation of the imprecatory Psalms, it is important to discuss at this stage the concept of enemies and African attitude to their enemies before the advent of Christianity. I will like to restrict my discussion to the Yoruba people of Nigeria.

Enemies in African Indigenous Tradition and Culture

The nature and process of dealing with enemies in African indigenous tradition is remarkably different from that of the Western world. This is because Africans living in the continent face some peculiar problems due to their perception of the world around them. To indigenous Africans the presence of evil, witches, sorcerers, evil spirits, and all kinds of enemies are painfully real. They believe that they are responsible for all the evil things that happen all over the world. In Africa indigenous tradition, all relations, children, and adult are taught the existence and the activities of enemies. The need to be protected from them is taken seriously. They use item such as animate and inanimate objects, (stones, sand, trees, leaves, human parts, animals, water, urine, and others) for protection.

Among the Yoruba people of Nigeria there is a belief that every person has at least one known or unknown enemy called *ota*. There are two types of enemies among the Yorubas of Nigeria. The first type is brought by some perennial quarrels, which come from variety of circumstances such as land disputes, property inheritance, chieftaincy titles disputes and constant rivalries among wives in polygamous homes. This type of enemy is called *orogun.* The second type is called *Aye* (literally means the world). These are sorcerers, witches and all persons who are inherently wicked and malicious by nature. They are more dreadful than the first group of enemies. They go to the extent of employing professional medicine person to deal with their enemies. Potent powerful words (so-called incantations) pronounced on charms such as *epe,* *(*curse), *isaasi, apeta, ironsi* and *eedi* are used.[25] The effect of such charms can be disastrous. It may be abnormal behavior, sudden loss of children and property, chronic illness and even death. To express how powerful and wicked the activities of witches, who are considered enemies of society can be, Primate J.O.S Ayelabola states the confession of a witch:

> We drink human blood in the day or night;
> We can prevent a sore from healing;
> We can make a person to lose a large sum of money;
> We can reduce a great man to nothing;
> We can send a small child to heaven suddenly;
> We can cause a woman to bear born-to-die children
> (*abiku*).[26]

Before the advent of Christianity, Africans had a cultural way of dealing with the problem of enemies and all evildoers. There were various techniques of making use of natural materials and potent powerful words. One of these cultural ways of protection against enemies is the use of imprecatory potent words (the so-called incantations) called *ogede* in Yoruba language. Traditionally when an African identifies an enemy and he/she himself/herself does not have the potent words or medicine to deal with such enemy, such a person consults a medicine man (*babalawo* or *onisegun* or *oologun* in Yoruba language) that prepares or teaches him/her some potent words or gives a charm for protection or for attacking the enemy. The words must be recited at certain place, at certain time of the day or night, and for certain number of times for such words to be effective. Usually, people who want protection at the time of travelling or hunting, for protection at home go to a particular priest called *babalawo* or *onisegun* or *oologun* (in Yoruba language), who are gifted and well disciplined in the art of medicine.

There are three major ways of dealing with enemies in African indigenous tradition. They are the use of potent words, called *ogede*, the use of medicine called *tira*, and other medicine for the body. A perfect example of the type of potent words used among the Yoruba society during the approach of an enemy.

O di oluworo-ji-woro	it becomes oluworo ji-woro
Odi oluworo-ji-woro	It becomes oluworo ji-woro
Oku aja kiigbo,	The dead dog does not bark
Oku agbo kiikan	the dead ram does no
Irawe t' osubu lu odo o di'egbe	The dried leaf that falls into the river is lost forever
Od'olu woro-ji-woro	It becomes oluworo ji-wo
Ki awon ota mi lo gbere	So let my enemies be lost
Oku aja niwon	They are dead dogs
Oku agbo niwon	They are dead rams
Ewe gbigbe niwon.	They are dried leaves.[27]

More examples of potent words for protection against witches and wizard who are considered arch enemies of society in the African indigenous tradition are numerous. However, it suffices to mention one more:

Igbagbe se oro ko lewe (3 times) Due to forgetfulness god did not
Igbagbe se afomo ko legbo (3 times) remember to separate

Igbagbe se Olodumare ko ranti la
 ese pepeye (3 times)
Nijo ti pepeye ba daran egba igbe   When the duck is beaten *it*

hoho ni imu bo 'nu cries hoho
Ki igbagbe se lagbaja omo lagbaja May forgetfullness come upon
                                             (name the name of the enemy)
                                             The daughter of mother, that is
                                             May he loose his senses that he
                                             May enter into the bush.
ko maa wogbo lo
*Tori t'odo ba nsan ki iwo ehin moo. . . ..*Because a flowing river does not
                              flow backward (and so on).[28]

These words when recited many times, would make the witches who are enemies trying to attack get lost in the bush or in the cities. It will make them forget all the evil actions planned against a person reciting the potent words.

    Another major way of obtaining protection against enemies in African societies is the use of charms or amulets. Amulets and charms are usually obtained from medicine men who are healers and diviners. They are called *tira* in Yoruba language of Nigeria. They are used for diverse purposes but mainly as protective devices to prevent witches and wizard, and evil spirits who are enemies, from entering a house and attacking a person. It is also used to nullify all the attempts of enemies or sorcerers. They are prepared with different ingredients according to the purpose of the charm or amulets. For example, a charm for the purpose of hanging on the doorframe for protection may be made of "seven leaves of some plants, and seven seed of alligator pepper." Charms to be tied around one's neck for protection against enemies may require alligator peppers, white and red cola-nuts, and the blood of a cock. Charms are wrapped with animal skin and sewn round. Others are wrapped inside pieces of cloth or paper and tied with some black and white threads. Some also require the recitation of some potent words and prayer to go along with the charms for their effectiveness.[29] Those words must be recited exactly according to the prescription of the medicine man otherwise it may not be efficacious.

The Use of Imprecatory Psalms for Defence and Protection against Enemies

When Christian missionaries arrived in Africa, the converts were forbidden to use African indigenous medicine, that is, potent words, talisman, and even herbal medicine for protection. They were told that it was abominable to Christianity. The missionaries, with good intention to promote the kingdom of Christ, did not only build schools, but they built maternities, dispensaries, and hospitals where orthodox medicine was dispensed against diseases. The truth is that those African Christians who had access to this orthodox medicine and were able to pay for them still had problems dealing with what they believed to be the source of the diseases, and misfortune (witches and wizards and other enemies, seen and unseen), and they sought protection from these. Orthodox medicine could not deal effectively with that aspect of African belief.

When they accepted Christianity and threw away their potent words, charms, and all kinds of medicine, they did that with the belief that there would be a better substitute for them for protection, healing, and success. The unfortunate thing however, is that the missionaries did not teach them the source of the white man's power which they thought must be present in the so called,

"White man's book," the Bible, (introduced to them). They were disappointed, and therefore, took laws into their own hands by using the Christian book and the traditional means for protection, healing and success. Many were excommunicated from the mainline churches. When others who remained in the missionary churches searched in vain for that substitute in the missionary Christianity that they accepted, they believed that the missionaries were hiding that power from them, and that they would never discover that power unless they broke away.[30] The inevitable result was the breaking away from the missionary churches with one of the major purpose of finding that greater power in Christianity. They search the Bible in their own way. [31]

The separation gave them the freedom to search the Bible in order to discover the supposedly hidden power. The book of Psalms became the favourite book read that contained that power for protection, and defence against known and unknown enemies. As discussed above, the most serious concern among Africans is power for protection against enemies, as a result of their strong and realistic belief in the existence of enemies who are to be attributed to witches, wizards, and evil spirits that fill African forest. They approached the Bible and used it with the same method that the indigenous African people used their indigenous medicine to deal with the problem of enemies and sought protection against enemies. They used mainly the imprecatory Psalms as they used potent words, charms, and medicine to combat evil forces and to protect themselves against forces of evil. Although this practice has spread all over African churches, including the missionary churches, African indigenous churches became the champion of this practice.

Imprecatory Psalms as Potent Words for Protection and Defence against Enemies

Mr. T. N. Adeboyejo was emphatic concerning the use of the Bible as potent words and shield for Christians. He says,

> I implore everybody to endeavour to read Holy Bible after this special arrangement especially every time because BIBLE is the word of Son of Mary, particularly it was incantation and shield for Christians. I beg you in the name of Merciful God to refrain from retaliation for yourself, because enemies will be foot for the children of God to reach the position of honor and glory.[32]

Psalm 10 which contains some imprecation (**10:15**) can be used for protection if one has enemies declaring war against him/her. Such a person must recite the Psalm, fast till twelve noon and pray three times, that is, in the morning, afternoon, and evening. The holy name *JARA TA AJAJA MOMIN* should be pronounced seven times.[33]

Evangelist Luke Jolugba who is the founder and pastor of Cherubim and Seraphim Church, Isanlu, Kogi State, Nigeria, considers reciting of Psalm **54** as the potent words to protect travellers.[34] However, Chief J.O Ogunfuye considers the reading of Psalms 17, in conjunction with Psalm 119:105-112 with some special prayers, as protection for travellers. According to him Psalm **17** should be recited when enemies are trying to make one's journey a failure and one has no defence. This Psalm must be read with the holy name *Jerora* with the following prayers:

> O God my Savior, I beseech Thee in Thy power to come down from Thy heavenly abode and deliver me from all my adversaries who now compass round about me to do me evil. O Thou that heareth prayers, arise in Thy wrath and fight my cause. Scare them away and render them powerless against me. Save me from their wicked designs and prevent them from blocking my way of success in my proposed travels. Let Thy holy angels and guard me throughout my journey. Give me Thy holy spirit to overcome all obstacles. Give me grace and favour and let all my wishes been granted for the sake of Thy adorable holy name, *Jehovah Jerora*. Amen.[35]

Psalm **109** which belongs to the Psalms of lament according to the Western classification is unquestionably one of the most difficult chapters in the scripture to read. This is because many readers tremble as they read this Psalm because of the Psalmist concern for vindictiveness toward other human being who has wronged the speaker. This Psalm is also the strongest example of imprecatory Psalms in the scripture. It is the voice of resentment and vengeance that will not be satisfied until God works retaliation on those who have done the wrong.

Psalms **109** and **9** also contain some imprecations (**9:19-20, 109:6-15, 17-20, 29**). In African context, when they are recited in conjunction with Psalm **51, 27, 91**, Genesis 11:1-9, and Matthew 15:29-38 they are potent words and powerful for protection against extravagance and wasteful spending that is usually caused by enemies.[36] This should include the recitation of the holy name *Jah-Jehova, Jehova Emmanuel, Jehova Lass* seven times.

Imprecatory Psalms as Amulets or Charms for Protection

I have stated above that the use of charms or amulets is one of the indigenous ways for seeking protection in Africa. The African Indigenous Churches make use of these methods in their approach to the interpretation of the imprecatory Psalms. Based on their belief in the power of words, the imprecatory Psalms are written on parchments, worn in the neck, hung on the doorpost of a house, or kept under a pillow overnight. Prayers are offered for the effectiveness of the charms.

The use of these imprecatory Psalms as protection against enemies, witches, and wizard is a common phenomenon in African Indigenous Churches in Nigeria. The Prophet J.O Ogunfuye seems to specialize in the use of the Bible, especially the book of Psalms, for protection, cure and success. For protection against "secret enemies, evil doers and trouble mongers,"[37] Psalm 7 should be written on a pure parchment and put in a special consecrated bag and kept under one's pillow. It should be written on the parchment with the special prayer below:

> O merciful Father, Almighty and everlasting King, I beseech Thee in the holy name of *Eel Elijon* to deliver me from all secret enemies and evil spirits that plan my destruction always. Protect me from their onslaught and let their evil forces be turned back upon them. Let their expectation come to naught and let them fail in their bid to injure me. Let their ways be dark and slippery and let thy holy angels disperse them so that they may not come nigh unto my dwelling place. Hear my prayer now for the sake of holy *Eel Elijon.* Amen.[38]

Psalms 83 and 9 are imprecatory Psalms and when used in conjunction with other Psalms such as 4, 32, 70, can be used as amulets to prevent all evils.[39] J. O Ogunfuye concludes his booklet on Psalms and their preparation.

> In this book you will read some Psalms, such as Psalms 4, 9, 32, and **70, 83**, and Psalm 127, etc. are recommended to be written on the pure parchment as an object for protection and success. The other Psalms, which are not included in the Psalms as recommended above, will also be found very useful and to give the desired results if they are also written on pure parchments in the same way as the Psalms mentioned above. This should be done in addition to the constant reading of such Psalms which are recommended in this book,

especially those Psalms for protection against evil spirits, evil
occurrences, enemies, and for good luck, grace and favour, progress
and for success in all undertakings.[40]

Imprecatory Psalms as Medicine for Protection

I have discussed above that one of the ways of mounting offensive and
defensive battle against the evil ones and enemies in the African indigenous
tradition is the use of herbal and non-herbal medicine. The reading and writing
of the word of God in conjunction with herbal and non-herbal medicine, and the
citing and reciting the holy names of God and angels to secure protection have
become a way of life in African indigenous churches.

T.N Adeboyejo prescribes Psalm 28, which also contains imprecation[41] to
be used as medicine for protection against evil people. Psalms 14, **24**, **34**, 50, 91,
110, 114, Isaiah 41:8-16, and 47 with special instruction are also good for
defence. Below are his exact words:

> On Wednesday a white candle in each corner of your room three or
> two white candles, one yellow candle in the middle of the room, read
> these Ps. **10**, 14, 110 and 114 each at the corner of the room in front
> of three candles at the middle, put bucket, pan or pot in which you
> have put palm front inside then. Put calabash of water near it, read Ps.
> 28, 91 and Isaiah 41:8-16 into the water in the bucket. Read
> Psalm.17, 50 and Isaiah 47 into the water inside calabash. After all
> these read Ps. 24 for the seal of it. Pray for redemption from all
> powers of Satan and all evildoers, in and outside of your body over
> the water in the bucket, and then pray for victory over all your
> enemies. Ask God to let them fall in spirit and physically let them be
> destroyed over the water in the calabash. After purification bathe
> with the water in the bucket and retain some for drinking, after that
> use incense of victory. Throw the water in the calabash outside or
> where you know that your enemies will step.[42]

For power over the evil spirit one should read Psalms **104**, three times, 71
once, 53, **54**, and, 55 once, 130 seven times and 137 three times for three
months. These Psalms must be read into water for bath for three months. The
water should be used for bathing every week. It could also be simply read
everyday as prayer. If one has the opportunity of using candles, for further
effectiveness, one should use two black candles, a yellow, orange, pink, and
three white candles for both prayer and reading into water. It will destroy all evil
spirit.[43] Protection against familiar spirits requires the reading of the Bible into a
big pot full of water, pour into that water a perfume called *bintu* and then read
Psalms, 3, 11, 23, **24**, and 51, Leviticus 26:6-7, Proverb 3:17-24, seven times,
with candles near the new pot for three days. On the third day, exactly at 12
noon, the pot should be taken to the bush where deep hole will be dug and a
person with the familiar spirit should enter that hole naked. Bathe such a person

in that hole and when he or she gets out of the hole, he or she should go home without looking back till he reaches his or her house. Break the pot in that hole and cover the hole. The same day a cake should be baked and the cake and some money should be given to the needy as alms. For seven days the one with the familiar spirit must not go to town and must not come out of his or her house after 7 P.M. for seven days when offering the prayers.[44]

Read Psalms **9**, 27, and **68** for protection for a pregnant woman who has the history of miscarriage. The pregnant woman will fast till 9 A.M. of the second day. For the first day, she should get stream water and put three-palm front inside it. She should read Ps. 9, 27 and 101 on the second day and Psalm 9, 68, and 101 on the third day. She should put some of the water in a cup. She would bath with the rest of the water. After the third day of bathing she should have a bucket of water, call seven or three prophets or even all the congregation, light four candles each on the four corners of the room or church for the prayers.

There should be the burning of incense and of singing seven songs of victory. Immediately they finish one song, they shall pray for victory, healing, redemption, and for easy and peaceful child bearing. After seven songs and seven prayers for her, read Psalms.30, **40**, and **70** to bless water for her to drink and to bathe at 9 P.M. [45]

Bolarinwa also prescribed Psalm 126 as a protection for a pregnant woman. According to him,

> When a woman with past experience of infant mortality becomes pregnant she should read this Psalm into the water for her bath, wash with it and drink a little from it daily throughout the period of gestation. Immediately after delivery, the same process should continue. The Psalm should be read into water to wash the baby until it is fully grown. The possibility of early death of the child becomes remote [46]

Psalm 4, 8, and 28 are recommended for protection for students against forgetfulness. Take some well or spring water. Put an unbroken egg and sugar cane inside the water. Read Psalms 4, 8, and **28** with the holy names *ELIALARO FAJA* sixteen times into it. Pray for protection over the water and put the egg into the fire to burn off completely and bathe with the water. If all students fail and if all students die, you will be successful and not die.[47]

Psalms **4**, **10**, **17**, and **12** are prescribed for protection against poverty. Adeboyejo gives his instructions:

> If you are in long term poverty, get a bucket of water, get ripe palm fruits, snail and dry pepper, if male, get nine, if female, seven, put all in the water, read Psalm .4, Genesis 1, read all verses, Psalms. **17**, **12**, **74** and **10**. Read them thrice each pray for victory over poverty. Pray this prayer: "God the father of host, God of the living not of the dead, God who changes poverty to happiness, God who changed the poverty of the Israelites when the people of Moab cursed them, that

God who changed curses to blessing, please change my poverty to
prosperity." (Take away the materials and use the water to bathe
always), until change occurs.[48]

Psalms **9**, 27, 51, 91, **109**, Genesis 11:1-9, and Matthew 15: 29-38 are
prescribed for protection against extravagance. The Prophet Samuel Adewole
prescribes the above passages with coconut. A hole should be made on it, pour
three to seven limewater, a spoonful of ocean water, and a perfume. "Burn
heavy incense and sprinkle perfume to enable the powerful angels descends."
Light a candle on the hole of the coconut which should be put on a rock. While
holding three other candles in one's hand sing three songs of forgiveness and
victory and seven songs of thanks and praises.[49] Recite the holy names *Jah-
Jehovah, Jah-Emmanuel, Jah-Michael* seven times.[50]

Page: 150

CONCLUSION

At a glance, the temptation is to condemn Africentric interpretation of
imprecatory Psalms as fetish, magical, and unchristian. However, a closer and
critical examination of this Africentric interpretation of imprecatory Psalms will
reveal some basic facts that make it legitimate, important, and Christian.

The use of imprecatory Psalms with the names of God shows African
tradition of the recognition of the power in names. African Christians, like the
Hebrews, revere the names of God and believe that these names in the Bible are
powerful when recited. The recitation of such names will achieve whatever is
desired.

The use of the imprecatory Psalms for protection against enemies and evil
spirit is also recognition of the fundamental belief in the power of words. The
belief in some potent words in African tradition is transferred to the belief
in the power in the Words of God in the scripture when memorized, and
recited and read. The fact is that the contents of some of these imprecatory
Psalms resemble some potent words (so-called incantation) in African tradition
and culture (The word of God is sharper than two edged sword Heb. 12:4). It has
the power to achieve whenever it is recited against the enemies who especially
are unrepentantly wicked. Unlike the Western world where the Bible is in doubt
and the Bible ceases to be the Word of God, African biblical scholars refuse to
study the Bible for academic sake.

The use of herbs and other material things in conjunction with the
imprecatory Psalms as a prescription for protection against enemies and evil
spirits also has root in African indigenous tradition. It demonstrates the belief in
God's power over nature and that whatever material things used in conjunction
with the names of God and His Words, must be potent because of the power of
words. In fact, reading the imprecatory Psalms is an act of faith in God's power,
name, and words.

African Christians use imprecatory Psalms not for the sake of their aesthetic value, but as an expression of God's righteous indignation against injustice. Praying the imprecatory Psalms is a platform from which the oppressed people can request God's fulfilment of His righteousness and justice. Although these Psalms truly express our humanness, it becomes an act of faith because despite the injustice suffered, every injustice suffered is left for God to respond to rather than the sufferer taking laws into his or her own hand. This action conforms to a Yoruba wise saying and teaching, *fi ija fun Olorun ja fi owo leran.* It means leave everything for God to fight for you. This also conforms to the New Testament teaching "Beloved, never avenge yourselves, but leave room for the wrath of God; for it is written, 'Vengeance is mine, I will repay, says the Lord' (Romans 12:19). The Psalmists addressed the problem to God who is the "final reference for all of life."[51] In fact, most African Christians will concur with McCann, when he said that the imprecatory Psalms which expressed vehement violent-sounding prayers is actually "an act of non-violence."[52]

Another closer look at the imprecatory Psalms teaches us about ourselves, that is, we are "vengeful creatures.[53]" It is indeed a reflection of what we are. To most African Christians, there is nothing morally inferior or un-Christian in the imprecatory Psalms. Praying the imprecatory Psalms is an expression of the "desire for an oppressor to be punished in proportion to the crime committed" (Psalms 109 and 137).[54] I personally conclude that there is nothing morally wrong in praying this prayer. I personally believe that so many Christians who condemn the praying of imprecatory Psalms are hypocritical. Such condemnation is sacerdotal. Not one will see an enemy biting him or her and will not respond with equal force. Why do Christians go to court? It is an attempt to punish the offender. Without pretension, it is better to pray to God to act rather than we doing the acting. When Africans pray the imprecatory Psalms, they believe that they are taking the offender or the enemies to the court of God. It is clearly acceptable in African Christianity and it is read in most churches in Africa.

Finally, the use of these imprecatory Psalms for defence and protection in African Churches is not limited to the African indigenous churches in the continent of Africa, the practice has spread all over the world where there is African Diaspora. Most missionary churches in the continent of Africa practice the reading of the imprecatory Psalms when all things are down. The efficacy of such practice is never doubted among these churches and among the people who use it. I am strongly convinced that reading the imprecatory Psalms by African Christians is better than going to the native priest for harmful medicine to destroy one's enemies.

Admittedly, care must be taken in the use of the imprecatory Psalms for evil intention. It should only be used for God's vengeance. It should not be read as a hobby. All things must be submitted to God with humility and understanding that God is a righteous God and that He is also a God of vengeance who will do justice when justice is necessary no matter how long.

Endnotes

1.   Prof. David Tuesday Adamo, was also a Research Fellow with Prof. Dick Human at the University of Pretoria, South Africa.
2.   John N. Day, "The Imprecatory Psalms and Christian Ethics," *Bibliotheca Sacra* 159 (April-June 2002) , 166-186.
3.   John Day.
4.   Erick Zenger, 1996. *A God of Vengeance? Understanding the Psalms of Divine Wrath.* trans. Linda M. Maloney (Louisville: Westminster John Knox Press, 1996), 13.
5.   Hicks, 1997,10
6.   Arthur Weiser, 1962. *The Psalms*, translated by Herbert Hartwell, (Philadelphia: The Westminster Press, 1962).
7.   Zenger, 46.
8.   Jackson, 2001, 1-4.
9.   Jackson, 1-4.
10. James L. Grenshaw, The Psalms: An Introduction (Grand Rapids, Michigan: William B Eerdmans Publishing Company, 2001), 65.
11. Grenshaw, 68.
12. Grenshaw.
13. Grenshaw.
14. Walter Brueggemann, *The Message of Pslams,* (Mineapolis: Augsburg Publishing House1984), 52.
15. Brueggemann, 52-53.
16. Brueggemann.
17. Brueggemann.
18. J. Clinton McCann,Jr, *A theological Introduction to the Book of Psalms* (Nashville, Tennesee: Abingdon Press, 1993), 116.
19. McCann Jr, 115.
20. McCann Jr.
21. Zenger, 37.
22. Grenshaw, 66.
23. I will like to acknowledge the fact that most of the materials in this section is taken from my book *Reading and Interpreting the Bible in African Indigenous Churches* (Eugene, Origen: WIPF and Stock Publishers, 2001). More details can be read in that book.
24. David Tuesday Adamo, *Reading and Interpreting the Bible in African Indigenous Churches* Eugene, Origen: WIPF and Stock Publishers, 2001.
25. P.A. Dopamu, " The Reality of Isaasi, Apeta, Ironsi and Efun as forces of Evil among the Yoruba," *Journal Arabic and Religious Studies* 4 (Dec. 1987) 50-61. "Epe: The Magic of Curse among the Yoruba," *Religions* 8, (Dec.1983), 1-11; Solomon Ademiluka, "The Use of Psalms in African Context", M.A Thesis, University of Ilorin, Ilorin, Nigeria, 1990.
26. *Esu: The Invisible Foe of Man* (Ijebu-Ode: Shebiotimo Publications, 1986).
27. Agoro, Tola, Delta State University, Abraka. Interviewed on 12/9/96
28. Ademiluka.
29. Ademiluka.

30. There are other important reasons for the emergence of African Indigenous churches: national feelings, struggles for authority and leadership disagreement over finance, breaches of church discipline, polygamy, lack of adequate attention paid to dreams, prophecy, and healing ministry of both body and soul.

31. Edward Blyden, a Dutch West Indies born Presbyterian, who rejected some of the claims of the anthropologists that white people were superior to black people, influenced the establishment of indigenous African churches. He further maintained that the evangelization of Africa would never be successful until it was taken from the hand of he White man who imposed alien forms of evangelization on Africans. The first noticeable indigenous church formed was the United Native African Church in Lagos, Nigeria in 1891. As a result of dissatisfaction with the dictatorial missionaries, foreign formalism which sometimes led to the quenching of the spirit, and against the foreign anti-African customs, laws, dancing, family, marriage, and etiquette, the African Church Organization was formed in 1901 and many prophetic figures emerged.

32. T.N Adeboyejo, *Saint Michael Prayer Book*, Lagos: Neye Ade &Sons, 1988),

33. Adeboyejo, 116)

34. Olatunji Joel, Israel O. Abe, and Samuel Jolugba, No Date. *Itan Igbesi Aye Ajihinrere Oni Luke Jolugba Ati aofin Ijo Pelu Awon Eto Isin Kerubu & Serafu*, (Isanlu: Kerubu ati Seraful), 39.

35. J.O Ogunfuye, *The Secrets of the Uses of Psalms*, Third Edition Ibadan: no name of the Publisher, no date), 17.

36. Adeboyejo, 45.

37. Ogunfuye, 51-52.

38. Ogunfuye, 7.

39. Ogunfuye, 98.

40. Ofunfuye.

41. Adeboyejo, 4.

42. Adeboyejo, 98.

43. Ogunfuye, 29.

44. Ogunfuye, 33.

45. Ogunfuye, 34.

46. J.A Bolarinwa, *Potency and Efficacy of Psalms* (Ibadan: Oluseyi Press no date),37.

47. Bolarinwa, 17.

48. Adeboyejo, 41.

49. Samuel Adewole, *Awake Celetians! Satan is Nearer*. Lagos: Celetial Church of Christ Publication, 1991, 42.

50. Adewole.

51. Brueggemann, 52.

CHAPTER IX

AFRICENTRIC BIBLICAL HERMENEUTICS ENROUTE: CHIEFTAINCY INSTITUTION IN POST-COLONIAL NIGERIA

Dapo F. Asaju

Introduction

Times are changing; so are traditional African Institutions. Chieftaincy Institutions have been in existence in virtually every part of Africa long before the colonial era. It persisted during the colonial era and continues to wax stronger in the post-colonial era. In contemporary times, new dimensions have become manifest which is significant for the Africentric biblical hermeneutical project. Two incidents will justify this. First, Nigeria's most prominent Biblical Scholar, Professor Samuel Abogunrin of the University of Ibadan (Nigeria's oldest University and pioneer Department of Religious Studies), who is also an eminent ordained Priest of the Evangelical Church of West Africa (formerly Sudan Interior Mission) was in May 2004 conferred with the chieftaincy title of *Esa* of Omu Aran, Kwara State Nigeria. This is the next position to the reigning King in hierarchy. Secondly, Venerable Joseph Adepoju, an Archdeacon in the Anglican Church of Nigeria as well as a postgraduate student of New Testament Studies was in June 2004 crowned traditional Ruler (King) of a prominent Yoruba town, Igbara Oke, near Akure, Nigeria. What interested these 'Christian Ministers and Biblical scholars to become chiefs and subjecting themselves to rites and customs that were hitherto perceived by Eurocentric scholars as incompatible with Christianity? Are there no contradictions? In the case of Abogunrin, he remains a practicing Pastor in addition to his chieftaincy responsibilities. This shows a changing paradigm in Africentric understanding of the Bible and indeed practice of African Christianity. Thus, I intend to comparatively examine the traditional chieftaincy system in Nigeria vis –a vis the Biblical perception. This study examines the Nigerian Chieftaincy Institutions as a bridgehead in Africentric Biblical hermeneutics. It finds parallels between the Biblical concept of Kingship and African Chieftaincy system, and canvasses this as means for to furthering Africentric methodology of Biblical Studies.

In colonial Nigeria, there were two main types of traditional government- Monarchy and a democratic form of gerontocracy. "The former featured in Kingdoms ruled by Obas, Emirs, Obongs, Obis and powerful tribal chieftains who wielded power in styles ranging from absolute dictatorship to near form of democratic gerontocracy were found among the Igbo and their neighbours."[1] Despite the overbearing and fundamental influences of colonialism, this Institution has remained solid virtually every nation in Sub-Sahara Africa.

Nigerian Biblical Scholars have joined their other African counterparts in various efforts to either 'decolonize Biblical Studies'.[2] or to 'Reconstruct African Christian Theology'.[3] Adamo has been very prominent in pursuit of Africentric Biblical Studies. He defines this as "the Biblical Interpretation that makes African Social cultural context a subject of interpretation."[4] a departure from the Eurocentric perspective to Biblical studies which have been inherited by African Theologians and Biblical Scholars trained in the West. He popularized the search for African models for Biblical hermeneutics, while Justin Ukpong's major contribution has been in the area of Inculturation methodologies in the African Hermeneutics. He argues that "colonialism is founded on an ideology derived from the classical idea of culture…In Africa as elsewhere; colonialism was seen as a "civilizing" process. If colonialism is fundamentally a cultural process, then the most fundamental process of decolonization must necessarily be cultural. African scholars all over the years have pointed this out."[5] Getui and Obeng's *Theology of Reconstruction,*[6] follows in this direction. In the meantime, Africa becomes increasingly marginalized. The theological metaphor of re-construction challenges African scholars to discern new insights to inspire a new movement, hopefully more vigorous than that of the 1970s –a movement that can help the people of this continent to regain their self-esteem and integrity, as they contribute towards the creation of a global community."[7] The basis for this emergent paradigm of deconstruction and reconstruction is the historical damage which colonialism had done to the total African psyche, which affects everything else. Nahashon Ndug'u restates this clearly: "The colonialists' main concern was to grab as much of Africa's wealth as possible in the colonies they had acquired. Together with the colonialists came the western Christian Missionaries, whose main concern was to control both the mind and the soul of the Africans. They considered themselves as having been given a divine mission to save the lost souls of

Africa. Thus from the beginning of the missionary enterprise, in tropical Africa, Christianity was presented to the Africans as part of European civilization, which was intended to replace the 'pagan' religion and 'primitive' way of life."[8] In the process, "the African culture had to be destroyed in order to have a *tabula rasa* on which the superior European culture was to be inscribed...The colonization of African mind has been the greatest damage that the west has caused on the Africans for they no longer have a basis for developing their African personality."[9] Leslie Newbigin concludes that "Western Christian Missions have been one of the greatest secularizing forces in history."[10]

African scientific Scholars such as Kihumbu Thairu, are even more severe by suspecting continued western colonialist interest in Africa's persistent economic and socio-political woes including the ravaging effects of the HIV/AIDS which he suspects might have been deliberately engineered to serve the ultimate capitalist interest of the globalizing Western powers who aspire to take over African continent some day. The back cover of his book

> The African and the AIDS Holocaust' states: Professor Kihumbu Thairu goes beyond the myths surrounding the spread of the pandemic, reviews historical antecedents and presents AIDS challenge to Africa in the perspective of racial survival...It is not simply a health issue- it is the survival of a people against whom the scales have been weighted for centuries, and whose extinction would benefit others....[11]

Desmond Tutu reiterates this damage further:

> The worst crime that can be laid at the door of the white man... is not our economic, social and political exploitation, however reprehensible that might be, no, it is that his policy succeeded in filling most of us with self-disgust and self-hatred[12]

Abogunrin agrees when he observes that,

> African elites are today unconsciously promoting foreign languages and culture to the almost total neglect of African languages, religion and culture and our children are gradually becoming foreigners in their own land. This is one reason for evaluating the colonial readings past and present in Africa, as well as the need to decolonize Bible interpretation.[13]

We argue in this paper that the chieftaincy institution has been one of the most resilient cultural systems to colonial eradication of African culture and is a potent factor for an African perception of contextual Biblical studies. We follow here, Gerald West's 'life interest approach' a departure from the common Eurocentric 'interpretative interest approach'. According to West,

> Interpretative interest is those dimensions of the *text* that are of interest to the interpreter, while life interests are those concerns and commitments that drive or motivate the interpreter to come to the text. Life interests come from our experience of the world and from out commitments to the world. With such interests, we come to the Bible to hear what it has to say concerning such things...African biblical interpretation has been dominated by socio-historical interpretative interests , though interest in the other dimensions of text can be detected...We need to begin to describe what is, rather than prescribe what ought to be. It is time to bracket the prescriptive paradigm; it is time to listen rather than to proclaim.[14]

This is the same approach that Manus has advocated in his *Intercultural Hermeneutics in Africa.* He argues:

> Intercultural Method I am canvassing is a vigorous approach in the decolonizing process of New Testament interpretation in Nigeria....This way of doing exegesis is another form of contextual theology that is derived from a critically cultural interface between the sacred texts of the Christian faith and the givens of the African life-world.[15]

Interestingly, Manus's book identifies the Chieftaincy institution as a potent factor in the decolonization project. He notes:

> "The missionaries, aware of the subjugation of the African peoples by the colonists, launched a crusade of 'christianising' the Africans they had encountered; especially their kings and paramount chiefs. The first targets of European missionary conversions and expansion in Africa were the rulers. chiefs. princes and members of the nobility. The Portuguese went as far as taking a Benin Prince (Nigeria) to Lisbon, educated him in Western values and handed him a Portuguese wife so that both could transform Benin culture and religious institutions."[16]

Traditional Chieftancy Institutions

The African people, contrary to Western Imperialist notions, have always been people with capability to organize and govern themselves. Contrary to widely held opinions of colonialism being the bedrock of African civilization, the African peoples have since the past one millennium demonstrated the independent system of local / native government as can be historically attested to in the now extinct Borno, Benin and Oyo Empires (in what has become known today as Nigeria). Till today, the chieftaincy institution has remained integrated in successive political and social arrangement; which confirms its crucial status in the African community. Okafor observes rightly that "whether in the North or South of Nigeria, the position of traditional authorities had been vitally important since pre-British era. Local rule developed around the traditional authorities. Generally, they were considered by their people as repositories of religious, executive, legislative as well as judicial function."[17] This made the Chiefs and local king become susceptible to colonial authorities' manipulation to suppress their people. The British colonists adopted indirect rule, that is, through native chiefs and traditional authorities who were regarded as integral part of the machinery of government, with well-defined powers and functions recognized by colonial government and by law. The Local Government structure in Nigeria still maintains this status quo. Many Chiefs are graded and on the pay roll of Government. The segments of society including churches have to deal with them. Here is, therefore, a meeting point between Biblical Christianity and Christian involvement in politics; a model for African Biblical hermeneutic in the direction of liberationist theology.

Our reference to Chieftaincy is to the institution of traditional rulers. Originally, the rulers or Kings were simply Chiefs but today so many other lower strata go by the title Chief (mostly honorific). We may at times interchange the terms 'Traditional Rulers' with 'Chief'. Nigeria is a culturally and religiously plural nation. The major ethnic configurations include the Hausa-Fulani (in the North), Yoruba (in the West) and Igbo (in the East). There are numerous sub –groups numbering about 250, each with distinct languages / dialects and peculiar Chieftaincy system. One thread that binds them all together is the operation of vibrant Chieftaincy Institution. This Institution is perhaps the only one remaining which has defied the colouring influence of colonialism and continues to enjoy support of the people and governments. What the Queen is to England, the Traditional Rulers (*Obas, Obis* and *Emirs*) are, to their respective domains in spite of the controlling force of elective governments. However, it has been noted that the chieftaincy Institutions have also acquired certain features which are consequent upon the effects of globalization, regionalization and modernization.

Emergent changes that have featured in the Nigerian Chieftaincy system since the Nigerian Independence on 1st October 1960, has religious dimensions. Chieftaincy in Africa is intrinsically and inseparably linked to religion. Amadi observes that there is a close relationship between religion and the chieftaincy institution. "...the real restraints on Rulers were religious. Even when a Ruler was not a Priest, he still had many rituals to perform. These rituals had taboos which the Ruler would dare not infringe."[18] Stackhouse also opines that :

> Religion must be reckoned with in politics...the idea that religion is and should be private and that the state is public and secular derive in large measure from the impact that a specific religion has had upon modern western social life. The idea or religion as being basically privatized is a socio-cultural product of the modern global circumstance, an aspect of the ordering involved in the rendering of the world as a single place.[19]

Prior to the amalgamation of the Northern and Southern Protectorates by Lord Lugard in 1914, each people were governed as independent nation states, bound together by similar culture and religion. While Islam held sway in the North among the Hausa- Fulani and the Kanuri, Indigenous African Religion was dominant in the South until Christianity appeared in official /formal presentation on 17th September 1842.[20] The Chiefs in Africa were not immune to the influences of these foreign religions but were indeed the common vehicles upon which the religions rode unto mass acceptance. It should be noted that religion and Chieftaincy world-wide have been intricately related. In England, the Queen is *primus interperes* over the Church of England. In Saudi Arabia, the ruling Caliphate also doubles as chief custodians of the most important symbols of Islam. We will always find religion as a tool of local governance because therein lie part of the relevance and power of the chieftaincy institution. Christianity and Islam support respect by people for constituted authorities, including local chiefs. Ladd agrees with St. Paul's Biblical admonition of submission to secular powers by stressing that "This attitude, even if it was authoritarian, should be kept because Rulers are agents of law and order."[1] We can say that such feelings have been responsible for Nigerian people's sustenance of the chieftaincy Institution through the colonial era and even after it. In every part of the country, the religious persuasion of a particular ruler does not disturb the respect to the Throne. Martin Luther shares this attitude -- "even if rulers are not Christian, they are placed as checks on the excesses of people who would be unruly and disturb the peace of the godly and law-abiding."[21]

Governance is fundamental to any society. The people of Nigeria have always respected their traditional institutions partially because of their respect for law and order and out of religious convictions. Chiefs are regarded as vice-gerents of God (the Supreme Being). They are often venerated as divine beings who are custodians of not only the traditional values and cultures of their people but also of the religious faith. In the past, some Chiefs were deified as gods and consequently added to the large pantheon of Indigenous Religion. That was the case with *Sango* (god of Thunder) and *Ogun* (god of iron and smith works) in Yoruba Indigenous Religion. The African Chiefs are the political Chief Priests working alongside the professional Priests in the religious activities of the Communities. As Bolaji Idowu has rightly stated of the Yoruba, they are "in all things religious."[22] They are the royal fathers of their people, a position that has sustained their respect even above the political leaders at any point in time. They are addressed variously as His Royal Highness or His Royal Majesty, and granted unique privileges which at times tantamount to immunity from the operative laws of the secular government.

Such was the aura they enjoyed in the pre-colonial era which often led to the Chiefs being easily used and manipulated as agents of the colonial subjugation of the once great African nations. During the slavery period, Chiefs were found to collaborate in the capturing, selling and exportation of their own people as slaves to Europe and Americas. This fact of history reveals the weaknesses and vulnerability of the Chieftaincy Institutions, then and now.

Some rulers were despotic. In a sense, many were evil, indulging in human sacrifices and other 'demonic' vices. Donald Guthrie agrees with this observation. "a good case can be made out of the view that political authorities were regarded in some ways in the contemporary world as representatives of the demonic powers which were believed to be the real authorities behind human affairs."[23]

During the colonial era, in the case of Nigeria, the British authorities ruled the Muslim North indirectly through the Emirs who had a strong control already. The *Alkali* courts were viable, and all it took for colonialism to succeed was to gain the co-operation and loyalty of the Emir. The unquestioning loyalties of their subjects were then guaranteed. The British Colonial authorities were prepared to jettison Christian interests in order to defend the Emirate co-operation in Northern Nigeria. This was demonstrated in the Colonial Government's ban on Christian Missionary activities in the Muslim North, for the larger part of the colonial era. In the West, which was more liberal and democratic in Chieftaincy Institutions, the method was that of direct occupation and control? The effect of these is the greater powers and influences which the Emirs have over their people than that of the Southern Traditional Rulers. In Yoruba land for instance, there were instances in the past where a despotic Oba, *Alaafin* of Oyo Kingdom was compelled by tradition, to abdicate the throne and to be beheaded, once he lost the support of his people as represented by the Traditional Council. This shows the many faces of the Chieftaincy Institution, such that it becomes rather difficult to generalize.

As the Chiefs are many, so do the cultures and traditions that characterize them differ. Yet, common strands can be traced, on the basis of which we shall examine the contemporary emergent trends in a general manner, but with particular emphasis on the Yoruba Chieftaincy system.

How much of the past have they retained and what innovations have come into the system in this global age of scientific, technological, religious and socio-political changes? In other words, what new *trends* are discernible in the contemporary Chieftaincy Institutions and how can these be compared with the Biblical portrait of Kingship?

Models and Trends of Kingship/Chieftaincy in Biblical and Nigerian Cultural Context

Historicity and Royal Lineage

The strongest linkage between African chieftaincy system and Biblical kingship is found in the Ethiopian royal history. Indeed, the origins of Christianity cannot be defined without the African presence. As stated earlier, Adamo has done much work in the area of Africans in the Bible. Indeed, from Moses' wife to Queen of Sheba, to Simon the Cyrene and the African s at the

Pentecost phenomenon (Acts 2), vigorous efforts have been made to advance the African claim as co-founders of the Christian faith. Our focus is on the Queen of Sheba story and the continued claim of her descendants to royalty in Ethiopia. The city of Axum remains in Ethiopia, the centre of the Sheba dynasty.

"The 1955 Constitution introduced by the late Emperor Haile Selassie reiterated what everybody then regarded as incontrovertible truth. It stated:

> The imperial dignity shall remain perpetually attached to the line of Haile Selasie I , whose line descends without interruption from the dynasty of Menelik I, son of the Queen of Ethiopia, the Queen of Sheba and King Solomon of Jerusalem.. By virtue of his imperial blood as well as by the anointing which he has received, the person of the Emperor is sacred. His divinity inviolable and His power indisputable.[24]

Emperor claimed to be the 225th monarch of the Solomon's line. This appeal to historical continuity was violated by Junior officers who staged a coup that removed and later killed the Emperor Selassie, putting an end to an imperial era steeped in Israelite root.

Noting the interrelationship between African nation states, pre-colonial times, and even much earlier, it is possible that African system of family lineage of succession was influenced by the Ethiopian model. In Benin tradition, a single royal family

Producing the Oba (King) who must be the first male of a reigning king was the same in Israelite monarchy. Following the abandonment of Theocracy in preference for Monarchy, Saul's family initially enjoyed exclusive rights to the throne but the lineage of David took this privilege over. In parts of Africa where the succession system is non-hereditary, intermittent chieftaincy competition and crisis do easily emerge. The same appeal to historicity is similar to the African appeal to oral historiography, tracing to the ancestral. This is common in Benin and Ile Ife royal myths and legends. Most major thrones in Yoruba land for instance trace to Oduduwa the progenitor of the race. It becomes easy for an African Biblical reader to understand, interpret, and apply the African custom to the Kingship in Israel. For instance, in the story of David, his son, Solomon and Rehoboam, inherited the throne of David.

Divine Kingship

Guthrie states that the idea of God as king is found in the New Testament. It comes into focus more because of the Kingdom of God concept. "Clearly the idea of a Kingdom implies a King and this furnishes a solid basis for the New Testament usage."[25] The Kingship of God derives from His creation of the earth. In Acts 4: 24, the disciples of Jesus in their prayer, addressed God as Sovereign Lord who made "the heaven and the earth, the sea, and everything that is in them." There are several throne images in the Bible portraying God as both King and Judge. African kingship / Chieftaincy are built upon the historical tradition of the people. One major basis for establishing and projecting the institution is the divinity attached to it. The Yoruba will readily address a reigning King as *Oluwa* (Lord), *Ikeji Orisa.* This second term means vice-regent to the gods. Perhaps this concept borrowed from Greek mythology, which attributes divinity to royalty. Like the Greek mythology, Kings are deified. This appears to have been the case of deification of Sango the Yoruba god of thunder. Indeed by virtue of their office, Chiefs or Kings are regarded as ruling on behalf of God the Supreme Being and ruler. They wield their judicial powers at the behest of God. Obas are therefore priests of their domain. But they recognize that they only reign on behalf of Olodumare the Supreme God. At social events of communal gatherings, or when in Church, the Chiefs or Kings are made to acknowledge their subsidiary position to the King of kings and the Lord of lords who is often welcome (albeit in *abstentia*). The Yoruba songs do frequently use the term *"Oba to ju Oba lo."* (a King that superseded others). This perception will help us interpret such texts as deal with God's response to Samuel when the people demanded for monarchy. Yahweh stated that he was the one they had rejected by asking for a king. In other words, like the African system, kingship and divinity are intricately intertwined. The divinities may play subtle roles but the ancestral cult does not. It is prominent in every Nigerian ethnic culture. Thulani Ndlazi resonates the feeling in East Africa, similar to that of Nigerian: "misinterpretation of ancestors 'living dead' in African culture is part of the tendency to demonize anything of African origin. The relationship between an African and his/her living dead is a real human experience of contact."[26] Conventional Eurocentric Christianity is yet to accommodate the theology of the ancestral cult in every African locale. The Chiefs or Kings are protectors of this cult which is the same manner as the Israelite Kings follow the traditions and religio-cultural heritages of their royal ancestral forebears. Moreover Israelites themselves never cease to refer to themselves as children of Abraham, Isaac and Jacob- their patriarchal ancestors! The genealogical presentation with which Matthew opens his Gospel provides ancestral base for the messianic ministry of Jesus Christ:

> The book of the generation of Jesus Christ, the son of David, the son of Abraham." (Mathew 1:1) "So all the generations from Abraham to David are fourteen generations; and from David until the carrying away into Babylon are fourteen generations; and from the carrying away into Babylon unto Christ are fourteen generations (Mathew 1:17).

Here is a conscious divinely calculated genealogical presentation of Jesus ancestral linkage that legitimatize his divine and messianic claims. In the same way, Kings and Chiefs in Africa derive their cultural\, spiritual and royal legitimacy from their ancestral roots. Whereas the Bible is a written documentation, that of African Chieftaincy remain in oral tradition. That, not withstanding, even the orature deserves respect as the literature.

King Politician

Kings are usually in charge of the political process of any community and nation. But because of the sensitive nature of politics they are usually expected to be non-partisan, This is because as fathers of their people, they should not be seen to support one political party against others. At best their intervention in governance is advisory or subterranean. But that was not the original role of Kings and Queens the world over. The Queen of England remains titular head of England but has little role over the political direction of the nation. But in the past, the King combined, presided over state functions. They were final authority on any issue. They had powers to sentence to death. The Israelite Kings throughout the Old Testament, wielded such powers although they were occasionally checked by equally powerful and politically-conscious prophets such as Nathan, Ahijah, Amos, and Isaiah. Nathan questioned David's seduction of Bath Sheba and the stage-managing of the husband (Uriah's) killing at war. His ironical parabolic condemnation of David as well as the prophetic judgment of the House of David for this unwarranted violence remains classic. Ahab stage-managed the execution of Naboth as advised by his evil and insolent Queen, Jezebel. This also called for prophetic judgment which became fulfilled with the death of both Jezebel and her weakling husband -King. In the New Testament, the execution of John the Baptizer was effected on the orders of King Herod, on very flimsy grounds, motivated to gratify the vengeful vendetta of a promiscuous Queen. John's reformist stance was fatally punished. This follows a trend of past persecutions of prophets like Jeremiah, in the hands of Kings. The modern era with democratic dispensation, brought control to the powers hitherto wielded by Kings; reducing their office to ceremonial status symbols rather than as Chief Executives.

In Africa, Kings and Chiefs wielded same powers as others in foreign countries. African legends tell of renowned Kings who were dreaded for their awesome powers. Some had to be forcefully dethroned as check to their extreme acts of terror. In Nigeria, in the First Democratic Republic, Kings were Active politicians. The *Ooni* of *Ife* (Yoruba's foremost King), Sir Aderemi Adesoji was not only a Legislator, but a Governor of Western Region, while serving as Traditional ruler. Today, Traditional Rulers have been integrated in the Local Government cadre. They preside over customary courts and have administrative, judicial and legislative powers- only at their community levels. Their decisions are still subject to that of the Constitution and Penal laws. Even the King can be arrested by the Police! The role that Israelite Prophets played as check to the Kings, are played by the Priests of the Traditional Religion of the Nigerian Peoples. In the case of the Yoruba, the diviner, using the divination instrument of *Ifa*, was always at hand to reveal to the council of Chiefs what the gods had to say or command, which were binding on the Kings. Even the selection of a ruler was in past times determined by the choice of *Ifa.*

The image of such kings as sitting on throne in the court is another area of similarity. There is a prominent throne imagery of God in the New Testament. This links the concept of King and Judge. There is also the idea of a court in heaven hinted in Luke 12: 8f, which predicts the Son of Man acknowledging men before the Angels. In the book of Revelation, the enthronement idea is marked in the vision of 4:2 (repeated in 5:1), where God is described as "the one sitting on the throne." In African context, every King has a courtyard in the palace, where the *Iwarefas* (council of Chiefs) meet. The *Kabiyesi* (King) is greeted respectfully as they bow at his entry. He discusses issues with them, seeks their advice, and calls the *Ifa* priest to consult the oracles if the matter is knotty, but always, the final decision on any matter lies with the King. His throne is set aside, and is reserved only for his use. When he dies, his son takes over where the system requires hereditary succession.

We have common grounds also in trying to interpret Biblical kingship from the African situation.

Prophet- King

David and Solomon typify the best showcase of a prophet-king model. Despite the burden of Kingship, they made their mark as repositories of wisdom, poetry, and inspirational spirituality. They combine political acumen with scholarly erudition. The Psalms of David and the Proverbs as well as Ecclesiastes of Solomon reminds the most consulted sources by Practicing Christians in areas of personal as well as communal study and worship. They thus represent a combination of the powers of rulership and the gift of God. That a King can also be a spiritual resource is a novelty introduced by these father and son royalty. This concept agrees with Plato's utopian conception of a philosopher king that should provide beneficial rule in human societies. The story of the visit of Queen of Sheba is relevant again. Her immediate motive (there could be some other remote interests) motive for visiting Solomon in Jerusalem was because of his famed wisdom, splendour and affluence; being a rich royalty herself, her attraction could chiefly have been the intellectual. African Chiefs and rulers are of a similar mould. They are all expected to be the chief repositories of the traditions and oral cultural verities of their communities. Readily found at every palace are court praise singers who orally recount not only the genealogy of the Kings and prominent families, but recall the history and past achievements of the community. Every family in Nigeria is traditionally expected to have praise poetry. From this, the past history and inclinations of the family are known. Aside from this, traditional rulers are regarded as chief priests of their communities. There are rites that only the ruler performs under the guidance of the vocational Chief priests. This trend persists. Even in cosmopolitan centres like Lagos, local indigenes still perform traditional rites. In Ojo area of Lagos, the College of Education had to close down momentarily in June 2004 because the host community was performing rites that women were forbidden from witnessing. They had to be indoors. No one dared take the risk to defy the traditional rulers orders, despite the secularity and modernity prevalent in the country.

Subjugated Autonomy

The subjugation of the autonomous powers of chieftaincy Institutions in Nigeria began with the Colonial powers but it is sustained even in the post-colonial era by the indigenous political /government authorities. The Colonialists used religion, in this case Christianity, to whittle down the effects of Traditional Religion over the people, from which the Chieftaincy Institution derived its potency.

Historically, the hierarchies, rituals and structures of the Church have been used to interpret and legitimatize social situations of mastery, patriarchy, colonization and capitalism by linking them to be ordained by God.[27]

The effects of this are the tendency by some Chiefs to demonstrate colonial mentality in their conduct of chieftaincy affairs. Some try to be modern and western in approach, rather than sustain the traditional values of their Stools. On the part of their subjects, the effects of Christianity and Islam have been adverse. This is because these two religions see many aspects of the Indigenous Religion as pagan, idolatry, heathen, etc. therefore they disobey them, and consequently reducing the control of the Chiefs over the community. Urbanization and the evolution of cosmopolitan and metropolitan cities have complicated matters. In most cities today, the residents are composed of people from different tribes. It is thus difficult to impose a single Chieftaincy tradition upon them. There is a trend now, whereby indigenes of particular tribe residents elsewhere do organize themselves in a manner that they appoint Chiefs over themselves in *Diaspora*. In Lagos, the Igbos has their *Eze*, while the Hausas in the city have their *Serikis*, despite the fact that Lagos is a Yoruba city. This is a new innovation in chieftaincy institution.

The traditional Chieftaincy institutions thrived because of the awe with which the subjects held it. It was virtually autonomous of the Political powers in so far as the running of its systems was concerned. For example, each local community had its system of appointment as well as succession of Chiefs. Among the Yoruba, four systems exist. Firstly, the traditional oracle *Orunmila* was consulted through *Ifa*, its divinatory instrument. Whoever was selected among the screened contenders was chosen. This system, though revered because of its religious process, could be manipulated. Definitely it was undemocratic. Secondly, the hereditary succession was common as is still practiced by the *Bini* royal dynasty. In this case, only one family produces the *Oba*.   The eldest male child of an *Oba* was sure to take the throne after his father. Some Emirs in Northern Nigeria operate the same system that is comparable to the British monarchy. It hardly left room for disputation, as the choice is obvious. The third system is hierarchical, as is the practice among the Ibadan people in Yoruba. The ruling *Oba* has deputies in their ranks. The most senior occupies the throne. The fourth system as is found among the *Okun* people of Southeast *Yoruba* is rotational. Selected families who were regarded historically as the earliest aborigines of the community form the group of Royal families. Each family produces the *Oba* in turns on a rotational basis. This system worked well before the colonial era.

Postcolonial era has witnessed the gradual erosion of the autonomy of the Chieftaincy Institutions by ruling political as well as military governments. The appointment of Chiefs have become very attractive and competitive, such that it draws the intervention of Political parties to install their cronies as a way of using the Chiefs as instrument of mobilization of their subjects to support such parties. Chiefs are ordinarily regarded as non-partisan because they are fathers of their subjects (who naturally may belong to various parties). There were instances where ruling Governments forcefully removed Chiefs from the throne because such Chiefs fell out of favour with the ruling Government. *The Alaafin* of Oyo was dethroned by the Western Regional Government led by Obafemi Awolowo in 1956 partly because of his support for the rivals of the ruling Government. The Emir of Kano, Alhaji Sanusi was also dethroned by the Northern Regional Government led by Sir Ahmadu Bello, the Premier. During the military era, in 1995 the Government of General Sanni Abacha dethroned, exiled and detained Alhaji Ibrahim Dasuki, the Sultan of Sokoto (one of the most powerful Traditional Chieftaincy Stools in Nigeria and traditional head of the Muslim Caliphate). These precedents on two of the nation's most respected Chieftaincy Stools signalled the decline of traditional immunity of the Institution.

Today, any Traditional Chief that is selected by traditional Kingmakers must receive the approval and official appointment by the Government. The Chiefs are put on Government pay roll, given official cars and receive their promotion and grading from the Governor who usually presents to them Staffs (sceptres) of office. Traditional Chiefs are required to be present at major Government public functions. At best, their significance is merely ceremonial, except in their limited domain where the local people accord them some respect. This emergent subjective status of Chiefs is a fall-out of the colonial era; governments now replacing colonial masters in their control of Chiefs as subjects and tools of indirect rule.

Secular Functionality

There have been attempts to modernize the Chieftaincy Institution by incorporating it within the secular superstructure of the society. Although the Chiefs had absolute executive, legislative and judicial powers prior to the colonial era, these powers was either totally taken away in some cases or they were greatly reduced. Today, each Chief has a traditional Council (cabinet) of lesser Chiefs. Together they try cases such as minor disagreements, marriage disagreements, land disputes, minor theft, etc. Cases that border on criminality are referred to the Police and the Magistrate or High Courts. No Chief is above the law. If the *Oba, Obi* or *Emir* fouls the law, he is subject to arrest, trial and possible imprisonment. In other words, the contemporary Chieftaincy institution operates as an arm in the government strata, which is another appendage of the public service. The above limited powers notwithstanding, Chiefs have been found as necessary stop-gaps in the crisis-management of the Nigerian communities. Whenever crisis broods, the Chiefs are found relevant in controlling the actions and reactions of their people. At times, they have failed or proved incapable to do this and at times they themselves were accused of being instrumental to crisis generation. In any case their roles have been useful a case in point is the government consultation with all major traditional rulers in 1999 during the crisis arising from the controversial annulment of the June 12 1993 Presidential elections. This threw the country into years of political turmoil. When religious crisis erupted, traditional rulers were appointed as part of the 'Advisory Council for Religious Affairs'. Other members included the topmost leaders of the two major religions in the country (Christianity and Islam).

As noted earlier, the Colonial authorities used the Chiefs for their indirect rule. In the Northern Nigeria, the Emirs were granted judicial powers at customary levels. Up till date, Customary Courts abound in every part of the nation to try cases which were not criminal but had to do with aspects of the customs of the people. That was the rationale for the permission by the Colonial authorities to have allowed the operation of *Sharia* (Islamic Judicial system) in Northern Nigeria. The *Sharia* Courts thrived in the North but were not totally independent of the normal civil courts. After the colonial era, the Northern Regional Government under Ahmadu Bello maintained the *Sharia* as penal code but not as criminal code. Unfortunately, in the current political dispensation this privilege has been used to enforce the adoption of *Sharia* as legal code in most States of Northern Nigeria, a development which led to public protests by non-Muslims who saw it as part of Islamisation process of the nation. The riots that arose from this claimed about 2000 lives in Kaduna city in 2000. In the whole unfolding events, the role of the Chiefs (in these case Emirs) has been pronounced because they stand to benefit from the use of religion to restore their waning powers and influence in the contemporary Nigerian society.

Capitalist Chieftaincy

One area in which the post-colonial chieftaincy institution in Nigeria has changed is in the introduction of capitalism into the system. Traditional African communities practiced communalism. The bi-polar struggles between capitalism and socialism were irrelevant to the African scene until the post-colonial era.

Western imperialist tendencies now characterize the Traditional stool. Writing about India which was another ex-British Colony, Panikkar observes that "The powerful cultural onslaught the Third World countries are experiencing today is an attempt to establish cultural imperialism-culture as imperialism-as a precursor to an all-embracing domination[2]

The original idea of Chieftaincy was simply for traditional governance. Although by their office and powers, Chiefs were not usually deprived in material terms, their choice was not usually dictated by their material affluence but by the laid down procedures for such appointments. It was the duty of subjects to provide for their Chiefs. Consequently they lacked no means of common sustenance. In fact, they were the traditional custodians, not only of the traditions of their people but also of the entire citizens, land and societal institutions. That was why a Chief could marry as many wives as he wishes, with little restraint when he desires a lady to be his wife. Some would even take-over the wife of another out of greed, like the Biblical David did of Uriah's wife (although with dire consequences). This traditional privilege was hardly tampered with by the colonial authorities. They allowed the Chiefs hold reins in their community in such mundane matters.

This privilege was carried over into the post-colonial era. This fact contributed to the larger- than- life images in which prominent Traditional rulers carry themselves in Nigeria today. They adorn themselves in peculiar royal garments, the Christians among them would not remove their caps in Church as is the custom for males, they drive in customized cars, usually the very sophisticated ones, their car registration plates are not the usual numbers but bear the name of such a Traditional ruler, for example OONI, SULTAN,OBI; they drive in a convoy of several accompanying cars, led by Police escorts blaring sirens to clear the way for an undisturbed traffic flow for the supreme Chief. The Chiefs have acquired this larger than life image that detaches them rather unfortunately from the people they govern.

The Traditional chieftaincy Institution today in Nigeria has become the exclusive preserve of the rich. Capitalism has characterized it. The throne is usually for the highest bidder. An eligible poor contender has little chance over a wealthy contender. Because of the aroma of power and affluence attached to the office, Chieftaincy disputes are common, often leading to fatal elimination of opponents. The educated elite have suddenly developed interest in Chieftaincy offices which were hitherto the preserve of elderly persons of the grassroots. In the Northern parts, virtually all the Emirs are educated and wealthy, some multi-millionaires. same goes for the prominent ones in the South and West. Some, like the Emir of Kano and the *Ooni* of Ile Ife are joint business associates who own and run international businesses. Many Traditional rulers today are big-time Contractors who are patronized by Government agencies. They use their royal offices to influence their personal business interests. In other words, Chieftaincy institution is an avenue for possible exploitation of privileges by the Chiefs.

Chiefs in the post-colonial Nigeria are often part-time rulers. They run their businesses alongside performing their royal functions as occasions demand. As sophisticated elite, some alternate their living overseas with their traditional duties at the Palace. This is a departure from the former situation whereby the Chief is mostly confined to his domain.

Most Nigerian Communities make it a policy that their Chiefs must be educated and well to do. One of the reasons for this is the role of the Chiefs as the spokesperson for their Communities before the government. In other words, Chieftaincy institution stands as lobby tool for community development. Wealthy Traditional rulers have initiated developmental projects that they or their business friends sponsor. Some have brought their influence to bear on Government agencies to establish industries and social infrastructure in their communities. It does not follow however those only wealthy rulers can achieve such feats. Wisdom and diplomacy is not always contingent upon one's material possession. Our conclusion from this new feature which is different from the colonial era is that this is a result of the economic and social -political benefits arising from the democratic and independent dispensation.

A notable phenomenon is the sale of Chieftaincy titles by traditional rulers, to selected persons who are regarded as of financial benefit to the throne. It is the tradition for Rulers to award honorary Chieftaincy titles (they go by various coined names) to persons of their pleasure. It has been a common practice that the poor are rarely so-honoured. Past and present leaders in Government, wealthy businessmen and foreign diplomats are awarded the titles. Sometimes this is motivated by the desire by the rulers to have such awardees become interested in the development of the community. However the question remains that must material status of a person determine his qualification for community leadership and award? Our opinion is no. The difficult knot in this phenomenon is the suspicion that awardees of Chieftaincy titles donate huge sums of money to the rulers in exchange for the awards. The awardees go by the title -- 'Chief...'. Some honorary Chiefs have been discovered to be fraudulent and of no good reputation. This commercialization of the Chieftaincy institution erodes the legendary respect given to it.

Chieftaincy and Religious Puritanism

The African Chiefs are traditionally the custodians of the Indigenous Religions of their people. This refers to the religion which was inspired, initiated and sustained by the African forebears and passed on to successive generations through oral tradition. This faith features the belief in the One Supreme Being who is serviced by a pantheon of Divinities as well as Spirits, belief in ancestors and, magic and medicine. The Chief is the patron of all gods (divinities) in the community and a superior priest to the particular patron god of the community. On special festival occasions, it was the duty of the Chief to perform the rituals stipulated for the gods. Not only the gods, got the Chief's attention. Also the representatives of esoteric forces that operate and rule over the town must be patronized and protected by the Chief. Because of the potency of their supernatural powers, the Chief inadvertently is expected to be initiated into cults and possess higher spiritual powers than his subjects. He was regarded as the 'husband' of the witches and a very magically artful person. At times, in times of crisis he is expected to be the last resort. For the foregoing reasons, the majorities of traditional rulers are dreaded for their *juju*. The Palace of the *Ooni* of Ile Ife for instance is believed to be occupied by more that 1000 gods each of which has its turn in occasional worship and rituals. There is one ritual sacrifice to one god or another in such palaces every day in the year. Some rulers are believed to still indulge in human sacrifices all in their search for superior powers and in keeping with age-long customs. These are part of the reasons why the rulers are treated with fear. The respected offered them are therefore compulsive rather than earned.

Today, a new trend is emerging in the Chieftaincy Institution. This is the introduction of religious Puritanism. The majority of the Traditional rulers today have joined new religions, mainly Christianity and Islam. Islam and Christianity are monotheistic faiths that are intolerant of African Indigenous Religion. When a Chief becomes a committed Christian or Muslim, a crisis of commitment arises because it becomes difficult for such a Ruler to remain faithful custodian and patron of the 'pagan' cults and practices. A choice has to be made, although several choose the option of least resistance- syncretism. Syncretism is the concurrent practice of essential elements of two normally incompatible religions. This is common. The same Chief who sacrifices to gods is found regularly in Church on Sunday or in the Mosque for the Friday *Jumat* prayers in the Mosque.

What is interesting today is the emergence of prominent Chiefs or Rulers who maintain puritanical commitment to their faith while on the throne. Rather than compromise such a commitment, they carry out a bold review of aspects of African Indigenous Religion, which are repulsive to their new-found faiths. Some contenders or selected candidates for the throne do give the precondition that their reigns will be in accordance with their chosen faiths that were contrary to the African Indigenous Religion. Upon such agreements, such Rulers are allowed to run the affairs of the community and palace according to the precepts of such religion. In the Western parts, some Rulers such as the *Alake* of Egbaland in Abeokuta hold daily Christian devotion in his palace before commencing the activities of the day. Some have Chapels or Mosques in their palaces. In the North, all Traditional Rulers, Emirs, are committed Muslim leaders as well.

The effects of this development are significant. First, it is an effect of the colonial influence, for colonialism rode upon the tide of religion in the conquest of Africa. Secondly, the Rulers are more popular with their people many of whom have also joined the foreign religions. Such religions as Christianity or Islam eventually become the official religion of the community. No meeting of the community will hold without opening prayers and closing prayers said in either or both of these religions. A typical Christian crusade, such as the one held monthly by the Redeemed Christian Church of God (which draws crowd of about 400,000), usually have in attendance an array of Traditional Rulers. Thirdly, the development is a threat to the continued relevance of the African Indigenous Religion which the Rulers are expected top patronises and protect. This is a reflection that post colonial era witnesses a continuation of the colonial influence upon the chieftaincy institution in the area of religion.

Conclusion

In conclusion, what we have attempted to do here is to identify and highlight aspects of the Chieftaincy institution in Nigeria which have changed in the post-colonial era. The effects of colonialism will ever remain with the colonized. The very fact that all African States speak *lingua franca* that were colonial in origin shows the inevitability of man living with heritage of the ancient and the modern. In the estimation of the emergent trends in the Chieftaincy institution, religion plays a crucial role. It is also in religion that the Institution will continue to find its most potent historical relevance and powers for the sustenance of the royal institution.

The Western world has much to learn from Africa in this aspect. The fact that despite modern civilization and technological development as well as political development, the Chieftaincy Institution still survives and is still being supported, patronized, and respected, shows that Africa is determined to retrace her identity and maintain its fundamental structures in spite of historical accidents such as colonialism. As Amadi asks: "is it possible to weld the traditional concepts of government into an instrument capable of coping with the running of a modern state? That is the possibility that African nations should explore."[28] Our opinion agrees with Amadi's above, We think that much of the colonial is still hanging around the Chiefs and the Chieftaincy Institutions in Africa, as demonstrated by the Nigerian situation. It is in remaining truly African and at the same time contemporary in the global world that the Chieftaincy Institution can survive and remain actively relevant. By and large, the African Chieftaincy institution is a vital model for exploring an Africentric biblical hermeneutic. It would be surprising how many similarities there are between the biblical and African worldview.

Endnotes

1. Elechi Amadi, Ethics in Nigerian Culture (Ibadan, Heinemann Pub. 1982), 94
2. Between 6th and 9th July 2004, African Biblical Scholars met at the Annual Meeting of the Nigeria Association for Biblical Studies (NABIS) to discuss the theme-Decolonizing Biblical Studies in Africa." It was held at the Lagos State University, Lagos, Nigeria, and hosted by the Department of Religions of the University. It drew participants from South Africa, and most Nigerian Universities.
3. See collection of essays on this current subject matter in Mary N. Getui and Emmanuel A. Obeng (eds.), Theology of Reconstruction (Nairobi: Acton Publishers, 1999).
4. D.T Adamo, Reading and Interpreting the Bible in African Indigenous Churches (Eugene, Oregon: WIPF Stock and Publishers, 2001); cf. "What is African Biblical Studies?" Paper presented at the Nigerian Association For Biblical Studies, Annual Conference, July 6-11, 2004, Lagos, Nigeria.
5. Justin Ukpong, "Inculturation as a Decolonisation of Biblical Studies", paper presented at NABIS conference, op.cit.
6. Getui and Obeng op. cit.
7. Jese Mugambi, 'Foreword' in Getui and Obeng op. cit.
8. Nahashan Ndung'u , "Towards the Recovery of African Identity" in Getup and Obeng eds., op.cit., 260
9. Op.cit.
10. Leslie Newbegin, quoted in P.G. Hiebert, "The Flaw of the excluded Middle," Missiology, 10 (1982), 44
11. Kihumbu Thairu, The African and the AIDS Holocaust : A Historical and Medical Perspective (Nairobi: Phoenix Pub., 2003), 5; Notes on back cover- page.
12. Desmond Tutu, quoted in G.S. Wilmore and J.H. Cone eds., Black Theology: A Documentary History (Maryknoll, New York : Orbis Books, 1979), 484
13. S.O. Abogunrin, "Decolonising New Testament Interpretation in Africa", paper presented at NABIS Conference, op. cit.
14. Gerald West, "Decolonising (South) African Biblical Scholarship: The Bible in (South) African History and Culture." Paper presented at The Annual Meeting of the Nigerian Association for Biblical Studies (NABIS), July 6-11 2004, Lagos, Nigeria, op.cit.
15. Ukachukwu Chris Manus, Intercultural Hermeneutics in Africa: Methods and Approaches (Nairobi: Acton Pub., 2003), 7.
16. Ibid.
17. S.O. Okafor, "Traditional Authorities and Local Government in Nigeria" in S. Olugbemi (ed.), Alternative Political Future for Nigeria (Lagos: Nigerian Political Science Association, 1990), 344
18. Max I. Stackhouse, "Politics and Religion" in Mircea Eliade (ed.), The Encyclopaedia of Religion Vol. 2 (New York: Macmillan, 1987), 410.
19. Ibid.
20. See D.F. Asaju, "Christian Evangelism in Badagry, Nigeria" in G.O. Ogunremi et.al (eds.), Badagry: History and Culture of an Ancient city (Lagos: RexCharles Press, 1994).
21. Martin Luther, "The Works of Martin Luther" in W.T. Jones et.al (eds), Approaches to Ethics (New York: McGraw-Hill, 1977), 170

22. Bolaji Idowu, Olodumare: God in Yoruba Belief (London: Longman. 1968), ix.
23. Donald Guthrie, New Testament Theology (Lancaster: Intervarsity Press, 1981), 132
24. Graham Hancock, The Beauty of Historic Ethiopia (Nairobi: Camerapix pub., 1977), 20.
25. Guthrie, Op.cit., 84
26. Thulani Ndlazi, "Bridging the Gap Between Christianity and African Culture" in Roswith Gerloff (ed.), Mission is Crossing Frontiers.(South Africa: Cluster Pub., 2003), 107.
27. Echoes, World Council of Churches publication, Vol. 18, (2000), 7.
28. Amadi, Op.cit.

CHAPTER X

UNITY IN EPHESIANS 4: 1-6 IN AFRICAN CONTEXT

Joseph Enuwosa

Introduction

In Ephesians, Paul unfolds for his readers the eternal purpose of God being worked out in history through Christ. Paul sees an alienated humanity being reconciled, a fractured mankind that is being united and a new humanity being created. He, thus, turns from exhortation to exposition of what God has done in his Son and what we must be and do in the Church. He moved from a mind-stretching theology to a concrete theology for the daily life of the Church. Paul's conviction and authority as an apostle of Christ undergird his exhortation.

The new society, the Church, which God has brought into being has two major characteristics. Firstly, it is one family made by Jews and Gentiles. Secondly, this society is a holy people. They are elected by God and set apart as God's property. Hence, the second Vatican Council declared that "the universal Church is seen to be a people brought into unity from the unity of the Father, Son and the Holy Spirit."1 Therefore, since God's people are called to be one people, they must manifest their unity. To this end, the article aims to show that the quest for Christian unity in Africa has its basis in the teaching of Apostle Paul. The study also intends to indicate the value of diversity in the Church which was well echoed by Paul. It is a strong stimulus to concern ourselves with

Christian unity and corrects a number of misleading notions on ecumenical issues. Rifts and secession arose in the Church which has been one, universal and undivided. It was at that time that a Church was truly universal. In this one and only Church of God from its very beginning, there arose certain rifts which the apostles regarded as damnable. But in subsequent centuries much more serious dissensions appeared and large communities became separated from full communion with the Catholic Church ..." (Vatican II, 455).2 All indeed profess to be followers of Christ but they differ in mind and go their different ways as if Christ himself is divided. In recent times divided Christians have started to show a sense of remorse over their divisions and longing for unity. Today almost everyone in different ways yearns for the one visible Church of God, a Church that is truly universal.

In the last half of this century, therefore, there have been great movements about the unity of the Church. Modern Christians' preoccupation with union matter in the Church may be traced to the Edinburgh Conference of 1910. Following this, the movement towards reunion gathered speed. Three notable milestones achieved in this effort are the inauguration of the Church of South India in 1947; the World Council of Churches in 1948 and the 1964 Vatican II decree on ecumenism. The Edinburgh Conference probably inspired the Calabar Conference of 1911 which agreed to be called Evangelical Union of Southern Nigeria. Since then some more united Churches have come into existence. It has, therefore, become important to look with fresh mind at Ephesians 4:1-16 since it is one of the two classic New Testament passages on Christian union.

The method used in this study is the Africentric approach to the study of Ephesians 4:1-6. By this, Ephesians 4:1-6 is examined in the context of the culture and the Church in Africa. The concept of unity in Ephesians is interpreted from the perspective of African culture. It is what D.T. Adamo referred to as "African Cultural Hermeneutics"3 which in J.S. Ukpong's phrase is "inculturation hermeneutics."4 This process engages the Bible with African social and cultural world-view. The basic feature of His method is that it derives data from primary sources. The text of Ephesians 4: 1-6 is explained by analogy (analogia entis).

This approach is distinct from Western biblical hermeneutics that works with secondary sources. The real meaning of a biblical text is drawn from a community of faith where it is practiced. Africa like ancient Israel is predominantly an illiterate and agrarian society where information is transmitted in oral tradition. This means that we have to search out the primary materials, locate, collect, and classify the oral history in our study. Here we encounter the same situation as it was in the kerygma of the early Church in Acts of the Apostles where the disciples proclaimed the salvation of God in Christ Jesus.

The disciples preached with joyful urgency that life can be radically different in Jesus. These oral proclamations of the life of Jesus in Jerusalem, Antioch and Samaria were the primary sources of data for the evangelists in the early Church. This is what forms a data in any study. It is original, realistic and more reliable than Western biblical hermeneutics that depends on literature and personal reasons. In Africa, biblical concepts are tested in practice. The contextual method is real, objective, existential and functional because it interprets biblical themes from *Sitz im leben* Africana, the actual life situation in Africa, since biblical tradition is a replica of African culture.

Western biblical interpretation is abstract and subjective. To be subjective is to interpret biblical passages from the perspective of oneself without due regard to the author's intention and the community of faith on which the text was based. The major disadvantage here is that it is a hermeneutics separated from life in the Church, what is at hand in the concrete situation in the Church and its environment. Hermeneutics in the West speaks in symbolic terms of "Q". Quelle, Special Matthew, Luke. Hence M.D. Goulder refers to it as the judgment of a non-existent "Q"5

These "Q, M, and L" hypotheses have no meaning for the ordinary man who wants to encounter Jesus that drove out demons, healed the sick, raised the dead, fed five thousand men and confronted the power of Satan. He seeks Jesus to drive away the witches, wizards and sorcerers that are haunting his life. This is a reality which contextual exegesis wishes to explore in African community and which Euro-American hermeneutics chose to ignore.6 For this reason, H.W. Turner concluded that "our Western studies of Christianity remain distorted in so far as they take little account of Christian forms in non-Western cultures.

Western hermeneutics can be helpful in the human dimension of religious reality. It can examine the phenomena embodied in religious expressions. But religious traditions are not only made of the observable or human elements, they include the manifestations of the sacred order, the "wholly order" from which rational approaches to the study of Scripture are deeply separated. "The task of understanding is thus doubly difficult" because Western hermeneutics is no longer attuned to the traditional forms of expression in myth, ritual and theology.8

Unity and Diversity in Paul's Concept

Scholars have drawn attention to the concept of unity in the letters of Paul, African tradition and the Church in Africa. This is the result of the fact that we have come to recognize that there is no strength and peace except in unity. We may appreciate this value "in the beauty of the rainbow precisely because of the emerging different colours."9 Thus, from African and Pauline perspective, unity may be defined as the arrangements of parts to form a complete whole in which each depends on one another for existence. Unity, therefore, is a peaceful co-existence.

Christian unity is a fact for Paul. Paul did not hold brief for a divided Church. So his major concern in Ephesians is the plan of God to bring men of all nations together in Christ. Paul explains the kind of unity which God intends to prevail in his Church. The apostle envisaged a form of unity in diversity, not uniformity. This readily brings to mind the form of unity which Christ recommended. He prayed "that they may be one, as we are one ..." (John 17:11). The emphasis is a Trinitarian unity. This is illustrated by Paul in Ephesians with two basic concepts.

The Unity of God

Christian unity arises from the unity of God. One is in fact touched by Paul's repetition of the word, "one" in Ephesians 4: 3-6. It occurs seven times in the four verses. Paul writes, "eager to maintain the unity of the Spirit in the bond of peace. There is one body and one Spirit, just as you were called to the one hope that belongs to your call, one Lord, one faith, one baptism, one God and Father of us all" (Eph. 4: 3-6). A careful reading discloses that three of these refer to the three persons in one God. The first four allude to our Christian experience in relation to the three persons of the Trinity. This theological fact is expressed in three simple affirmations"

(i) *One Body, One Spirit*
Paul's metaphor of body is used in different forms to explain the unity of the Church. In 1Corinthians, the body with many parts is identified with the Church that has many branches (12:12). This is more explicit in Colossians (1: 18,24). In Romans, Paul used the metaphor to show how different gifts can exist within the one Church for the benefit of every member (12:4-8). This image of the *ekklesia* is more developed in Ephesians (1:2, 23; 4:1-12, 15-16; 5:23). It is typically Pauline. For Paul the identification between Christ and his Church was the first lesson he learnt about Christianity: "Saul, Saul, why are you persecuting me" (Acts 9:4). Paul expanded this teaching in Romans 12:5 1 Corinthians 12:12 and Colossians 1:18.

In this body, Christ is the head, the believers are members, and the Holy Spirit is the Soul (1 Cor. 12:11-12; Eph. 2:22). There is one body because there is only one Spirit. The one body is the Church, the body of Christ which is formed by Jews and Gentiles (Eph. 1:23). Its cohesion depends on the Holy Spirit who dwells and animates it (1 Cor.12:13). The totality of believers constitute the one body of Christ irrespective of denominational inclination.10

(ii) *One Hope*
Hope in ordinary parlance is the manner by which we expect and desire something in the future with the confidence that we will have it. It is called the anchor of faith in Hebrew 6:19. In New Testament theology, hope is a gift of God by which we firmly trust that we will have eternal life through the merits of

Jesus Christ. It is, thus, a desire and expectation of salvation with an assured confidence of obtaining it through the infinite goodness, power and mercy of God in Christ Jesus.11 The object of Christian hope is God Himself whom we look forward to possess for eternity. Hope does not exist after death. It is the living alone that can maintain hope. We also do not know or see what we hope for. Paul, then, said "hope that is seen is not hope: for what a man seeth, why does he hope for" (Rom. 8:24). The opposite of hope is despair and presumptions.

The hope of Christians is one. Believers set their eyes on the kingdom of God through Christ. This is the tenet or the goal of all Christian pilgrims. Thus, for Paul, all Christians share this one hope, one faith and one baptism either by immersion or aspersion because there is only one Lord (Eph. 4:5). Jesus is the centre of Christian faith, hope and baptism. Through him, the goal of eternal life in God's kingdom can be achieved. We have to wait for the coming of Christ with expectant hope of joining him in his glory.

(iii) *The Metaphor of a Building*

Paul also utilized the notion of a building to explain the unity of the Church. This concept of Paul has its parallel in Matthew 16:18: "Thou art Peter, and upon this rock I will build my Church." In 1 Corinthians, Paul said that the Corinthian were God's building (1Cor. 3:9). In this house, God is the builder, Christ is the foundation and the Holy Spirit dwells in it. According to D. Guthrie, this passage is interpreted in verse 16 and in 6:19 where they refer to God's temple.12 Here the totality of believers form the abode of the Spirit. Thus, the Spirit dwells in the assembly or the congregation of God's people. The individual Christian that constitutes the "ekklesia" is also a dwelling place of the Holy Spirit.

The concept of the temple as God's dwelling place has an Old Testament background. For 'the ancient Jews, God dwells in the temple in Jerusalem. Paul did not completely concede to this view of God dwelling in a man-made mansion or a physical temple, but he did not infer less. He transformed the concept from a sacred building into a spiritual building. The spiritual meaning of building is illustrated in Ephesians 2: 19-22. Paul said, "the whole structure being joined together and growing into a holy temple in the Lord; in whom you also are built into it for a dwelling place of God in the Spirit."

By this interpretation, the whole Church, the Christian community is the temple of God. Each part of the structure represents the different Churches or denominations. The Churches like the parts of a building are important in so far as they are an integral part of the whole. The function of all the separate Christian communities was to form an observable part of the whole Church."13 Christ, the foundation of the building, is the source of unity for the different parts on the whole. The work of the Holy Spirit here is obvious. The Church, then, is the abode of God in Spirit. The denominations would never become a united whole without the work of the Holy Spirit. Consequently all believers for Paul are members of a spiritual household or family of God.

(iv) One Family

There is one Christian family. Paul maintained that there is "one God and Father of us all who is above all and through all and in all" (Eph. 4:6). This implies that God is the father of all Christians. Some ancient manuscripts read "in you all". A Robinson thinks that the addition of the word "you" is "a timid gloss"14. Certainly many ancient versions omit it. However, the gloss is correct. For the "all above, through and in" whom God is Father are his family or household. The result of this notion of divine household is the concept of the people of God.

Israel was the chosen and elected people of God. Israel as God's people rest on a theocratic view-point. "Israel was a people chosen by God and watched over him."15. She retained her identity on the basis of God's might, not her own strength. For Paul, therefore, the Church as the people of God "was foreshadowed from the beginning of the world and had a marvelous preparation in the history of Israel."16. People as it is used in this study are collective. It is the totality of God's people, the collectivity of God's people (Eph. 1:4; Rom. 11:5).

(vi) *African Concept of Unity*

The prevailing meaning of the concept of unity in African tradition and the Church in Africa is similar to Pauline concept of unity. Unity in African perspective is the act of living together peacefully with mutual respect and accommodation of individual differences. According to P. Esiri, unity in Urhobo is *ekuekugbe* meaning "joining together." This means coming together, co-existence. Unity is also explained in Africa by symbols. African concept of unity is based on clan structure.

African tradition is built on a spirituality of belonging. People belong together in a community or the family. The clan is a close kinship group of an extended family system centered on the ancestors. People are seen as a member of a single family of one ancestral descent. The head of the clan and the founder-ancestor are the rallying point of unity in the clan. An annual festival is designed in honour of the great ancestor to foster unity. Under the clan head are village heads. In Nigeria, the clan heads are called Oba, Obi, Ovie,, Eze and Emir. The names differ from place to place because of differences in dialect. The head is the king and he treats every member of the clan as people of one household, one family.

According to C. du Toit," African societies are family-centered."17 The entire clan is an extended family. "Life is shared with all for whom you have to take responsibility."[18] C. du Toit used the South African word *Ubuntu* to explain the unity in African clan structure. *Ubuntu* for Toit means to participate in clan activity for the purpose of unity. In Africa, a person is identified by his or her interpersonal relationship, not individualistic tendency." The identity of the person is found in his or her place in the community. Without this sense of belonging a human is more than half dead."[19] In Africa it is a matter of "I participate, therefore, I am."[20]

Thus, to live in Africa, ultimately means to participate in the unity of the clan structure. An African is a being-in-communion; he is a non-solitary being because he works in unity with others. In discussing unity and social relation of man in African community, Benjamin Ray noted that the belief in Africa is "I am because we are and since we are, I am. I exist and since I am not alone, I realize that I am alive or I exist."[21] In this way, the clan is the center of unity as a people, a family or a household. The Pauline concept of the people of God, one family and a household is already embedded in African culture. African Christian is, therefore, familiar with these Pauline symbols used to express unity.

While an African believes that he is a communal being and his brother's keeper, he recognizes himself as an individual in his own right. He is aware of his unique personality shaped by his destiny. The recognition of individual implies diversity. Though unity and communal life are accepted pattern of life, the right of one person precludes the right of the other.

The larger society of the clan is the tribe. Each tribe in Africa is made up of several clans with a loose federalism. The importance of this cultural pattern in our discussion of unity in Ephesians and the Church in Africa is immense. The concept of tribe operates all over Africa. The characteristics of the tribal and clan structures are similar to Pauline concept of the Church as the body of Christ. As the body or the building is made up of different parts, the tribe is made up of different clans. The different parts and clans represent the different denominations. While the body is held together in unity by the head, the clans are held together in unity by the tribe. The tribe provides the unity for the diverse clans. This partially explains the amazing success of the Church in Africa because it has bred new tribes and clans in Christ.

In summary, therefore as the one Father creates the one family, the one Lord provides the one faith, hope and baptism. The one family of faith, forms the body of Christ sustained by the Holy Spirit. Since the unity of God is inviolable, the unity of the Church is also inviolable. It is indestructible as the unity of God himself because we cannot multiply or split the God head. This, however, might have been stated too dogmatically. Scholars may oppose this view that we cannot split the Church because it contradicts our experience since the divisions in the Church is self-evident. How, then, can we reconcile the obvious divisions of the Church with the insistence on the indestructibility of its unity?

At this point a necessary distinction has to be made. It is not just between the visible and the invisible Church. Though this distinction is correct, but the concept of the invisible Church whose members are known only to God has been misused. It has been employed by some scholars as an excuse for opting out of responsible membership in the visible Church.

So the distinction needs to be somewhat refined. The distinction is between the Church's unity as an invisible reality present in the mind of God. What appears as visible disunity is only diversity like the trunk of a tree and its branches before God (John 15:5f). In the mind of God, therefore, we are one. In inter-denominational congresses we sense our underlying unity in Christ. But outwardly and visibly we belong to different Churches and different traditions. Some are not even in communion with one another, while others have even strayed far from New Testament Christianity.

Paul himself saw this paradox of the unity and diversity in the Church. This can be explained better with the human family. Mr. Eze Okafor and Mrs. Ayo Okafor are couple with three children: Efe, Odafe and Ibrahim. They constitute one family. Marriage and parenthood has made them one and a united family. If Eze's family disintegrated because of divorce and quarrel, can we not regard Efe, Odafe and Ibrahim as a member of the same family between the children. It will be quite correct to regard them as one family in spite of the disastrous disintegration.

Mr. And Mrs. Okafor remain indestructibly parents of their three sons who are still brothers despite the severed relationship. For simply nothing can alter the fundamental basis of this family which the circumstances of marriage and birth have imposed on it. This also applies to the Church. Nothing can really disturb the basic unity of the Church because it rests on one fundamental principle of the saving plan of God in Christ. Though the Churches may have some theological aspects in which they are radically different, the Christ-event is the core doctrines. The extended family members of Mr. Eze, however, may not acquiesce to this situation. They would urge them to maintain the unity of the family by means of the bond of peace in spite of individual differences.

We cannot acquiesce in the same way to the tragedy of apparent disunity in the Church at the cost of its indestructible unity. For this reason, Paul tells us to be "eager to maintain the unity of the Spirit" (Eph. 4:4). The Greek verb, *spoudazontes*, eager is emphatically used in this verse. The force of this word is clearly brought out in the New English Bible translation as "spare no effort." The word requires a conscious and diligent effort to sustain the unity of the Church. According to M. Barth we cannot exactly bring out the urgency contained in this Greek verb by translation. The word does not only show haste and passion, but the total effort of the members of the Church. Members' whole attitude would be involved, their will, reason, emotion and physical strength.[22] Barth concluded thus:

> The imperative mood of the participle found in the Greek text excludes
> passivity, quietism, a wait-an-see attitude or a diligence tempered by all

deliberate speed. Yours is the initiative! Do it now! … Such are the overtones in this verse.[23]

Ephesians may have been a letter addressed to several Churches. Perhaps, there were many Christians who met in small units in Ephesus, house Churches. Aquilla and Priscilla for example had a Church in their house in Rome (Rom. 16:3-5). Probably they developed the same when they came to Ephesus (Acts 18:26). Hence Paul had in mind the unity between and within the Churches. This concern of the apostle still holds for inter and intra-church relationship today. There is room for differences of opinion about the precise form of Christian unity and the nature of the Church.

But we should all be eager for some visible expression of Christian unity provided fundamental Christian concepts are not sacrificed to achieve it.[24] Christian unity is based on our belief of one Father, one Lord and one Divine Spirit. Thus we cannot attain unity in the Church if we reject the doctrine of the Trinity. "Authentic Christian unity in truth, life and love is far more important than union schemes of a structural kind although ideally the latter should be a visible expression of the former."[25] The way we behave towards our fellow Christian will foster unity.

The Charity of Our Behaviour

Good behaviour is the basis of Christian unity. In Ephesians 4:2, Paul believes that Christian unity rests on the charity of our conduct. This unity of the Church is characterized by four qualities of human behaviour. These qualities are meekness, lowliness, patience and love. This shows that Christian unity depends on moral qualities. Modern scholars often argue from the structure of the Church.[26] J.R. Stott also sees it from the moral point of view. He said "certainly in the quest for Christian unity … we must say that the moral is more important than the structural."[27]

(i) Meekness

Meekness is a virtue applauded by Aristotle. Aristotle hated extremes and loved "the golden means"[28] Meekness gives a man the quality of moderation. It is the middle way between too much anger and weakness. On the contrary meekness is the character of a strong man whose power is under control. He exercises self-restrain on his power. It is the quality of a strong personality who is master of himself and servant of others. According to G.G. Findlay, meekness is the absence of the disposition to assert personal rights either in the presence of God or men (1 Cor. 4:21;2 Tim. 2:25).[29]

(ii) Lowliness

Lowliness was much despised in the ancient world. The Greeks never used their word for humility and still less of any admiration. For them, humility (*tapeinotes*) is an abject, servile, subservient attitude "the crouching submissiveness of a slave."[30] The value of humility came to be known through Christ. He humbled himself and used the model of a child for his ethical and behavioural teachings. Paul used the Greek word *tapeinophrosyne*, for "lowliness of mind" (Phil. 2:3-8). The humble man recognizes the worth and value of other people, this attitude led Christ to employ himself and become a servant (Phil. 2:3-8).

Lowliness and meekness are naturally related. The meek man thinks as little of his personal claims as the humble man of his personal merits. They blend together in the character of Christ who described himself as gentle and lowly in heart. Matthew used the phrase *"praos ... Kai tapeinos"* meaning gentle and lowly (Mt. 11:29).

(iii) Patience and Love

Both words form a natural pair. For patience, *makrothymia* (Rom. 2:4; 1 Tim. 1:6) is long suffering towards aggravating people as God in Christ has shown towards us. This leads to forbearing one another that encourages mutual tolerance in peace. Love is the final quality, it embraces the preceding two. It is the crown and sum of all virtues, because to love is constructively to seek welfare of others and the good of the Christian community. The binding quality of love is celebrated in Colossians 3:14. The passage reads: "And above all these put on love which binds everything together in perfect harmony."

These are therefore, the foundation stones of Christian unity. External structure of unity cannot stand if these ethical behaviors are absent in the church. When this strong base is laid, it is then that a visible unity can be built. No unity is pleasing to God if it is not a product of charity. Humility is essential to unity. While pride sows discord, humility, patience and love are the greatest single secret of concord. This can be explained by our experience. We move with those we love and we treat those we do not love like dirt. Then there must be unity in the relationship with those we love and disunity with those we hate. In the words of Stott "personal vanity is a key factor in all our relationships."[31] If instead of pride we give others our respect by recognizing their intrinsic God-given worth, we shall be promoting harmony in God's Church.

The Significance of Ephesians 4 for the Church in Africa

What does unity in Ephesians imply for the church in Africa? Paul goes on to elaborate the outcome of unity in the church. It leads to "the unity of the faith and of the knowledge of the Son of God, mature manhood and the measure of the stature of the fullness of Christ" (Ephesians 4:13-16). This is the goal to which the church in Africa should tend and attain.

The Maturity of the Church in Africa

The verb attains means "to come, to meet, and to pass from potency to actuality". The first two phrases in Ephesians 4:13-16 refers to Jesus Christ. M. Barth thinks that "mature manhood" also refers to Christ. He translates it as "the Perfect Man"[32]. This meaning is forced on these terms because what we are expected to attain is not Jesus himself, but maturity in our knowledge about Jesus. In other words, the goal of the Church is its maturity in unity which comes from knowing, trusting and growing up into Christ. The problem is not easily resolved because if unity already as a gift and inviolable, how can it be attained as a goal? Probably the answer to this question is to regard unity as something progressive. It is capable of full development. This complete unity will be realized when everything comes together under Christ. J.R.W Stott, thus, remarked, "the unity to which we are to come one day is that full unity which a full faith and knowledge of the Son of God will make possible."[33]

The phrase, "mature manhood" has also been interpreted by some scholars as individual Christian who is growing into maturity in Christ. This is certainly the concept in the New Testament. But this concept seems to demand that we interpret it as a corporate concept. Though the unity depends on the maturity of the individual members, it refers to the Church growing in unity as a whole. Paul in his passage (Eph. 4:14) sees the Church as a single organism, which is the body of Christ. The church is to grow up into an adult stature. The apostle referred to it as the new humanity which God is creating, the "one new man" (Eph. 2:15). We may even drop the body metaphor and inquire exactly how the Church grows into maturity. In contrast to doctrinal instability, which is more of immaturity, Paul emphasized:

> Speaking the truth in love … in order that we may grow up in every way into him who is the head, into Christ, from whom the whole body, joint and knit together by every joint with which it is supplied when each part is working properly, makes bodily growth and up-builds itself in love 4:15-16).

For Paul, therefore, the Church grows by truth and love. "To allow ourselves to be hurled hither and thither by the force blasts of false teaching is to condemn ourselves and the Church to perpetual immaturity" (4:14).[34] To him we need the truth which should be taught in love (4:15). The unity of the Church in Africa can only grow and build itself up in love.

This maturity in Ephesians can be manifested in three areas of co-operation among Churches in Africa. The Church can co-operate at the spiritual, theological and practical levels. The scheme of unity at the spiritual level must evolve interior conversion, faithfulness and a change of heart of the members of the different Churches. It also includes fellowship, worship, revival, prayer, praises and other devotional exercises.

At theological level, the desire for unity must be ecumenical. Students in theological colleges should study the works of theologians of the varying Christian traditions. As a product, theology is still in the making in Africa. Productive theology reflects upon and states the central themes of the Christian faith in a way that comes to grip with African culture.

Many Churches in Africa will find co-operation in social actions. In this direction, unity can be very successful. This has to do with efforts of Churches to meet social demands. They are not strictly religious matter. They are secular in nature: IMF loan, globalization, and economic exploitation of Africa, oppression, social injustice, poverty, corruption, education, health services and religious intolerance.

At this level, Christian unity in Africa is seen only in the Church service and the very ideal of life-work dictum: "doctrine divides, service unites." The Church in Africa has no other task than to serve God and man. This is her mission especially in this continent where we have the highest percentage of the poor in the whole world. This poverty is perpetuated by Euro-American policy of deregulation, globalization, and competitiveness. The Church is a servant as Jesus was a servant. This argument has led D. Bonhoeffer to think that the unity of the Church is the unity of those who believe that the Church exists primarily to serve the world.[34] Questions regarding the Church's nature, true marks, structure and authority remain important, but they cannot be antecedent to the prior and essential question of the Church's mission or purpose.[35]

Efforts geared towards ecclesiastical unity in social action have greater impact on the populace than spiritual and theological unity. This is because practical actions usually involve the generality of the Christian population. It enjoys grassroots participation because it is easy to carry the ordinary faithful along in matters concerning their health, the education of their children and economic fair-play.

Unity is very important for the deep desire for peace and fidelity to the gospel. Christ wants unity. He prayed "that they may be one ... as we are one" (John 17:20). The missionary activities of the Pentecostal Churches have multiplied denominations. Each mission tries to extend its area of influence. The mission field, therefore, breeds rivalry. In this situation, unity will help the Churches to come together to discuss, resolve and minimize rivalry. It leads to co-operation, tolerance and peaceful co-existence.[36] Unity among Christians provides a good environment for effective witnessing by avoiding unhealthy denominational rivalry.

Similarly, unity among believers is capable of repudiating the arrogant aggression and negativism of Christian fundamentalists. Their pride obscures the good news of Christ and portrays Christianity as a militant religion. It dispels in us the negative attitude we have towards other Churches and shakes us out of our false sense of security. This attitude makes the proclamation of the gospel ineffective and irrelevant. Unity among Christians removes prejudice and create a conducive atmosphere for proclaim Christ.

Moreover, Christian unity is essential in this age when the search for African Christianity is intensified. This would help us to discover the real African face of Jesus. It will give the Church a true African character so that the Church can be freed from institutional self-interest and foreign theology.[37]

Conclusion

Thus, the Church of Christ for Paul must show charity, unity, diversity and growing sense of maturity. This is the type of society God wants his Church to be. We may be dissatisfied with present ecclesiastical status quo in which denominations antagonize one another. We may not be satisfied with things as they are but rather the Churches should work together as a team in Africa for total renewal.

Though there are African Christians who are determined at all cost to defend and uphold God's revealed truth concerning his church. But sometime they lack the spirit of love and tolerance of another denomination. Others' behaviors are antithetical to this point of view. They are eager to maintain and exhibit brotherly love. But in order to achieve this, they are prepared to sacrifice the central truth of God's Church.

Thus, while some African Christians are very conservative, complacent, ready to acquiesce to the present situation and resist change, others are too radical wanting to dispense with the individual Church on ecumenical matter. These tendencies are not part of Pauline attitude to the issue of unity and diversity in the Church. Stott's dictum may be correct when he said: "Truth becomes hard if it is not softened by love; love becomes soft if it is not strengthened by truth." The apostle calls us to hold the two together. Paul's primary concern is not structural unity, but ethical unity. The Church should become a truly caring community marked by humility, meekness, long suffering forbearance and love. This will prevent the African Church from smugness, or complacency.

Endnotes

1.   A Flannery (ed.), "Dogmatic Constitution on the Church," *Vatican Council II* (New York: Costello Publishing Co. 1975), 352.

2.   Ibid, 455.

3.   D.T. Adamo, "African Cultural Hermeneutics," Lecture Note, Delta State University, (Abraka, 1998), 1-2.

4.   J.S. Ukpong, "Rereading the Bible with African Eyes: Inculturation and Hermeneutics," *Journal of Theology for Southern Africa*, Vol. 18, No. 2, (Cape Town, June 1995), 4, 8.

5.   M.D. Goulder, "Is Q a Juggernaunt? Journal of Biblical Literature, Vol. 15, No. 4. (New York, Winter 1996) 3.

6.   Ukpong, "Rereading the Bible with African Eyes."

7.   H.W. Turner, "The Contribution of Studies on Religion in Africa to Western Religious Studies" in *African Theology En Route*, (London: SCM Press, 1982), 65.

8.   D.E. Klemm, *Hermeneutical Inquiry*, Vol. 1 (Atlanta: Scholars Press, 1986). 2.

9.   U.Ofei, "The Ethnicity Question," *Guardian,* No. 11620, (Lagos, Thursday, February 15, 2001), 63.

10.   D. Guthrie, *New Testament Theology*, (London: Intervarsity Press, 1981). 746.

11.   C. Hart, *Students Catholic Doctrine* (London: Burns & Qates, 1959) 129.

12.   Gutherie, *New Testament Theology*, 848.

13.   Ibid.

14.   A. Robinson, *Paul's Epsitle to the Ephesians with Exposition and Notes*, (London: Macmillan, 1950), 93.

15.   P.J. Kobelski, "Ephesians", *New Jerome Biblical Commentary* (London, 1993), 889.

16.   Flannery (ed), "Lumen Gentium," *Vatican Council II*, 350

17.   C. du Toit, "African Spirituality and the Poverty of Western Religious Experiences", *Journal of Theology for Southern Africa*, (Cape Town, March 1998), 49.

18.   Ibid.

19.   Ibid.

20.   Ibid. 49

21.   B. Ray, *African Religions*, (Englewood Cliff: Prentice Hall, 1979), 132.

22.   M. Barth, *The Broken Wall: A Study of the Epistle to the Ephesians*, (London: Collins, 1960) 428.

23.   Ibid.

24.   J.R. Stott, *God's New Society: The Messenger of Ephesians*, (Illinois: Intrer-Varsity Press, 1973), 155.

25.   Ibid. 155.

26.   B. R istan, *T he E pistles o f t he N ew Testament*, (Michigan, E ardmans, 1963), 86.
        Stott, *God's New Society*, 148.
27.   G. Adler, *History of Great Ideas*, Vol 3,(London: Epworth Press, 1972), 37.
28.   G.G. Findlay, "The Epistles to the Ephesians," *Expositor's Bible*, (New York: Hodder & Stoughton, 1992), 265.
29.   F.F. Bruce, *The Epistle to the Ephesians*, (London: Pickering and Inglis, 1961), 88.
30.   Stott, *God's New Society*.
31.   Barth, *The Broken Wall*, 484.
32.   Stott, *God's New Society*, 169.
33.   Ibid.
34.   D. B onhoeffer, *L etters a nd P apers f rom P rison*, e d. E B ethge, (New York: Macmillan, 1971), 197.
35.   S.B. Mala, "Principles of Dialogue: Texts and Notations,: *Notes*, University of Ibadan, (Ibadan, 1989), p. 10.
36.   M. Talbi, "Islam and Dialogue: Some Reflections on a Current Topic" *Encounter*, No 11 & 12, (London, Jan. 1975). 12.
37.   E.A.Ayandele, *The Missionary Impact on Modern Nigeria*, 1842-1914, (London: Longmans, 1966), 18.

CHAPTER XI

RE-READING ROM 12, 3-21 WITH THE AFRICAN CULTURAL EYES

Professor Ukachukwu Chris Manus

Introduction

Over the years, Paul's Epistle to the Romans has been read from the perspectives and lenses of many peoples and cultures. The Eurocentric perspectives have made the letter function as a presentation of the Apostle "Paul to generations of readers from Augustine in the fifth century, through the Reformation era, down to the present day."[1] Besides, there have been several interpretative problems associated with the controversy over "the meaning of righteousness by faith and the interplay of faith and works in Christian life" *à la Martin Luther's* epoch-making exegesis in the *Römerbrief*. Karl Birth's Commentary on Romans that was published after World War II has, to my mind, set the pace for the privileged reading and *reconstruction* of the New Testament theology of early Pauline Christianity which has continued to influence contemporary Euro-American cultures and spirituality. The Barthian paradigm had continued to set the tone for a Western cultural reading of Paul's epistle to the Romans.

But as the European and American missionaries set foot on the shores of Africa, the good news transmitted in Paul's epistle to the Romans alongside the rest of the canonical books of the New Testament had been received as part of the gospel faith brought to converted Africans. Rom 13,1-7 and its prescriptions, among others, on obedience and docility to persons in authority despite its cultural context in the later days of Emperor Nero, had been made a big issue in the colonial churches in Africa. Since then, evangelization and mission by the mainline churches have read the Epistle in the views provided by the *sola scriptura* slogan of the Reformation and early Protestantism. But can there be in this age another vision or horizon of looking at the message of Paul in Romans? Can African culture/s provide exegetes another perspective at understanding Paul's good news to the Roman Church and by implication to African Christianity or Christianities in view of the explosion of adherents to Christianity in modern Africa? This paper makes bold to provide an African perspective.

My Working Methodology

In contemporary times, African Biblical hermeneutics has come on stage. As had been indicated in a number of my recent studies, the Intercultural Hermeneutics is adopted in this study. Working with African critical resources, Intercultural Hermeneutics seeks to make the Bible and its message address grassroots Christians in their actual contexts in Africa.[2] Since the historical critical method has raised problems to the interpretation of Romans and while many European and American exegetes have sought alternative approaches to reading Romans, I wish to employ the Intercultural Hermeneutical approach to seek out the cultural factors that had influenced Paul's message in this portion of the letter; namely Rom 12,3-21 that can be married with the African cultures or to demonstrate how Paul's message can, with the African religio-cultural or social cultural resources be *re-read* to address human experiences as lived out in the African real life experiences. The approach will, from the standpoint of African socio-cultural perspective, provide insight into Paul's mind and the spirit of his message of the text in order to let contemporary African Christians in turn understand the letter as clearly as it could have been assimilated by the Roman addressees in the mid-first-century Rome. The objective character of the approach is its ability to go far beyond the settings of both author and audience for as a written text transmitted in the canon, it has a life and meaning of its own derived from a specific culture zone of the ancient world, that is, to reflect, as one commentator remarks, on the "actual historical situation obtaining in the Roman community in relation to Paul" at the time of composition (Byrne :6).[3] Thus, Intercultural Hermeneutics is, for me, a reconstructive method. Made aware of this actual situation, the African readers as "implied readers" will become able to make their own interpretive input.

The method asserts that every interpretation is concretely rooted in and influenced by the specific context out of which it arises and for which it is devised.[4] It is not merely an art of doing exegesis that is solely influenced by the textual context rather it is a hermeneutics in which rigorous comparative analysis of the contexts (The Bible's + the Nigerian Culture) remains an integral portion of the interpretive process. By the method, I wish to re-read Paul's message in Roman 12, 3-21 in the light of the African culture. Intercultural Hermeneutics, as I use it, presupposes that there is nothing primitive, irreligious and impious in the receptor culture (African) that may not have parallels in the biblical stories. It thus affirms that the Bible must therefore be interpreted interculturally with the aid of other cultures for easier comparison, assimilation and articulation in other peoples' own cultural settings or life-world. The approach compares the Roman socio-cultural milieu with the African symbolic universe. In short, the African culture is employed as the base through which Paul's message in the passage is to be given meaning from the African Christian faith experiences. This enterprise is, as Justin Ukpong terms it, "*re-reading* with and through the African eyes"; that is, through the African cultures and social contexts.

It is the belief of most African Biblical scholars that the study of the Bible from the perspective of Africans produces dimensions of biblical scholarship which non-Western cultures and traditions do not bring to the exegetical profession. The cultural conditions and the contemporary African peoples' shared "symbolic universe" produce different horizons in so far as the tools used in the analysis and interpretation promote the emergence of some morale that can yield into some African specific autochthonous theological verbalizations and distinctive expressions. This is the approach being adopted in this paper.

African Culture as Context of Interpretation

In Romans 12, 3-21, African Christians are gratified to read Paul's instruction on the Church as a leveler, as a body with many members endowed with different chasms. In the text itself, the body is depicted as composed of many limbs each operating a different function with respect to other limbs for the body's common good. In African cultures, trees that branches out into many branches are significant symbols of unity and togetherness of the people. Such trees are held as sacred and this is testified in several African narratives and myths of origin.[5] Before the advent of Christianity in Africa, most communities had their community squares set under huge multi-branched trees. Among the Igbo of southeastern Nigeria, though ascephalous in nature, the Elders constituted a conciliar ruling class (Isichei 1976:1-16). In this patriarchal society, *Ndi-Ichie,* the Elders gather either under the shade of an *Edo* tree (a short thick-branched shrub), or under an *Oji* (Iroko tree), or an *Udara* (a hard-stemmed apple tree found in many parts of the rainforest regions of West Africa) or under an *Ugba* tree (African salad-producing tree) and or under the *Kola-nut tree (oji)* to deliberate on the commonwealth of the community. The shade of the communal tree provided roof for the gathering of the villagers. During moonlight nights, the community orators told their oral narratives and verses whose morale helped to mould the character of the youth and to refresh the experiences of the elder persons.[6] On certain market days, such as *Eke* or

Nkwo (among the Igbo), Oha, the community gathering took place under the shaded tree. The Elders led the deliberations. Domestic disputes, land cases, marital problems and other such consanguine altercations were adjudicated and settled in order to ensure peace and unity in the village. Prayers to the spirits and some particular deities were said by the priests and the holders of *ofo* (the Igbo symbol of truth and justice). Under the shade of the Iroko tree (*Ukwu oji*) or the shade of the Kola-nut tree *(Okpuru ojii)* cases are taken and judgment passed. The Kolanut is a stimulant that grows best in Yorubaland of southwestern Nigeria. It is believed to be best used in ritual ceremonies by the Igbo of southeastern Nigeria. Kolanut is needed for pouring libation and saying prayers through the ancestral spirits to the Supreme Being variously known in African Traditional Religion.[7] According to a well-spread Igbo proverb (*kama okpe ghara ichiri, eburu ya ga n'ukwu ojii*), that is, (if a case cannot hold because there is no kolanut, it is taken to *okpuru ojii – the Kolanut shade)* where Kola-nuts would readily be available as a pod may fall before the gathering rises.

Under the Sacred Tree the people take cases such as those on divorce, cases of marital infidelity, incestuous offenses, and crimes considered the desecration of the community's sacrosanctity.[8] Like in Nriland, a priestly Igbo community, their Priest-King presides over the clerical village group under such shades. From there, he charges his community to go out to the wide Igboland to *persuade* the Igbo to live in peace and to purify the earth polluted by violence and blood-letting.[9] Usually these kinds of trees do not produce big pods that can fall and kill any one. The central position these trees occupy in most of the communities and their outspread branches make them a rallying point for the people. Both the living and the living-dead (ancestral spirits) are believed to assemble under their sheds for specific purposes. Here, *Umu-ama,* the youths also gather at their own times to hold deliberations on issues that affect their age-grades, unions and their cleaning and policing roles in the community. In some communities, bamboo bunks are constructed and mounted under the trees and in some other places heaps of sand are raised at some corners for children to enjoy their sand-games when the Elders are not gathered for deliberations. Once the families, age-grades, unions, youth groups and also settlers in the community gather under the Sacred Tree all the people see themselves as one and no longer as separate families. As a gathered people, they make up one body under the one tree and under the tutorship of the Elders. This is where the Fathers form the minds of the "sons of the soil". This is where values such as initiation which teaches Master. "Nobody" demands to move up on the social ladder to become a Master "Somebody" is inculcated.[10] "This is where traditional values like respect for old age, the observance of the New Moon and Harvest Festivals, the mourning of the dead, purification rites and the celebration of marriage customs, the custom of seclusion of menstruating women are hammered into the ears of the audience.[11] As observed by some Western anthropologists, this is where laws stipulating penalties for adulterers and the abhorrence of witches are imparted to the youth and reminded the old ones.[12] This is where the web of social relationships and the "extended" notion of brotherhood, for example, among the

Igbo are strengthened. This is where the Elders and other gifted orators usually speak figuratively to demonstrate their epideictic prowess in persuading their audience to reject postmodern values and harmful foreign influences that pollute cherished traditional customs.[13] Generally, such trees are held as the channels from which ancestral spirits come to be re-incarnated in the community. It is a great taboo to cut any portion of such trees as knifing or axing the trees is tantamount to inflicting wounds and pain to the spirits of the living-dead members of the community whose abode is believed to be in the trees.

Among the Wakamba of Kenya, the community is a corporate entity. Naming ceremony initiates a child into the community. At such a ceremony, the entire community is involved as it is a necessary step in the preparation of the child to fit into the communal ethos. There are other institutions where the training of a Mukamba (one individual Wakamba) takes place. The *thome*, a leafy and shaded tree with large branches provides the official place of assembly of the community elders and young men in Akambaland. It is under the *thome* tree that important issues concerning the family and society are deliberated upon. Boys received traditional couching and education under the *thome* from their fathers. Sacrifices and libations are offered and poured under the shade of this sacred tree. Of this official place of assembly, Charles Dundas, a European traveler who had visited East African region in the first decade of the 20th century had this to say:

> Outside the enclosure is an open space, generally shaded by a tree. This space called *thome* is one of great importance. The natives are very fond of sitting here for a few hours after dark by a large fire for which there is always a stack of wood and it therefore becomes a great place of gossip and talk; it is also the workshop of the village. The members of *thome* hang very closely together and form almost a little state by themselves, perhaps the only form of state known to the Mukamba.[14]

The *thome* was so central in the Akamba family life-world. It was under its shade that the father took time off to let his sons into the secrets of his wealth, how he acquired it and how it can be increased. It was here that he diligently explained the family tree (genealogy) to his sons and who, among the kiths and kin, within the family was enslaved, abroad or dead. The Ukambani elders discussed problems that arose in the village under the *thome*. Even bride-wealth and other matters concerned with the well-being of the extended family were thoroughly trashed out. It can be argued that the *thome* became a miniature school where elders and the gurus of the community prepared „the sons of the soil" for life. Under the *thome* flowed out the final authority to the families that make up the community. Since decisions reached at the *thome* were given the stamp of authority by the Akamba family heads, the elders made it a point to introduce their sons to the sacrificial lore of the society. While the boys received traditional education at the *thome*, the girls were tutored in their roles as future wives by their mothers in the kitchen.[15]

Among the traditional Abagusii, the Kisii people of western Kenya, conflicts and oath taking are heard and resolved on a large field under a huge sacred tree, the *Omotembe,* with large branches. When conflicts arise, the *Omoruoti*, the head of the clan Elders summons a gathering of all the villages in a *Ritongo* (the clan council), composed of Elders from various villages. When either party feels that judgment given is unjust, the two are made to swear an oath. Each person holds the trunk of the sacred tree. What obliges them to this submission is the belief in the power of the ancestral spirits that inhabit the tree. The tree is held as the final judge and witness of the sincerity or otherwise of the complainants.

In sum, I would say that under these sacred trees, the African sense of unity in diversity is best lived out. The events at the shades invite the responsibility of all and sundry. The shades constitute the rallying-points of the communities. It was here that Elders dished out their counsels in narratives of oral discourse to the people either in praises or as reprimands and even sometimes in curses to those who violate the customs of the community. It was here that the communities received tutoring in the values of the society. It was here that the people heard persuasive speeches cast in traditional rhetoric aimed at admonishing them to remain attached to their traditional values system. It was here that the blood-bond of love, and the spirit of solidarity were reinforced and handed on as they were received from generations to generation. The spirit of industry and nationalism were encouraged. Robbery, violence and murder were despised and reprehended. Tolerance was taught as the hallmark of communal existence. It can therefore be concluded that the African 'symbolic universe' readily provides ingredients that parallel Paul's rationale for the exhortations he gives out to the Roman Christians in this portion of the Letter.

The Social Cultural and Historical Context of the Roman Church

Because Paul's Epistles to the Romans was written to persons of faith in a living community with diverse cultures to address certain issues, the Roman social and historical contexts require to be briefly investigated in order re-addressed in the new situations raised by the African cultural contexts. Commentators agree that the Epistle was written in the early spring of 58 AD, in short, in the early period of Nero's regime.[16] It is through this Epistle that the most accurate information about the constitution of the Church in Rome is made available to contemporary readers. There is no doubt that some significant features of the history of Rome can provide the background information without which Paul's aims for writing to the Roman Christians may not be concretely understood by the African audience.

We are well informed that Rome was the cosmopolitan city of the west; indeed a then world power of its own.[17] People of all nationalities flocked and inhabited the city. For example, there was a substantial number of Jews who had engaged themselves in commerce and business in the city. For the Jews, Rome ranked third after Alexandria and Babylon as a world business center of that era. According to Brown, Rome was "the first city in Europe known to have had a Jewish presence."[18] The city's inhabitants included immigrants from Palestine as slaves and captives; especially those brought to Rome by Pompey in 65 BC when he overran Palestine. The population of Jews in Rome at that time had been estimated to have numbered about 40,000 to 50,000 persons.[19] In spite of their secular engagements, the Jews were strict adherents of the Law, a fanaticism that had won them nothing but hatred from their neighbors.[20]

The Roman emperors however maintained a liberal and judicious policy towards the Jews. A Jewish historian records that they were allowed to freely practice their religion.[21] In spite of the presence of many poor Jews in the trans-Tiber quarters, there however lived in the city many Jews of rank and position; many of them big time merchants. Even Cicero attests to the presence of some Jews with remarkable political clouts in Rome (*Cicero, Pro Flacco 28*). The wealthy among them were even called "father" or "mother" of the local synagogues.[22] However, one characteristic of the Roman Jews had been observed by Raymond Brown. He admits that the "Roman Jewry looked to Jerusalem for guidance" in religious matters.[23] This may explain why they put on airs, were haughty and exhibited supercilious attitudes in their relationships with other races in the Christian community.

Christianity in Rome

Given this preponderant number of Jews in Rome, and not to talk of itinerary Jewish converts to Christianity, one can see why Paul expressed intense desire to visit Rome considered "a promising missionary field" (Brown-Meier:97). Even Luke, the author of the Acts depicts Paul's intense desire to reach Rome with the good-news (Acts 19,21; 23,11). Christianity had existed in Rome for some years, perhaps, a decade earlier about the 40s before Paul's epistle to the church was composed. This is one reason why he had desired for a long time to visit the church (Rom 15,23). Much earlier in the epistle, Paul confirms his intention when he writes that "the faith of the Romans is being reported all over the world" (Rom 1,8), a statement which some authors agree suggests that a strong church had already come into existence in Rome. According to Ambrosiaster, a fourth century Christian commentator, and perhaps a member of the Roman Church himself, the church was not founded by an apostle but by some persons "among the Jews of Rome."[24] Besides, Brown opines that those who largely composed the Roman church were people of Jewish extraction associated with the "pillar apostles," namely Peter and James in spite of the presence of a large ethnic *incolae* of gentile origins. Others believe that some of Paul's own converts had found their way to Rome. For Paul, the Church of Rome falls within his jurisdiction as an apostle of the Gentiles, thus he finds no objection to writing to them (Rom 1,6, 14-15). Brown maintains that the earliest *body* of the Roman church would appear to have been "Christians who kept up some Jewish observances and remained faithful to part of the heritage of the Jewish Law and cult, without insisting on circumcision."[25] Sunday and Headlam note that, the Roman church was a mixed bag; "a community not all of one color but embracing in substantial proportions both Jews and Gentiles."[26] As stated before, the Jewish members of the community did not constitute a significant majority. The non-Jews seemed to have been in the majority and had wielded greater influence especially when the Jewish members who had previously held ascendancy in the community had gone along with those forcibly expelled by Emperor Claudius.

But as one reads Romans 11,18/12,3, it becomes noticeable that there had occurred a great rift between the Gentile Christians of Rome and the Jewish Christians when they came back. Paul asks for tolerance even though by all standards, the Roman church was mainly a Gentile church as he describes it in Rom 1, 5-7. It is this Jewish/Gentile complex altercation in the Roman church that made him to wish to smoothen the two *bodies* into an ecclesiology of the church as *one body* with many branches. Besides, Paul's extended greetings in Rom 16, 3-16 is quite indicative of the composition of that church.[27] The listing of the people - native-born Jews 8, Latins 4, and Greeks 10 - draws attention to an admixture of nationalities in the Roman church. Despite the racial backgrounds of the members of the congregation, their social status are largely of slaves and freedmen and women (the *libertini),* proselytes of pagan origin, other non-Jews of varying levels of attachment to Judaism, perhaps the *phoboumenoi* of Luke's Acts. There were also people from such noble households as those of Narcissus and Aristobulus, a descendant of the House of Herod, king of Judaea. Since many of the members were not Romans, Greek was the *lingua franca* in the community. The audience, though preponderantly Gentile, had an acquaintance with the scriptures of Israel, which they had learnt in the synagogues. This may explain the willingness of the community to be moved by the distinctively Jewish persuasive art of speech Paul employs in the letter. It has been observed that this heterogeneous community lived with a crisis, a crisis of agreement concerning the messianic status of Jesus of Nazareth.[28] The disturbing messianic claims by groups in the church put the unity of the community asunder and things were no longer at ease. Paul wrote to persuade them to come together as *body* of Christ.

The Context of the Text

Canonically, chapter 12,3-21 is located within chaps. 12,1-15,13 in which Paul dishes out general exhortations to the quarreling Roman Christians.[29] The parentheses are given "from a general point of view" and do not address "any special circumstances." Further on, Sunday-Headlam comment that there is no "definite logical order" in the unit. In their *Commentary,* the duo had devised a structure which runs as follows:

(a)   12, 1-2 a general introduction on the character of Christian life
(b)   12, 3-8 the right use of spiritual gifts in relation to church order
(c)   12, 9-21 a series of maxims essentially illustrating the Christian principle of love.
(d)   13, 1-7 Christian duties towards rulers and people in authority.
(e)   13, 8-10 a special exhortation on love as inclusive of all other commandments.

(f)   13, 11-14 the injunction to embrace spiritual life as preparation for the near approach of the love.

According to this structure, the central theme of the passage under study, 12, 3-21 revolves on the spiritual gifts and the significance of love in the Christian community. Much as the above structure is wide and extensive including 12,1-15,13 with its summons to the members of the church of Rome to live according to the gospel,[30] I will limit my analysis to 12, 3-21.

Text Analysis

The passage, informs us of Paul's injunctions to the members of the Roman church to abide by the basic demands of Christian living.

V. 3 is an exhortation to the faithful to think soberly. In a characteristic Hellenistic oratorical style, Paul directs the members to reflect on the practical aspects of life in a community under Christ.

In vv. 4-5 the church is described as One Body with many parts, where each part functions differently. In other words, the Roman church is composed of many members. There are Romans (Latins), Jews, and Gentiles. All these races are described as *One Body* in Christ though they be individually different. They are members of one another; that is, a community founded on unity in diversity; a community that should be caring and loving.

In vv. 6-8 attention is drawn to the chasms given to members. Each member has his or her own different gifts. The chasms must be used for the common good and to the advantage of the community's up-building and well-being. In the light of individualized gifts, members are called to function as:

(a) Prophets who are to speak forth the mind of God according to the level of the individual's faith and understanding.

(b) ministers (*diakonia*) who serve the community to the best of their ability.

(c) Teachers who pass on the good news to neophytes to the best of their ability.

(d) Exhorters who preach the good news well with all the possible skills of communication.

(e) Contributors who in their generosity give out in cash and kind.

(f) Overseers who take care of members' needs with a sense of duty and dedication.

(g) Benefactors who readily come to the material needs of members with all cheerfulness.

Vv. 9-21 is a Paraenesis. In this section, Paul issues *thirty pieces* of counsel. Top on the list is his injunction to the community to show *love* in all sincerity in order to build up the congregation as One Body with many branches. For the Romans, it is under this *One Body* that the community members fellowship together in the spirit of *koinonia,* prayer, and love in all practical terms of it in order to await the *parousia* of the Lord.

Given the features exposed in this analysis one logic behind the text that would fascinate both the untrained and trained readers in Africa is that Rom 12,3-21 is enclosed within Paul's exhortation on the essential character of Christian life and the call to embrace spiritual life in readiness of the imminent *parousia* in 13,11-14. In Paul's writings, this sort of invitation is quite commonplace (1 Thess 4,16-20). The reality of love remains, for Paul, the hallmark of Christian existence. For him, Christ exuded love to all and sundry: Jews, Samaritans, Romans and other Gentiles. Likewise, all who follow him must expend this limitless love to others. The passage enunciates themes that embody, like in the African contexts, the central principles of the Elders' didactic tales on people's negligence of the spirit of *Umunna wu ike* (power is in the Community) as a necessary philosophy in healing the wounds inflicted by disunity and conflicts among members. All the injunctions by Paul are, as in the African setting, concerned with the preservation and promotion of life. Paul nuances his exhortation to focus on life lived in Christ in readiness for his coming while for Africans, it is life lived to prosper the future of the community till they received the gospel of Christ from the missionaries.

Interpretation

In this section, I present an interpretation of the passage under study in the light of what has been exposed in the discussion above; especially as the African "ordinary readers" or "implied audience" would wish it be read to them. Here, I would be making some contributions towards reading "Romans Through History and Cultures". My contribution is, in order words, an interpretation mediated through the Intercultural Hermeneutics, a methodology that uses African cultural resources as "the base through which the biblical gospel must be transmitted to the African people." [31] The approach is applied in such a way that what is presented cannot but remain faithful to Pauline tradition.

V. 3: *Introduction to Rom 12,3-21 as an Instrument of Persuasion*

In this introductory verse, Paul turns "to the social reality of the Christian congregation in its interrelationships" (Dunn 1988:732). He admonishes the community members to take an inward and critical self-appraisal of themselves. He draws their attention to the need to wear a sober attitude of mind as a necessary step towards the establishment of the right sort of relationships that characterize effective community living. The key to achieving this attitude is located in the right understanding of the specific gift *–charis –* God has given to each member and its good use afterwards. He advises that each member refrain from wearing a haughty attitude, that is, they should avoid any thoughts of superiority above others but rather that they should think in a manner that leads to a sober understanding of the self. The attitude Paul canvasses finds its root and parallel in Greek philosophy of the day. Christianizing the values of the day, Paul advises that a sober self-assessment of Christians depends on the way they perceive themselves to have been gifted by God since their conversion to the gospel. They should avoid whatever divides Jews and Gentiles. No one should consider himself or herself favored by God as he or she displays his or her charismatic prowess. Such a pride should be leveled. It posed the greatest danger to the unity and the corporate identity of the members of the people of God. What counts is one's own gift as a Christian and how one uses it for the promotion of the community's common good. With these well-chosen words, Paul sets the scene for the people to listen to his instructions.

Instead of the Greco-Roman rhetorical style of address, I wish to read with the African audience here the influence of Hebrew biblical rhetorical style on Paul's preaching profile. This is proven as Talbert admits that the use of a number of OT citations suggest "that Paul and the Church of Rome had exclusive use of the LXX, The Testaments of the Twelve Patriarchs."[32] Here we encounter a Semitic technique of persuasion close to the potency of oral discourse in Africa. In Africa we are not able to consult Aristotle, Cicero and Quintilian and the classical authors to seek the form and structures of Paul's letter–kind within the science of rhetoric. Our libraries are found in our folklore and massive orature that has been bequeathed to posterity by the ancients. Besides, our readers are not trained to recognize the use of classical literary devices by a biblical author. They cannot even see their influence in Paul's speech, talk of their bearing and significance in their every day lives. What is closest to their mind and perception is persuasive oral discourse like the Semitic art of persuasion where the speech-maker makes extensive use of the lore and wisdom sayings of the people. Like *Baba*, the African Elder or Priest-king, who, when he speaks under the Sacred Tree, dots his address with proverbs, songs, anecdotes and idioms to capture the attention of his hearers and to convey the message of his speech so would Paul be understood as he makes regular references to Hebrew scriptures. The *Baba* (father) would enjoin his audience to re-live in the community values inherent in African communitarian life that build up the unity of the community. Much as he would enjoin them to promote their cherished cultural values, he would also advise them to eschew bitterness, rancor, hatred and gossips and all anti-social behaviors that tear apart than unify the community (and so Elder Laban Marang'a, April 7th, 2003). Unlike Paul who couches his parenesis in Hellenistic rhetorical tradition, the African Elder uses figurative expressions such as *Umunna wu ike (*power is in the brethren), *Igwe bu ike* (power is in the multitude), *riri wu ujo* (fear is in the multitude) and praise-songs of the proto-ancestors, progenitors and heroes of the race such as: *Oji agu Ndu, Kwee nu!, Yaa* (people whose fathers catch live lions, say, Yaa), *Onwa na etiri oha, Kwee nu!, Yaa* (people whose Grandfather is the moon that lights up the night for all to see, say, Yaa), and *Eze di ora mma* (people who produce the best and generally accepted king, say, *Yaa*) - all to excite the sentiments of the people. He would enjoin them to appreciate the need to live as one people whose power is in the 'brethren'. He would remind them of a popular African philosophy: "I am, because we are; and since we are, therefore I am (powerful)."[33] This popular philosophy spurs the addressees both young and old to revitalize and hold fast to their unity and solidarity.

Now, in the Church, the community of believers in Jesus Christ, especially among the Yoruba of southwestern Nigeria, the Elder is known as *Baba Ijo* (Church Father). He is invested with the authority to exhort the congregation whenever the opportunity arises. Whenever there is crisis, he, like Paul but illustrating from ancestral affiliation narratives, enjoins the people of God to stay together, live together in spite of ethnic differences, pray together, dine and celebrate together at the table of the Lord for such was the ideal in traditional community life. For the *Baba Ijo* (father of the church) this is the good news Paul asks him to convey to the Christian community whenever he reads Rom 12,3-21 with them; namely to sermonize on the very business of unity of mind and purpose.

Vv 4-5 *The Church as One Body*

The image of the community with a "new corporate identity appropriate for the eschatological people of God" is described as a *One Body*[34]. The term, *body* that was very much used in the ancient world to designate the cooperation and collaboration with human groups was well known in popular philosophy. Each person has a body that is one piece, a unity. This one body has many limbs. The body image is a usual Pauline metaphor. In 1 Corinthian 12,12-27, believers constitute the *Body of Christ.* In Eph 4,15, Christ is the head of the body. In its Pauline anthropology, the *body* has many parts but each part does its own thing in different ways all to the progress of and the *health* of the *one body.* The analogy, taken from the "symbolic universe" which both Paul and the Roman Christians shared is strong and quite significant. Paul employs it to "give his readers a sense of coherence and identity which would sustain them over against the larger body politic in which they lived and worked" where national and racial solidarity counted more than any other value.[35] The metaphor rings a bell to the Roman Christians that the church should be all-inclusive; with "the

Gentiles as equal citizens in the eschatological people of God ....”[36] It is used to reinforce the notion of Christian community as a corporate entity in which Gentiles have equal share. It therefore, serves to define the values and the diversity of gifts operative within the overall oneness of a community ruled by the Law of Christ. Dunn correctly opines that “Paul saw it as one of the best means of encouraging the right sort of community spirit in Diaspora congregations.”[37]

The image finds parallels in many African peoples, folk narratives, and idioms of life. Among others, I have chosen the *Oha (Community) Gathering* under the *Sacred Tree* in most community centers to bring home the significance of the Pauline *body* symbol to the African audience. The *Thome,* the *Edo* or the *Ojii* shaded trees with lush foliage and many interlocking branches provide the *forums* where the *Oha* gathers to sort out its problems, thrash out disturbing issues and educate the people in their communal lore, wisdom and traditions. The people themselves, though from one agnate origin, but now many, live in different homesteads and many a time under the same neighborhood with strangers and settlers from other villages. But when the “sons of the soil” come under the shade of the *One Tree* to receive tutoring in their traditional values of community life, their differences sink and they translate themselves into *one body* protected and provided for by the benevolence of the spirits of the “living-dead” members and the community’s earth Mother goddess.[38] They make up the *one body* under the *One Tree* and the tutorship of the Elders. This is where the Fathers form the sons. This is where the web of brotherhood is strengthened. This is where the Elders and the orators demonstrate their epideictic prowess as it had earlier on been noted. The *Oha* is the life-wire of the African community. Hence, like the Roman Church made up of various peoples yet instructed by Paul to constitute the *One Body* in Christ in order to protect the gospel values in spite of individual differences, African Christians in their various ethnic backgrounds see themselves offered the opportunity by Paul’s ecclesiology of the *One Body* to convert freely into the Church of Christ with all their experiences of a high sense of solidarity, and unity in diversity and adherence to communal values system. It is apt to assert that the spirit of the verses speaks loud of a preaching of the gospel in parallel lines with the teaching of African traditional morals in their epideictic forms. In both traditions, the goal is to celebrate values held in common, to develop a sense of attachment and adherence to traditional and gospel values as well as to sensitize the audience on the need to abhor the inroads brought about by competing values of postmodernism.

Vv. 6-8: Appropriate Use of Christian Chasm

Paul raps on the importance of chasm given to each member of the Roman Church and directs them to cling to their appropriate use for the benefit of others in the Church. He enumerates *seven gifts,* God’s graciousness outreach to humankind which serves as "a means of grace." This is grace that gifted persons communicate to others through the exercise of their own particular gifts. Potentially it stands to promote the progress and unity of the community. As Dunn remarks, "the body of the Church of Christ in Rome is by definition a charismatic community where members function charismatically."[39]

In traditional African communities, certain functionaries exist who with others work together to stabilize the communities and to ensure the survival of the process of internalization of the communal ethos. While Paul recognizes the role of prophets as persons who, under inspiration, can see forth and declare God's intervention in various events and his will for the Church,[40] African communities have priests who function as diviners – the go-between men and the gods, the Hermes of the people.[41] As has been noted by some commentators, the essential role of the prophets is to enhance faith of the believers and thus that of the communities.[42] In the African religio-cultural contexts, the prophets were clairvoyant persons who said-forth the mind of the divinities to the Elders and the fathers who speak under the shade of the Sacred Trees. Paul espouses the role of persons who serve as ministers (*diakonia*) in the community.[43] In African communities, persons who function so, though not called *ministers,* do exist. They take the errands from the Elders to various family heads and see that order, peace and respect for community traditions and customs are kept alive and undiluted. Among the Igbo, this task falls upon the shoulders of the errand-men of *Ndi-amala*. Paul saw the need for *teachers* whose sole business was to teach the good news to new converts and to consolidate their faith and that of the community. Such were the likes who produced the *Didache* in the early church (Talbert:88). In traditional African societies, certain wise men and women fulfilled this social role quite significantly. They passed on, to the best of their ability, the wisdom and traditions of the Fathers orally and in tales and narratives. Each of their tales, anecdotes and parables is didactic, that is, each has a morale, a lesson on life to teach to youngsters (Oranekwu:49, n. 141). These people often doubled as *exhorters*. In large community gatherings, such persons exhorted powerfully with words. Their use of the choicest proverbs in Igbo gatherings have graphically been x-rayed and documented by Chinua Achebe in his novel, *Things Fall Apart*.[44]

In pre-colonial African communities, there were well-to-do persons who fulfilled the role of the *contributor*. Among the Igbo communities, the *di-ji* (rich yam farmers) and *Ndi ogaranya* (the big landed-property persons) had, in sedentary agrarian communities spent their wealth on public support. In contemporary modern economy, some of the big-time traders, tycoons and money-bags nowadays known as *Aka ji aku(s)* fit Paul's category. Most of them give out generously to the upkeep of the Church and other charities. There are also a developing crop of *Ndi Enyem' aka* – contributors who give out their cash for mercy causes and for the care of the unfortunate members of the community, the bereaved people, the orphans, widows, people struck by one natural disaster or the other and for school children and students whose parents are unable to pay their school fees as life in the jungle is often quite precarious.[45] The *Overseer* who, as Paul enjoins, would take care of the community find their types in the role of the Elders and the Fathers from the various family homesteads. These *gurus* virtually run the original African states from the shade of the Sacred Trees (the *Thome, Edo, Ojii or the Ukpaka)* or from the *Oha Nyiki* (an ubiquitous elitist club that virtually determined social codes of action in sedentary Igbo communities).[46] They are custodians of the mores of the communities. Without their vigilance and guidance, the communal ethos derails.

In this light Paul's gospel in this unit would readily be understandable in the African Churches where African Christians have been accustomed to living with the different social roles of people. Building up the community is a teamwork well enshrined in an African proverb loosely translatable as *united we stand, divided we fall.* For example, George Oranekwu observes, "it is the duty of the community to make, create or produce the individual" in most African societies.[47] Having said this, it can be argued that already in most African communities, there had been an εκκλφσιαι, as known in its Greek social-world or the συναγογοι in the Hellenistic Jewish communities. The message of Paul and his *One Body* ecclesiology reflect the African experience of the community gatherings.

Vv. 9-21: Exhortations On Unanimity and Love

In this section Paul issues *thirty pieces* of counsel, qualities that should make operational the exercise of gifts in the Christian community. Reproducing the early Christian tradition which had taken over the OT wisdom traditions, the Jesus tradition of the earliest Christian communities and the ethical Sophia maxims of popular Greco-Roman philosophy as observed in v.3.[48] Paul composed this unit, again to persuade his audience. Top on the list of his agenda is that the community should show αγαπφ ανυποκριτοφ *genuine love* in all its sincerity (1 Cor 13,13; 2 Cor 6,6). For Paul, genuine love is "the quality of relationship distinctive of Believers."[49] This is essential to build the congregation as One Body with many branches. The love that motivated God's action in Christ is divine love (5,5,8; 8,39//8,35). On the horizontal level, it translates into human love that includes strangers, foreigners as well as the enemy, one that overcomes evil with good (v.21). This is the type of love Paul asks of Christians (13,10; 14,15). It has been observed that in the eastern Mediterranean culture, a family works as a unit, each member defending the honor of the other.[50] Paul adapts that notion to address the issues of relationships within the Roman Church.[51] So, for Paul, where there is love, there will be no destructive competitive spirit; each person does her/his own thing freely while she/he respects someone else (1 Cor 13,4-6; Phil 2,3-4).

On the African culture, the Igbo parallel may provide some insights in which the lesson on love may be appreciated. In Igbo language, the term *ihunanya* (translated love) is a tricky compound word. It is derived from a contraction of *Ihu* (face) and *anya* (eyes) conjoined with the particle, *na* (and) to mean a visual encounter; a face-to-face meeting of the eyes of two persons or that between more than two persons. From the face-to-face encounter of persons, there can develop an acquaintance that, over a period, may translate into *ihunanya* (face-to-face-occasioned relationship). In other words, what the eyes can see or behold can become relational. This sort of relationship is not necessarily from *Obi*, the heart, the powerhouse of emotion. Of course, *Ihunanya* cannot be equated with the term, *Obioma*, the good dispositions of the heart. It is rather *Obioma* that sustains *Ihunanya*. For the Igbo, love is not strictly speaking an inner cordial experience as in its non-biblical Greek notion of εροω or its Latin equivalent, *amor, amoris* used to denote the conjugal love between man and woman. For the Igbo, *Ihunanya* does not convey any intimacy between persons. It refers to an associative acquaintance made as a result of visual meeting with another person(s)[52]. It is Western ideas associated with εροω love) that have led many to give *ihunanya* an amorous connotation. So, when the Igbo and some other *Kwa-speaking* African peoples read Paul in this unit, their perception of this reality is only made sublime by his use of the qualifier, ανυποκριτοω (genuine, that is, *ihunanaya nke si n'obi* – love that hails from the heart). For the Igbo then, this sort of face-to-face encounter oiled by emotions from the heart would mean the love that motivates people to live in unity supportive of one another in spite of whatever divides them. This is the love that makes Christians co-exist in the spirit of *koinonia,* sharing and prayer till the parousia of the Lord comes (Rom 13,11-14).

Conclusion

This disquisition on Rom 12,3-21 from an intercultural hermeneutical approach has much to commend itself. Most commentators agree that Romans 12,3-21 has its context within Romans 12,1-15,13 where exhortatory materials of a general and particular nature are outlined.[53] The structure offered by earlier commentators, such as that of Sanday-Headlam reveals that the central theme in Rom 12,3-21 is the value Paul places on the charismata of individual Christians as the foundation on which αγαπφ is based in the Church. In v. 3, I see an introductory exhortation cast speech-wise in Hellenistic oratory. Paul employs the device to draw attention of his audience to the need for a sober self-appraisal towards attitudinal change from the members of the congregation. In vv.4-5, the image of the Church as One Body with many limbs comes to the fore. The values of the gospel are hamstrung into the ears of the audience. The message is sent across with the use of the epideictic discourse in which celebration of values held in common are stressed. And vv. 9-21 are written to focus on the importance of various degrees of charismata graciously given to each Christian to enable him or her execute a specific task for the good of the community. Seven of such functions are enumerated.

In my analysis and interpretation, I have confronted the text with ideas gathered from African cultural resources, thus introducing insights proffered by intercultural hermeneutics. My objectives are twofold: (a) to indicate how African "trained readers" (like me) would read this portion of Romans in Bible Sharing Group Meetings "with" and "for" the African "untrained readers"; that is, the "ordinary readers" and (b), to demonstrate an alternative approach of interpreting Romans from a different social historical and cultural context.

Paul stresses the fact that Christian charismata are necessary ingredients for maintaining ecclesial growth and stability. I want to agree that there is no other place this injunction is so much relevant than in the young churches of Africa. Love is the solid foundation upon which the One Body of Christ must be founded. Where genuine love prevails, individual charisma will be harnessed towards building up the community. Such a community becomes a place where people realize themselves as humans who are given chance to make contributions towards its growth and progress as One Body. Having viewed Romans 12,3-21 from the African perspective or having read it with the African eyes, it is discovered that African Elders use epideictic discourse to motivate the audience to adhere to the traditional values of community life. It is acknowledged that Paul's image of the people of God as One Body under Christ is quite at home in the African peoples' experience of the interactive unity among the kin-groups that assemble under the shade of the One Tree. Over the years, these basic communities had been oriented towards the promotion of the spiritual, social, political and economic survival of its members and as such had existed as *One Family* under the wisdom of the Elders as the custodians of the community ethos. Thus Paul's One Body image brings in a message of encouragement that enriches the social and cultural contexts contemporary mission and evangelization require in order to advance the aspirations and progress of the Church in modern Africa.

Endnotes

1. B. Byrne, *Romans, Sacra Pagina Series*, Vol. 6, Harrington, D.J. (ed.), (Collegeville, Minnesota: The Liturgical Press, Michael Glazier, 1996).
2. C.U Manus, *Intercultural Hermeneutics in Africa: Methods and Approaches*, (Nairobi: Acton Publishers, 2003).
3. Byme, 6.
4. Manus, *Intercultural Hermeneutics*, 37.
5. G. Parrinder, *African Mythology* (London: Oxford University Press, 1975).
6. R.N. Egudu, *The Calabash of Wisdom and Other Igbo Stories* (Enugu, Nigeria: Nok Publishers, Enugu, Nigeria, 1983), 13.
7. F.N. Nwahaghi, F.N 1996, "The Meaning of Kolanut Ritual Symbol Among the Igbo of Nigeria" in *Sevartham*, Vol. 21(1996), 93-104 cited by Oranekwu, 61, note 147.
8. Mama Dorothy Chikere, aged 84, interviewed 3rd May, 2003 at Uzoagba, Ikeduru, Imo State, Nigeria.
9. E.E.Uzukwu, A Listening Church: Autonomy and Communion in African Churches (New York: Orbis Books, 1996), 25.
10. G.N Oranekwu, "The Significant Role of Initiation in the Traditional Igbo Culture and Religion: An Inculturation Basis for Pastoral Catechesis of Christian Initiation." An Inaugural-Dissertation zur Erlangung des theologischen Doktorgrades, Albert-Ludwigs-Universität Freiburg im Breisgau, Fakultät für Katholische Theologie, Freiburg, Germany.
11. Ogbalu, F.C. (ND), *Igbo Institutions and Customs* (Onitsha, Nigeria), 21.
12. G. T. Basden, *Niger Ibos* (London: Frank Cass, 1966), 415-418.
13. Pauline Osuji, (Mrs.), aged 50; interviewed at Ile-Ife, Nigeria, 8th May, 2003.
14. M. A Kyalo, "An Investigation on Traditional *Akamba* Marriage: Implications for Christian Marriage," MA Thesis, Department of Religious Studies, Catholic University of Eastern Africa, Nairobi, Kenya (work supervised by me), 75.
15. Kyalo, P.M. 2003, An Investigation on Traditional *Akamba* Marriage: Implications for Christian Marriage," MA Thesis, Department of Religious Studies, Catholic University of Eastern Africa, Nairobi, Kenya (work supervised by me), 79.
16. W. Sanday, & A.G Headlam, *Romans: The International Critical Commentary*, (Edinburgh: T & T Clark (Latest Impression, 1998), xiii-xiv; Brown, R.E. & Meier, J.P. 1983, *Antioch and Rome* (New York: Paulist Press, 1983), 98; Byme, 11.
17. Brown and Meier, 98.
18. Brown and Meier, 93.
19. Brown-Meier:94.
20. Sanday-Headlam, xxiv.
21. Josephus, Antiquities XIV, 10.
22. Sanday-Headlam:xxiii.
23. Brown-Meier, 97.
24. Sanday-Headlam: xxv.
25. Brown-Meier:104.
26. Sunday and Headlam, xxvi

27. Here is the rationale to understand church as the *body* with many branches as African Christians are wont to see the Sacred Tree in their communities with many branches under which reconciliation and other matters affecting the well-being of the people are discussed and resolved.

28. There is evidence enough to warrant the belief that the church of Rome was founded on house-churches (Rom 16,5;7,10b,11,14) with perhaps all the Christians occasionally meeting together (Byrne 11).

29. Sanday-Headlam, 351.

30. Byrne, 28.

31. Musa W.Dube, 2002, „'What I have written, I have written'" (John 19:22), in Katongole, E. (ed.), *African Theology Today*, AthTS 1, (Scranton: The University of Scanton Press, 2002, Dube, Musa W. 2002,).

32. See for sure, *Wisd. of Sol. 8,7; 4 Macc 5,23; Philo, Immut. 164 and Josephus* as contemporary literatures. C.H.Talbert, 1969/70, "Tradition and Redaction in Romans 12,9-21", *NTS* (1969/70) 16, 83-93.

33. J.S. Mbiti, *African Religions and Philosophy* (London, Heinemann, 1975), 108-109.

34. D.G. Dunn, *Romans 9-16, in Word Biblical Commentary*, Vol. 38 (Dallas, Texas: Word Books).

35. Dunn:733.

36. Byrne: 19.

37. Dunn:733.

38. Obiukwu 1978

39. Dunn:734.

40. Byrne: 370.

41. Manus 2003:30-32.

42. D.E.Aune, *Prophecy in Early Christianity and the Ancient Mediterranean World* (Grand Rapids, Michigan, Eerdmans, 1983), 198-217.

43. J.N Collins, *Diakonia. Re-interpreting the Ancient Sources* (New York & Oxford University Press, 1990), 232-234.

44. Chinua Achebe, Chinua, *Things Fall Apart*, (Ibadan: Heinemann Educational Books, Anchor Books reprinted 1995).

45. O.U. Kalu, Precarious Vision: African Cultural Development (Enugu: Nigeria, Fourth Dimension, 1982).

46. Note that the cultures being described reflect the order of things in the pre-contact era of African civilization. Of course, the situation is not commonplace. While it is so with the rather ascephalous communities like those of the Igbo, the Luo and the Wakamba, the more royal kingdoms, like those of the Yoruba, the Ashanti and the Ganda had palaces where the Royal Fathers gave their Chiefs the tutoring who would pass them on to the subjects (See, Manus 1993).

47. Oranekwu, 48.

48. Ellis 1957;Talbert 1969/70:88.

49. Byrne: 375.

50. Byrne: 376.

51. C. Spicq, 1958-59, *Agape dans le Nouveau Testament*, Vol. 2, EB (Gabalda, Paris, 1958-59), 22-27.

52. Even dependable sources indicate that the sudden explosion of the use of αγαπφ ∀in the earliest Christian author, Paul (75x) is sufficient indication that the

Christians found it necessary to make a fresh minting of a previously little-used word; ..." (Dunn, 739).
53. Sanday-Headlam:351;Byrne:13.

CHAPTER XIII

CELIBACY AND THE BIBLE IN AFRICA

Oyeronke Olajubu

Introduction

Celibacy as a doctrine has been a subject of controversy among scholars over the years. Some see it as one significant way of serving God; for example, the Roman Catholic Church Clergy views celibacy as a spiritual option that gives the individual more time to attend to the things of God. Some Protestants, on the other hand, see celibacy as nothing short of hypocrisy[1] and that marriage is the course for man. However, not much has been offered as a justification for the option of celibacy by its advocates as opposed to those who do not practice it.

The aim of this paper has three dimensions. First, to give the highlights of the doctrine of celibacy. In doing this, we shall define the term celibacy taking into cognizance the views of some scholars. Secondly, we look into what the bible teaches about celibacy. This dimension is essential because of some questions that are often raised on the issue. Such questions include: Why celibacy? Is celibacy of any relevance to being favoured by God? Is the option to go celibate of any importance in the judgment of God? These questions represent essentially the background research of this work. Thirdly, we shall attempt to offer a conclusion that will adequately represent a new perspective of understanding on the issue.

The Concept and Definition of Celibacy

Celibacy has always existed in history for different reasons and in different world religions. For example, celibacy is practiced in Buddhism, Hinduism, and to a certain extent, in African Traditional Religion.

One of its earliest manifestations was during the institution of monasticism. Monastic system can be traced back in history of the middle Ages (100-1400 B. C) when there was the belief that man's work could be divided into two, namely the natural and the spiritual[2]. It was then believed that only the spiritual work of man was pleasing to God. Withdrawal from the society to loose oneself in mystical contemplation was consequently thought to be the higher life[3]. The natural work of man which includes eating, dancing, and sexual relations were to be rejected. Boettner speaks on two principles upon which celibacy was initially based. First, that celibacy was a holier state than matrimony, and second, that total withdrawal from social intercourse and business of the world was conducive to true religion.[4] The validity of such principles is of course doubtful. There seem to be expressed in these principles opinion that an individual cannot serve God while living in the social community. It is also clear that the individual can serve God as well while choosing to be withdrawn from the social community: for example, the Roman Catholic priests and nuns who stay in mission and convents and yet serve God in his vineyard. The point being made here is that it is not the mode or place of living that is important in the service of God but the individual's faithfulness to God.

The natural world, to these ascetic, is evil and sinful in itself, hence they avoid it as much as possible. This led to their living in secluded areas, which gave rise to Church, but there is the possibility that the practice of celibacy in the Roman Catholic Church might owe its origin to Monasticism.[5]

Celibacy as a doctrine in Christianity can only be found among the Roman Catholic Church clergy. It is compulsory for priest and nuns to go celibate. Requirements for admission into the Roman Catholic Church clergy include a good religious background, fitness, especially sexual fitness of the aspiring priest or nun to ensure that a sacrifice is actually being made for the sake of the service of God. The concept of celibacy essentially predicates on the option to remain unmarried for the purpose of serving God. It is the option to renounce marriage and recognize this as a sacrifice to God. It is an appeal to God on a serious note that activities of sexual relationship both in marriage and outside it are outside the will of God for those who serve Him at the altar. Our expressions will be more specific when we examine the definition of celibacy.

The Definition of Celibacy

In the Oxford Dictionary, celibacy is defined as the state of being unmarried especially as a result of a religious promise.[6] A religious promise not stated here, but which obviously involves the service of God. According to Donald Goergen, in his books, *The Sexual Celibate*, celibacy, comes from Latin word "caelebs meaning 'alone' or single '[7].He goes further to say that celibacy is a possible choice of single life for the sake of Christ, in response to the call of God.

Goergen is of the view that celibacy is a form of reaction to the call of god, giving a picture that implies that the decision of the individual to go celibate depends exclusively on the call of God. Loraine Boettner also provides another view in his book *Roman Catholicism*. He is of the opinion that celibacy is the abstinence from marriage. He goes further to distinquish celibacy from chastity, which is the abstinence from sexual relations[8]. His definition points to the difference between a vow of celibacy and a vow of chastity, though most often, the individual who chooses celibacy as a way of life also takes the vow of chastity. *Chambers Twentieth Century Dictionary* defines celibacy as a state of being unmarried under a vow. It is not clear what vow this is but we can assume with some measure of certainty that it is religious. When these definitions are carefully considered, three points come out clear on the meaning of celibacy. These are:

(1)   That it involves the state of being unmarried.
(2)   It is by choice, and
(3)   It is not for the sake of being single but purposely for religious reasons.

If we use these highlights as raw materials usable for the purpose of defining celibacy, it can be defined as a state of choosing to be unmarried for sole purpose of deep devotion to the service of God. Celibacy is therefore a standard of life freely chosen, an option that work only with the will and not with correction. We shall now proceed to examine how well this definition is supported by the Bible.

Biblical Perspective on Celibacy

In the Old Testament, there are examples that show the great importance placed on marriage by the Jews. For example, we have the marriage of Isaac and Rebecca in Genesis 24, and that of Hosea being asked by God to take an adulterous wife in Hosea 1. Both examples show how important marriage was viewed in the Old Testament. Moreover, we cannot find any injunction on celibacy for the believer in the Old Testament. Celibacy can therefore be said to be without support in the Old Testament, rather marriage is advocated for.[9] It can, therefore, be submitted that withdrawal from society as a prerequisite to the study of the word of God was without support in the Old Testament.

However, during the inter-testamental period, there existed groups that practiced asceticism, which include the practice of celibacy. One of such groups was the Qumraan Community that believed strongly in the imminent coming of

the reign of God. There were also the Essenes who believed that they could serve God better by withdrawing from the society into the wilderness.

The New Testament does not offer much teaching on celibacy. There are however two passages that deserve some brief comment. The first passage is Matthew 19:12, which is a discussion on celibacy by Jesus. It says:

> For some are eunuchs because they were born that way: others were made that way by man: and others have renounced marriage because of the kingdom of Heaven. The one who can accept this should accept it.

Scholars agree that this passage is an authentic saying of Jesus[10] even though they have given different interpretations to it. Some see it as a clear comment from Jesus to his disciples to go celibate while others view it as a mere recognition of celibacy as a way of serving God for those who can. We shall examine the views of some scholars who hold these different views to facilitate our understanding of the passage.

Gaebelein sees the passage as Jesus freely conceding that for those, to whom it is given, it is better not to marry and "the one who can accept it should accept it." Jesus, in Gaebelein's opinion, did not see celibacy as a holier state than marriage (cf. 1 Timothy 4:13). He saw it as a special calling granted to one for greater usefulness in the kingdom of God. This commentary reminds those who impose this discipline on themselves of Paul's conclusion that "it is better to marry than to burn with passion." Gaebelein's view can be surmised as stressing the voluntary nature of the celibate way of life.[11]

Filson's[12] comments are slightly distinct from those already mentioned above. In his view, celibacy is not for all men. Only a minority and those by personal choice can and should go celibate. Marriage belongs to God's created order and it is sacred. Children who issue out marriage are the blessings of God. Jesus blessed children and likened them to the kind of persons who belong to the kingdom of God[13]. Filson presents marriage as the normal course for humanity as expected by God, though a minority may opt for celibacy out of personal choice. According to Filson, the issue of celibacy being a holier state than marriage does not even arise because marriage to him is sacred.

Schaff[14] sees the third group of eunuchs as enumerated by Jesus in the passage as those who, being married, yet for the sake of the kingdom are as if they are ready to sacrifice their conjugal enjoyment for the sake of their spiritual calling.

Other scholars are of the opinion that this passage is most likely gentile in origin,[15] because celibacy was not favoured by Judaism. Celibacy is seen as existing only for those who can accept it.

Another group of scholars[16] see the passage as meaning that Jesus made room for both celibacy and marriage as honourable and proper to discipleship. Jesus did not see one as spiritually higher than the other. Celibacy is only for those who are able to practice it. It is sanctioned as a vocational choice but not for ascetic reasons. Both marriage and celibacy are seen as demanding much from the individual. The issue of one state being better or holier than the other does not arise.

From the above consideration of the different interpretation of Matthew 19:12, some conclusions become possible. Jesus did recognize celibacy as a positive way of serving God. Celibacy as far as Jesus was concerned was not for all men but only for those who can accept it. That celibacy is not superior to marriage; both are gift from God with high demand from individual.

Can we then say that Mathew 19:12 is a biblical basis for celibacy? It will be wrong to answer this question in the affirmative because Jesus did not command his disciples to go celibate. He merely stated the possibility of some individuals going celibate voluntarily but quickly added that for those who can not, it is better to marry. But to answer the question in the negative will not be right either, because Matthew 19;12 does not forbid whoever can practice celibacy, neither is it a command for the Christian to avoid going celibate. The Matthew 19:12 passage should therefore be seen as Jesus' recognition to both marriage and celibacy as possible ways of serving God depending on individual choice. The second passage that deserves examination in the consideration of biblical basis for celibacy is 1 Corinthians 7:1-10. The authenticity of the passage as belonging to Paul is undisputed.

Paul recognized marriage as a divine and good institution and as the normal and proper state in which men and women should live together. So in 1Corinthians 7:2 he advises every man to have his own wife. He advocates marriage for younger widows in 1 Timothy 5:14. In Ephesians 5:3, Paul subscribes to the fact that a man should marry. It is the same for a woman. These views of Paul show that he recognizes and recommends the institution of marriage for individual. In spite of these views, Paul seems to suggest that marriage is a concession rather than the normal and proper status expected of man by God. 1 Corinthians 7 1-10 has been suggested as a biblical basis for celibacy by some scholars. On the subject of marriage and celibacy, Paul states clearly that his reaction is his own views on the issue. He, however, feels that these views should be adequate because of his status as an apostle through the grace of God. (Cf. 1 Corinthians 7:25). The eschatological framework in which Paul lived also affected his discussion on marriage and celibacy. To Paul, both celibacy and marriage are gifts from God. However, because of distress, tribulation of the flesh (passion), the fact that time is running out, the Parousia is imminent, it is better for the Christian to be single. This will give the Christian time to attend the things of the kingdom of God before advent of the day of tribulation. Jesus gave his disciple the duty to spread the gospel of salvation to all the nations, before his second coming. An unmarried individual will be free of any family ties to travel and preach the gospel, which must be done quickly because of the imminent coming of the Lord Jesus Christ. The single person by his status is seen as representing the heavenly state of man, because on the day of the Lord, they will neither marry nor be given in marriage.[17]

I Corinthians7: 7 is a verse in the passage under consideration that has been interpreted in various ways by scholars. The verse says:

> I wish that all men were as I am, But each man has his own gift from God; one has this gift, another has that.

Paul's status being referred to in this passage is controversial. Was Paul a celibate or a widower? The possibility of Paul having married at a certain time in his life is high because of his membership of the Pharisaic group, which required its members to be married. So it is possible that Paul resolved to live a celibate life dedicating his time and energy totally to the propagation of the gospel after the death of his wife. In this case he will be a widower. The probability of Paul being a single man who never married cannot be totally ruled out, however, because nowhere in his writings or in the writings of other apostles about him do we have any mention of his wife. Whichever way this question is answered, the important thing as far as this paper is concerned is that the state being referred to here by Paul is a single state. He wished that all men could remain single like him. His state of being single may be due to the practice of celibacy, or the death of his wife. Others even argue that Paul was a eunuch.

Some scholars view this passage as expressing the opinion that there are benefit in living celibate life.[18] Far from exalting celibacy over marriage, Paul rather recognizes the fact that not all men have to marry. It is much better to marry and satisfy the sexual desire of the individual than to remain unmarried and "burn with passion." The phrase "burn with passion" here implies the inward thirst for sexual satisfaction in the individual. This is better understood in the light of Jesus' discussion on how the sin of adultery can be committed by the individual.[19]It is not limited to the actual act of having sexual relations outside marriage but include harboring erotic and sensual fantasies about the opposite sex in one's mind. Now such fantasies are not evident outwardly, yet it is passion. Paul's warning is against such fantasies. He can thus be said to hold the view that marriage is a concession for the weak. While we have specific instructions in the Bible for the Christians to marry (ref. Ephesians 5:31), the same cannot be said of celibacy. We therefore wonder why marriage should be considered for the weak.

Scott[20], on his own part, says Paul's advice is for those who are single to remain as they are. This however has no apostolic authority behind it. "I say this by way of concession not command" (cf.1 Corinthians 7:6). According to him, Paul saw both celibacy and marriage as manifestations of the grace of God, to be undertaken and to be sustained purely in the strength, which they daily supply. The best situation according to him is that of an unmarried person, who is under pressure to marry, followed by one who physically expresses his sexuality within marriage. The least desirable person is the person who needs marriage as a means of expressing his sexuality but is compelled to do without it. The main issue worthy of consideration as far as Scott is concerned is the emphasis on the voluntary aspect of the individual becoming celibate. A case where celibacy is imposed on the individual should be avoided.

Conzelmann[21] is another scholar who views the passage differently. He is of the opinion that sexual asceticism, which is the direct exercise of the negation of the flesh, is certainly not a way of salvation. The wish of Paul that all men remain like him is not made into principle. He used the word (*thelo*) which means 'wish'. Celibacy is an individual gift, which cannot be acquired by training. He does not see any connection between celibacy and salvation, though it is a gift. He warns against people trying to acquire the gift of celibacy by training. The point being made by conzelmann is of considerable importance in our opinion. It speaks to the fact that the option of celibacy cannot be achieved through acquisition of knowledge but only through commitment seems to outclass epistemological understanding of celibacy because it has connection with desire and the best option that can be chosen by the individual.

Another view, which has been expressed on the passage under discussion, is its domination by the expectation of the imminent parousia.[22] Paul's reaction here is seen as potraying marriage as little more than legalized cohabitation. Though marriage is no sin, celibacy is to be preferred. Marriage is presented as interfering with individual allegiance to the Lord; hence Paul saw marriage as a less desirable choice. As explained above, it is not right to see celibacy as a state holier than marriage. Marriage belongs to God's own created order. It can therefore not be seen as being inferior to celibacy. Rather than hindering the individual from serving God effectively marriage gives him/her the serene atmosphere necessary for the individual's peace of mind. The presence of a partner, as is true of marriage, gives the individual the advantage of consultation with a second person of a different psychological composition. Like a popular adage says two heads are better than one. The view of these scholars that celibacy is superior to marriage can therefore not be accepted.

Driver [23] interprets the passage as saying that celibacy is good but marriage is natural. Not everybody possesses the gift of celibacy. The passage should also be understood in the framework of the imminent Parousia, according to him, hence Paul's advice to the Corinthians not to burden themselves with marriage (CF 1 Corinthian 7:8). We will examine the view of one more scholar on the passage.[24]

Schaff opines that Paul advocates celibacy but advises marriage for those who do not have the ability and grace to cope with the celibate life. Paul's view on marriage here is seen as not being total by him.

Certain facts can be deduced from God and not by training. Everybody cannot lay claim to the gift of celibacy, only those given the grace by God can practice it. The interpretation given to 1 Corinthians 7:1-10, especially verse 7, on the discussion of celibacy by scholars would appear to be Paul's personal views. It will however be proper to state also that such an insight have the backing the Holy Spirit. Paul preferred singleness for at least two reasons. First, because it gives the individual the opportunity to devote his/her undivided attention to the propagation of the gospel without the distraction of worldly cares. Secondly, there was a strong belief in an imminent Parousia, so why burden oneself with the cares of the world? Bearing both reasons in mind, Paul's argument for celibacy can easily be understood. But Paul's argument still be valid? Is the situation still the same? The fact that Christ is still expected by the Christians today is undefeatable. But Christian today realizes that nobody can claim to know the exact time of the parousia. Jesus Christ may be back today, tomorrow or in the next One Hundred years but he will surely come. At the time Paul was writing, the parousian was conveyed as being so imminent that some individuals actually expected the second coming of Christ before their death. Can 1 Corinthians 7:1-10 then be cited as a scriptural basis for celibacy? I do not hesitate to answer in the negative. Paul himself states clearly that his advice is a concession and not a command, but that his views should be adequate as it is based on his status as an apostle of God. We have also made mention of the possibility of such an injunction being made with the backing of the Holy Spirit.

Can we then say that celibacy is with or without scriptural basis? From the above examination of both Matthew 19:12 and 1 Corinthians 7:1-10, it is clear that neither passage can be said to have given divine sanction to celibacy, though as a Church discipline, celibacy can draw support from these scriptures.

Salvation and the Option for Celibacy

Prominent in our discussion above is the issue of imminent parousia, which is one of the reasons why Paul preferred celibacy. This belief has however receded to the background though Jesus Christ is still expected to come back. The claim by Paul that the celibate Christian is free from the cares of the world and so direct his individual attention and energy to the service of God is debatable. The married man or woman utilizing his/her time, even if not all, faithfully to the propagation of the gospel is to be preferred to a celibate who is never faithful to his/her celibate vow. The yardstick therefore, is not as much as the single or married state of the individual, but the level of faithfulness to God in whichever of the states an individual finds himself, or herself. We are of the opinion that Paul's preference for celibacy is most likely due to his great zeal for the service of God. As far as Paul is concerned nothing mattered so far the gospel of Christ was preached to the people and souls were saved for the kingdom of God. From all indications, he would have loved a situation where everyone has no other business but the preaching of the gospel. Such was his zeal, he therefore, encouraged celibacy if this will result in a wider spread of the gospel. Nowhere in his discussion did Paul say that celibate will be specially favoured by God for living a single life as compared to his married counterpart. The celibate and the non-celibate Christian are therefore completed by Jesus Christ on the cross of Calvary.

The fact that one is single or married not withstanding, it is the belief in the name of Jesus and the acknowledgement of his death, resurrection and ascension that guarantees salvation. When the disciples asked Jesus "who is the greatest in heaven?" he compared the humility of those who will enter the kingdom of God to that of a little child (Matthew 18:1-3). Neither celibacy nor marriage is a criterion for entering the kingdom of heaven. All promises in the Bible are for all Christians who have accepted Jesus Christ as their Lord and Saviour. The Bible does not hold any special promise for the celibates. (Such promises as "No weapon forged against you shall prevail and you will refute every tongue that accuses you"(Isaiah 54:17) and those in 1 Peter 2:24 and John 4:19 seem to serve only as a basis on which the Christian may base his / her claim to security, healing and general well-being from God during prayer).

If nothing makes the celibate special in his relationship with God as compared to the non-celibate, why then will an individual opt for celibacy? An individual might decide to go celibate because of his level of commitment to the service of God. But is this true in reality? Can a single man serve God in the single state better than a married man? Is the execution and planning of policies easier for one who is alone or for one who has a companion? If man can serve God better in the single state, why did God bother to create with him a helper? (Genesis 1:27). (God says that it is not good for man to be alone. Is God not knowledgeable enough about the creatures of his hands to know their needs?). On our part, we will like to submit that it is better and easier for two people to plan and execute policies than for a single man or woman. But then we must not loose sight of the fact that the individual is free to choose either of the two possible states in which man can serve God i.e. the celibate state or the married state celibacy therefore, can be due to voluntary choice. So long as this is not seen as placing the celibate individual higher than his married counterpart, the freedom of choice should be recognized and respected. Celibacy may also be practiced for the purpose of population control since the celibate is not expected to have children. Within the church, celibacy may also be seen as a way of spending one's life on the community.[25] The important fact to note about celibacy is that it is entirely voluntary. Celibacy does not hold extra-ordinary promise for the individual. Neither celibacy nor marriage per se makes an individual a better Christian. The faithfulness of the individual to God is what counts.

Celibacy in Africa

As mentioned above, celibacy is practiced only by the Roman Catholic Church clergy in Christianity. A serious challenge to this practice is the value placed on procreation in Africa. Children are clearly the lifelines of African societies as they guarantee conformity of the family line as well as ensure the continuum of ancestors into the living space. Children therefore fulfil both physical and spiritual needs. In the African community, emphasis, most often than not, is on sons as female are viewed as transitional members of the family due to the norm that all females will marry. Though celibacy to a certain extent is present in African Traditional Religions, such occurs usually at old age when expectations of family life would have been met or early in life prior to the individual's family life experience. A situation where the individual is exclusively celibate in African Traditional Religion is an exception, if a possibility at all.

The celibate person, female or male, of African origin with an African consciousness will want to be convinced of failing in societal expectations. This is for obvious reasons as he or she can neither marry nor procreate. Among the Yoruba, refusal to marry and procreate by a matured female or male translates to irresponsibility for which the family, clan, and community suffers ridicule and other implications. Because the philosophical level of culture[26] constitutes the most potent of cultural levels, evidence pointing to the unsatisfactory practice of celibacy by the African person abound. Reported cases of celibate persons with "hidden Children" are open secrets while report of sexual relations between celibate males and females are not unknown in Africa.

We are persuaded that exclusive celibate is not compatible with the Africa cosmic view or philosophical stand. Celibacyin Africa is a foreign imposition on the African Catholic church in Africa. It therefore, becomes understandable that celibacy will be "modified" in face of African realities of life. We submit that the Roman Catholic Church in Africa has enough reasons to reconcile the practice of celibacy. This is truer than ever if the gospel is to avoid a state of self-embarrassment in Africa via the Roman Catholic Church.

Conclusion

In this paper, an attempt has been made to define celibacy. Scholars' views on celibacy and its definition were also considered. We have also examined the possibility of celibacy laying claim to any divine sanction in the Bible. We saw that celibacy was a church discipline that can draw support from the Bible though backed with no divine sanction (CF Mathew 19:12 and 1 Corinthians 7:1-10). The relationship of the celibate v is-à-vis that of the n on-celibate w as also examined. We discovered that both were equal before God. It was also stated that an individual is free to choose whether to serve God in the celibate or married state, since both are recognized as possible ways to serve God.

The freedom of choice of the individual was also mentioned. We also stressed that for no reason should the celibate be seen as being closer to God or higher spiritually than the married. We noted how erroneous it would be for an individual to see celibacy as a way to be specially favoured by God. Celibacy or marriage does not determine faithfulness to God by the individual. We will therefore like to submit that both the celibate and non-celibate Christian are equal before God. Some promises were cited in the Bible meant for the Christian irrespective of the state in which he/she is serving God.

It can be submitted therefore, that celibacy offers no special privilege to the Christian. But an individual may choose to serve God in the celibate state. This is based mainly on personal conviction and the grace of God and not because the celibate expects to be elevated above his married counterpart on the ground of being celibate. Celibacy is not a guarantee for salvation.

ENDNOTES

1.   Dr. B.U. Enyioha, a lecturer at the Nigerian Baptist Seminary, Ogbomoso. Interview on the 10th of May, 1989.
2.   I. Boettner, *Roman Catholicism* (London: The Banner of Trust London, 1966), 383
3.   Ibid., 384
4.   Ibid,.385
5.   W. Walker, *A History of the Christian Church,* Edinburgh: T & T Clark, 1959), 9
6.   A. S. Hornby et al., *Oxford Advanced Learner's Dictionary of Current English*, (Oxford University Press (1974), 135.
7.   D. Goergen, *The Sexual Celibate* (New York, 1979), 108.
8.   L. Boettner, op. Cit., 381.
9.   Genesis 2.24.
10.   F.V. Filson, *A Commentary on the Gospel of Mathew* (London: 1960, 207.
11.   F.E. Gaebelein (ed.), *The Expositors Bible Commentary*, Vol. 8, (Grand Rapids: WM B Eerdmans Publ, 1984), 212.
12.   F.V. Filson, Op. Cit., pp. 206-208.
13.   Matthew 18:3.
14.   P. Schaff (ed.), *Langes Commentary on the Holy Scriptures,* Vol.8 (Michigan,WM B Eerdmans Publishers, 1960), 338.
15.   See *The Interpreters Bible* – A Commentary in Twelve Volumes, Vol.7 (New York: Abingdon Press, 1953), 480-482.
16.   See. *The Broadman Bible Commentary*, Vol. 10, (Nashville, Tenessee: Broadman Publishing House, 1970), 188.
17.   Matthew 22:30.
18.   *The Broadman Bible Commentary*, Vol.10 (Nashville, Ten: B roadman P ress, 1970), 328-329.
19.   Matthew 5:28.
20.   J.R. Scott (ed.), *The Bible Speaks Today – The Message of 1 Corinthians* (England: 1985), 118-121.
21.   H. Conzelmann, I *Corinthians*, (Philadelphia: 1975), 114.
22.   See *The Interpreters Bible – A Commentary in Twelve volumes*, Vol.10, (Nashville: Abingdon Press, 1953), 212.
23.   S. R. Driver et al. (eds.), *1 Corinthians –The International Critical Commentary*, 2nd edition (Edinburgh: T & T Clark, 1963), 130-133.
24.   P. Schaff (ed), *Langes Commentary on The Holy Scriptures*, Vol.10, (Grand Rapids, Michigan: WM Eerdmans Publishers 1960), 216.
25.   Interview w ith Rev. Father Peter Otubusi of The Holy Cross Catholic Church, Ikire, Oyo State, on the 2nd of January, 1989.
26.   B. H. Kato, *African Cultural Revolution and the Christian Faith*, (Jos: Challenge Publication, 1976), 15

CHAPTER XII

POVERTY IN THE OLD TESTAMENT IN AFRICAN PERSPECTIVES

Robert Wafawanaka

Introduction

The problem of poverty[1] in Africa is somewhat astounding given the fact that Africa is the world's richest continent in terms of natural resources. According to *The Economist* of September 14, 1996, Africa has 40% of the world's hydro-electric power; most of the world's diamonds and chromium; 50% of the world's gold; 70% of cocoa; 60% of coffee; 50% of palm oil, etc.[2] Yet despite such wealth, Africa is grappling with grinding poverty, misery, political and economic instability. The two greatest ironies are that Africans are worse off today than they were at independence, and that many countries can no longer afford to export food, let alone feed themselves. Something must be seriously wrong.

The existence of poverty in Africa has a long history. The extent of poverty in Africa is so widespread that one does not need to question its existence. One only needs to visit the continent or read reports by the International Labor Office, the World Bank, the IMF, or the Carnegie Inquiry into Poverty and Development in Southern Africa. Despite Africa's richness in mineral resources, poverty continues to increase on the continent.

Causes of Poverty

Several causes of poverty may be identified. Among them is unemployment, inflation, overpopulation, or landlessness. My research indicates that while poverty has always existed in Africa, it is surely worsened in the modern context by corruption, political and economic instability, lack of democracy, quest for political power, as well as the spread of disease particularly HIV/AIDS. The evidence from my research implicates African government leadership, not the African people in general, as the major cause of much suffering and poverty in modern Africa.[3] In the foreword to *Africa Betrayed,* Makaziwe Mandela writes, "Although external factors beyond the control of Africans played a role, Ayitteh asserts that the policies of African leaders contributed in no small measure to the grinding poverty, appalling human misery, and deterioration in social conditions that are evident across much of Africa."[4]

However, my interest is not to measure how poor Africa is, but to unravel some of the causes of this problem, and above all, to demonstrate how traditional Africans have confronted this problem and how modern Africans might learn from it. I believe that a brief comparative look at poverty in the Bible reveals some of the similarities between Africa and the Bible in so far as the subject of poverty is concerned. In addition, a critical reading of the Bible reveals the candid strokes with which the ancient Israelites wrote their story. One only needs to take a look at the legal section of the Bible or some of the prophets of the 8th century BCE.

The other major cause of poverty in Africa is the rise of AIDS/HIV in Africa particularly in sub-Saharan Africa.[5] This region has been so devastated by this epidemic that health officials are at a loss. According to recent statistics from UNAIDS, 34.3 million people in the world have contracted AIDS. 24.5 million of them live in sub-Saharan Africa. These figure show that over 70% of all reported cases are in sub-Saharan Africa. In addition, nearly 19 million people have died of AIDS, 3.8 million of them children under the age of 15. The 1999 statistics indicate that there were over 4 million new cases of AIDS in Africa. In the same year, 85% of those who died of AIDS were in Africa. Similarly, 12.1 million children were orphaned by AIDS in sub-Saharan Africa. This is estimated to reduce life expectancy in sub-Saharan Africa from 59 to 45 years between 2005 and 2010.[6] Currently, in the worst affected African countries such as Botswana and Zimbabwe, 1 in every 4 persons is thought to be infected. According to the U.S. Census Bureau, this has led to the "zero growth" because "people are dying in their young adult years, not after leading full livers and then dying."[7] In January 2000, U.S. Ambassador to the United Nations, silence, Richard Holbrooke suggested working with the Africans around the critical issues in Africa, or risks a more expensive operation in the future.

A number of factors contributing to this epidemic may be identified. Some of them are shame, stigma, separation of families due to migrant labor patterns, the conspiracy of poverty and prostitution, ignorance, expensive drugs, or lack of leadership. While Uganda once topped the list of AIDS infections, the aggressive awareness campaign by the government of President Yoweri Museveni and NGOs has produced a decline in AIDS cases. By contrast, *The Associated Press* reports that it is only recently (1999) that the Zimbabwean government has publicly acknowledged the problem of AIDS and taken specific measures to address it.[8]

While a disease like AIDS may partly be caused by poverty, it also leads to poverty in another way. Oftentimes the victims are so incapacitated by their illness that they cannot afford to care for themselves. In addition, AIDS destroys the basic fabric of society, the extended family. Moreover, children are left without the basic necessities of life—food, shelter, and clothing. Without traditional support systems, such children will not achieve their maximum potential. The World Development Movement puts it as follows, "Although there are numerous factors in the spread of HIV/AIDS, it is largely recognized as a disease of poverty, hitting hardest where people are marginalized and suffer economic hardship. IMF designed Structural Adjustment Programmes (SAPs), adopted by debtor countries as a condition of debt relief, are hurting, and not working. By pushing poor people even deeper into poverty, SAPs may be increasing their vulnerability to HIV infection, and reinforcing conditions where the scourge of HIV/AIDS can flourish."[9] Short of a miracle or the invention of a cure, the future looks very gloomy for Africa. And consequently, the state of poverty in Africa is sure to be aggravated by HIV/AIDS.

Another factor that has contributed to the increase of poverty in Africa is the devaluation of the agricultural economy in Africa. While land is the basis of most African economies, not everyone wants to work on the land because of the low status assigned to such labor. In a paper entitled "The Complexities and Consequent Neglect of Agricultural Development," Douglas Ensminger identifies ten complicating factors. Among these factors are the low socio-economic and political status assigned to agriculture by developing countries, mistrust of government, favoring commercial farmers, low prices, and limited technology.[10] He writes, "This low status assigned to agriculture is deeply rooted, dating back to the colonial era . . . . Farm families want to educate their children for a government job or work in the cities. They do not want them to do the drudgery work of farming. Government workers look down on rural people as being incompetent to make decisions. Young people seeking entrance to a university will go to an agricultural college as a last resort."[11]

Other factors also contributed to the existence of poverty on the African continent and elsewhere. Poverty can also be caused by natural phenomena (such as weather patterns or soil quality, among others). It can also be caused by human design (for example, oppression, exploitation, laziness), or lack of good health. In some cases, the causes are not obvious. Reginald Herbold Green argues that although the existence of poverty in Sub-Saharan Africa is an historical fact, there was no golden age when the land flowed with wealth and everyone w as w ell fed. He also cautions it is equally false to treat poverty as primordial, unchanging, and inevitable.[12] Given these facts, it is worthwhile to try to assess the history of poverty in order to predict future trends.

The colonial argument has been one of the most cited reasons for the existence of poverty in modern Africa. Ironically, the suffering that Africa has endured in the post-colonial p eriod is quite u nlike that of the colonial period. While some are quick to blame colonialism or western imperialism for their problems, it is apparent that the problem is largely rooted at home. True, colonial masters did not train or educate Africans to rule themselves but rather to serve them. Nor did they believe that Africans were capable of ruling themselves. This s entiment i s c learly r eflected i n a n i nfamous st atement o nce made by the former Rhodesian Prime Minister, Ian Douglas Smith. At the height of British obstinacy, Smith declared that majority rule would come "not in a thousand years." When majority rule came to Zimbabwe in 1980, the appropriately titled book, *A Short Thousand Years,* appeared. It is also true that centuries of colonial rule cannot be undone by a mere four decades of independence. However, the evidence does not suggest an honest effort to eradicate the colonial past but rather to emulate it. Some scholars have even seen it as a new form of colonialism. This explains the call for a "second liberation," or the ludicrous call for "re-colonization" in some circles due to the belief that Africans can't rule themselves.

Despite these sentiments, it is clear that Africans can indeed rule themselves as evidenced by the greatness of Africa's ancient Empires like Egypt, Nubia, Ethiopia, Libya, Mali, Songhai, Ghana, Benin, or Great Zimbabwe. This fact has been amply demonstrated by historians like Basil Davidson in books such as *The African Past, Lost Cities of Africa, African Kingdoms,* and *Africa in History.* In his book, *African Saga,* professor Stanlake Samkange writes, "Long before Europeans dominated Africa, Africans had organized large empires with a high civilization, great cities, and a flourishing economy based on agriculture, mining and trade."[13] In addition, traditional Africa's indigenous institutions also demonstrate how Africans were capable of managing their affairs.[14]

Historical Overview

The phenomenon of poverty in Africa is not new. Poverty has existed from antiquity to the present, and continues to increase. Despite its existence in Africa, it is arguable that by and large, people thrive in its midst with spirit and dignity. Central to the survival of poor Africans are the traditional values of social solidarity, communal responsibility, mutual caring, and above all, the institution of the extended family.

Structural and Conjunctural Poverty

Perhaps the most comprehensive treatment of the subject of poverty in Africa has been undertaken by John Iliffe. Iliffe's use of the categories of "structural" and "conjunctural" poverty in defining the nature of poverty in Africa is of profound importance. Iliffe defines structural poverty as "the long-term poverty of individuals due to their personal or social circumstances," and conjunctural poverty as "the temporary poverty into which ordinarily self-sufficient people may be thrown by crisis."[15] This definition of structural poverty centers upon the physical condition of the poor and their ability to provide for themselves. It also hinges on the social situation in which they find themselves. These are situations beyond their control. Hence their poverty is "long-term." The condition of the conjunctural poor dependents on an external force. The conjunctural poor are physically able to provide for themselves but may also be facing circumstances beyond their control. These could be natural or human-engineered. Their poverty is "temporary" because their circumstances could change of themselves or be reversed by human will.

Iliffe's definition centers around the issue of land, the main "economic mode" or basis of sustenance for traditional Africans. In land-rich societies, the structural poor were at a disadvantage primarily because of their inability to exploit the land. This situation was worsened by the lack of family or relatives to provide for them. In land-scarce societies, these types of poor continued to exist, but were obviously outnumbered by the new poor, that is, those without land. Due to urbanization and overcrowding, the new poor were not only the landless but also the homeless and the unemployed who lacked the necessary skills to compete at the job market. Although these were physically able and willing to provide for themselves, they were faced with the problem of lack of land or other resources, as well as insufficient pay. Similarly, their poverty would be exacerbated by lack of family or relatives. From Iliffe's survey, it is evident that it is the structural poor who were most adversely affected, especially if they lacked family, relatives, or even land[16]

These categories and differentiations are of primary importance for our understanding of poverty not only in Africa but also in other societies. I contend that they have a universal significance and application which enables one to understand the subject of poverty in general. I shall refer to them in my comparative approach to the subject of poverty in traditional Africa and in ancient Israel.

Categories of the Poor

Green divides the poor into the absolute poor and the relative poor. The absolute poor are landless (or nearly so) and have no other source of income. The relative poor are the peasants who may occasionally hold jobs.[17] According to Green, absolute poverty affects one third of the people of Sub-Saharan Africa.[18] While this figure might be interpreted to mean that the remaining two thirds are not the absolute poor, it does not mean that they are rich either. In fact, the majority of these people are the relative poor. Charles Elliott's study is quite revealing. He observes that although many people have enough to eat (and therefore survive), "Other needs go largely or wholly unmet."[19] While budget studies often point to basic needs, other non-essential items are ignored. After analyzing these studies in relation to Africa, Elliott concludes, "the great majority of rural dwellers must be considered to be poor in absolute terms, and that a high proportion live [*sic*] in extreme poverty."[20] He further observes that well over half of the African rural population has incomes, consumption patterns, foods, and goods that in any society would be regarded as unacceptable.[21] These are the absolute poor, and it may be helpful to identify them.

The Absolute Poor

Green identifies eight classes of the absolute poor.[22] First, there are the landless or near-landless people without substantial regular remittances from urban working household members. The landless top the list because land is the basis of subsistence for rural Africans. Without it and without income from the city, one can be desperately poor unless he or she is engaged in some kind of trade. This situation can be exacerbated if such a person has no relative or household member to provide for him or her.

Female-headed households are part of the absolute poor because women have fewer hours available for the production of marketable goods other than those for household consumption. Women are also affected by unequal access to services and the division of labor along gender lines.

Aged and crippled-headed households are also impoverished because of their lack of productivity. Green also sees this as "evidence of a general poverty situation eroding extended family and communal solidarity mechanisms."[23] This is so because traditionally, the handicapped were always protected and provided for by their families.

Another group of the absolute poor are those who are isolated physically and socio-politically. For example, they may be far from transportation routes, which lower access to services and markets.

Those without significant sources of cash income other than food crops also fall into Green's group of the absolute poor. These usually have only food crops to sell because of ecological, access, or market availability reasons.

The absolute poor are also located in hostile ecological zones such as drought-prone areas of low soil fertility and areas prone to soil erosion. Because of many people's dependence on land, such a situation would ensure the continuation of poverty.

Victims of natural disasters like flood or drought are likely to remain in the group of the absolute poor after the disaster has passed. This is especially so if the victims have to abandon their homes and land and relocate elsewhere.

The last group of the absolute poor that Green identifies is victims of war. Again, these may be uprooted and forced to become refugees in a new location.

The Relative Poor

Green also identifies six urban groups that are likely to suffer from relative poverty. Some categories overlap. I shall merely enumerate them. The households of the relative poor are: on only one income; lacking any formal sector wage earner; female-headed; aged or crippled-headed; victims of natural disasters like sacking and war; and gaining primary income from informal sector employment or urban petty commodity production.[24]

Green's categorization seems to give the impression that the absolute poor are found only in rural areas and the relative poor in urban areas. However, by rural standards, some rural folk are better off, if not outright rich.[25] Conversely, some urban dwellers fit in the group of the absolute poor. Although some of the categories overlap, it is far worse to be an absolute poor person in an urban area than in a rural area. This is so because in urban areas, the social or kinship circles are comparatively weaker. This may also explain why one never sees a beggar in rural areas, whereas begging is synonymous with the urban poor. Another reason why the absolute poor are worse off in urban areas is because everything in the city has to be bought or is sold. If there is over-crowding or unemployment, the problem worsens.

According to Charles Elliott, a small minority (about five percent and sometimes less than one percent) of the rural population are, even by urban standards, wealthy.[26] He delineates two extremes: 1) the wealthy, such as civil servants, teachers, skilled and semi-skilled workers, wholesalers, retailers, and well-established farmers with export crops and ties to cooperatives; 2) "peasant farmers," composed of "those who seek to produce a surplus for sale, though they may not always be successful in that intention."[27] This group is in an extremely vulnerable position because they have neither the security of a subsistence producer, nor the security that comes from the financial resources of the "successful 'progressive' farmer."[28]

The rural poor therefore, whether subsistence or peasant farmers, depend largely on crop sales and the sale of livestock like cattle, goats, sheep, pigs, or chicken. Elliott calls the latter the second major source of cash income.[29]

While the rural poor in Africa are either the absolute or relative poor, the distinction between the two can be fluid. One may move from one state to another, depending on prevailing circumstances. However, Elliott argues that there are sometimes mechanisms that make it difficult to break the cycle of poverty. He singles out land, climate, altitude, and soil structure as factors that influence poverty. Because of the colonial legacy, he rightly points out that few Africans live in areas of great agricultural potential.[30]

Since poverty is not only an economic state but also a process, the poor are always striving to better their economic condition. In this light, Elliott cites an apt example during the days of the Federation of Rhodesia and Nyasaland in the 1950s:

> The Shona that moved into Southern and Central Zambia in the days of the Federation and immediately afterwards was almost certainly not the lowest income stratum of the population . . . . Rather they were those who were sufficiently highly motivated and sufficiently able to identify--and respond to--an opportunity to break out of the constraints imposed by the racial allocation of land in Rhodesia. To that extent, their migration did not represent a way of escape for the poorest but rather a more rapid transit to prosperity for the progressive.[31]

While this may have been true for a few lucky ones, the very poor could not afford such an escape. Because of the transitory nature of poverty, Elliott concludes, "for some of the rural population poverty has increased. For some, it has diminished. For some it has not much changed."[32]

It would perhaps be fitting to add to Green's picture of the absolute and relative poor the fact that some of the very poor are children. Stewart MacPherson shows in alarming detail the plight of poor children and women in developing countries.[33] Despite special rights accorded to children, they can be vulnerable to neglect, abuse, or curable diseases. In some societies, boys get preferential treatment over girls, a situation that might harm the latter emotionally and psychologically.[34]

John Iliffe's Model

While the above categories of the poor in Africa are helpful, I find Iliffe's categories most useful. According to Iliffe, the poor of pre-colonial Africa were mostly children, adolescents, the incapacitated (the sick, dying, blind, or insane), or outcasts (structural poor, due to personal circumstances), as well as victims of climatic or political insecurity (conjunctural poor).[35] Because pre-colonial Africa was land-rich, Iliffe contends that its poor were not landless but mainly the incapacitated.

In Iliffe's historical view of poverty in Africa, colonialism unleashed new forms of poverty. The scramble for Africa necessarily led to the displacement of the poor to undesirable and infertile areas, as well as to urban areas. Thus the new poor suddenly became the landless and homeless.

The post-colonial or independence era also had its own categories of the poor. While the traditional poor were still there, the new poor were the unemployed youths, and unmarried and old women, in crowded urban areas.[36] Because of these dynamics, Iliffe concludes, "poverty in Africa has been a cumulative phenomenon."[37]

African Traditional Beliefs, Religion, and Ethics

The Family

The family is one of the strongest institutions in African tradition.[38] This extended family is the nucleus of social norms, customs, and conventions. It is from this central unit that one is introduced to the issues of kinship, religion, and morality.

According to John S. Mbiti, the African family also includes the unborn and departed relatives, or what he terms "the living-dead."[39] The living-dead are one's recently departed relatives who are still "'alive' in the memories of their surviving families, and are thought to be still interested [*sic*] in the affairs of the family to which they . . . belonged in their physical life."[40] Mbiti also points out that since the living-dead are still part of the family, they have to be fed and offered libations, otherwise they will bring misfortune upon the family.[41] Hence "the living-dead solidify and mystically bind together the whole family."[42] Since there is close unity in families, one does not exist as an individual, but as part of a group. Mbiti renders it more aptly when he says, "In traditional life, the individual does not and cannot exist alone except corporately. He owes his existence to other people, including those of past generations and his contemporaries. He is simply part of the whole."[43] Therefore, it makes sense that one suffers or rejoices corporately, for "whatever happens to the individual happens to the whole group, and whatever happens to the whole group happens to the individual."[44] Like the ancient Israelites, Africans also believe in corporate responsibility.

Kinship Circles

Branching from the family unit, Africans always have kinship ties of some sort among themselves. Whole villages are related in one way or another, such that society as a whole is built on strong kinship ties. According to Mbiti, "The deep sense of kinship, with all it implies, has been one of the strongest forces in African traditional life. Kinship is reckoned through blood and betrothal."[45] Kinship controls social relationships, binds people together, and even extends to cover animals, plants, and non-living objects through the totemic system. Kinship embraces everybody such that "everybody is related to everybody else."[46] Hence, when strangers meet, they first determine how they are related, and then behave to each other accordingly. Because of this, one has literally hundreds of fathers, mothers, wives, and children.[47] The totem is the visible symbol of unity, kinship, belonging, togetherness, and common affinity. A totem therefore acquires sacred status such that it may neither be harmed, killed, nor eaten[48]

Society and Culture

African traditional society has a strong cultural heritage. It has a system of values, beliefs, ways of thinking, indeed a philosophy. It is also important to point out that each group of African people has its own cultural heritage. Some things are similar, yet others are different. Therefore, while using the generic term "African culture," one should always be mindful of the varieties that exist. These serve to enrich the reader's experience, or to provide an opportunity for comparison and contrast.

African society is a closely-knit unit. It consists of families, clans, tribes, leaders, and a variety of individuals whose services are essential to the community. Vast reserves of knowledge are contained in oral tradition. As Mbiti points out, this legacy is expressed in literature, dance, music, drama, social organizations, religion, ethics, philosophy, and economic life.[49] These are the building blocks of society. Individuals draw from this wealth of information in their daily lives. Although many issues pertain to African society and culture, we will only list a few that are most relevant to our discussion. These are values like altruism, hospitality, sharing, and communal spirit.

Scholars of African culture have established that Africans are a very hospitable people. They usually put the other first; and in many situations, the well-being of the other usually takes precedence over one's own. A person would go out of his or her own way to ensure that the other person has been taken c are o f first. T his i s c losely r elated t o t he i ssue o f generosity, which i s strength of African people. Temba Mafico succinctly describes how traditional ethics dictate that Africans should take care of strangers and the poor.[50] Writing on the Yoruba of Nigeria, Bolaji Idowu clarifies this point:

> The Yoruba are by nature a hospitable race and are particularly hospitable to strangers. Before life became as artificial and sophisticated as it is today in many parts of the country, a traveler need have no fear where to lodge or what to eat if benighted; he was sure to find ready hospitality wherever he called. The Yoruba teach that o ne s hould b e h ospitable b ecause it is right t o be so, as also because one can never tell when one might be in need of hospitality oneself.[51]

Although Idowu's study focuses on a particular group, his observations apply to a great many African people.

Another cultural value of African society is the idea of sharing. Even if resources are limited, people will always want to share what they have. This sharing can take place in families, villages, or tribes. Needless to say, sharing with strangers is considered a great virtue. To illustrate this point, the Shona people of Zimbabwe have a proverb which says *nzara ishuramweni* (hunger forecasts [the coming of] a stranger). In their collaborative work, Albert B. Plangger translates Mordikai A. Hamutyinei's explanation of this saying as follows: "It often happens that visitors turn up just at a time when the host is least prepared with provisions. But even so, the h ost w ill t ry his level best to satisfy his guest and the whole family."[52]

Finally, Africans have a very communal cultural heritage. A spirit of community is evident in their day to day relations. People often come together in good and bad times. For example, if a celebration takes place, it often brings the whole village together. So also in times of sadness, people gather to comfort one another, mourn the loss of a loved one, or simply lend a supportive hand.

From this brief survey, we can conclude that African society has some very strong cultural values. In essence, these are deeply humanistic in nature. Such values enable people to confront any problem facing them with confidence and determination. They basically know that they can support one another and confront any situation, be it disease, hunger, death, or poverty.

Religion and Ethics

The term "religion" is used here to refer to African Traditional Religion.[53] Bolaji Idowu gives a philosophical definition of African Traditional Religion:

> Religion results from man's spontaneous awareness of, and spontaneous reaction to, his immediate awareness of a Living Power, 'Wholly Other' and infinitely greater than himself; a Power mysterious because unseen, yet a present and urgent Reality, seeking to bring man into communion with Himself . . . . Religion in its essence is the means by which God as Spirit and man's essential self communicate.[54]

On a s impler n ote, J. Omosade Awolalu explains A frican Traditional Religion thus:

> When we speak of African Traditional Religion we mean the indigenous r eligion of t he A fricans. I t i s t he r eligion t hat has b een handed down from generation to generation by the forbearers of the present generation of Africans. It is not a fossil religion (a thing of the past), but a religion that Africans today have made theirs by living it and practicing it.[55]

Prominent scholars of African Traditional Religion agree on the close connection between religion and ethics. Idowu describes the Yoruba in the following manner: "In all things, they are religious. Religion forms the foundation and the all-governing principle of life for them . . . . The religion of the Yoruba permeates their lives so much that it expresses itself in multifarious ways . . . and is the basis of philosophy."[56] John Mbiti basically agrees with him when he states that "Africans are notoriously religious, and each people have its own religious system with a set of beliefs and practices. Religion permeates into all the departments of life so fully that it is not easy or possible always to isolate it."[57]

If such is the case, it follows that religion plays a central role in people's lives, their practices, and interpersonal relationships. Since religion is so pervasive, it logically follows that there is no distinction between the sacred and the secular, the spiritual and the mundane. Any distinctions people might make are merely artificial. Consequently, one cannot claim to be non-religious, strictly speaking. To Mbiti, "Religion is the strongest element in traditional background, and exerts probably the greatest influence u pon the thinking and living of the people concerned."[58]

While religion is present everywhere and in everything, Mbiti lists five specific parts of African culture in which religion can be seen.[59] For the purposes of this study, we shall only pursue the connection between religion and ethics in African ways of thinking.

The subject of ethics or morality is a broad one. However, it is one of the cornerstones of our study. We shall therefore examine how the relationship between religion and ethics impacts social relationships.

Ethics is the "science" of good and bad, or right and wrong conduct. It is the study of those universal principles of human conduct which are common to all people. Motlhabi contends that while ethics refers to the theory of morals, morality refers to the practice of morals or moral principles.[60] It is the latter definition that we are mainly concerned with in this study. We shall therefore consider what morality means in an African setting.

Bolaji Idowu undertakes a comprehensive study of African morality by focusing on the Yoruba people of Nigeria. His view is that morality is the product of religion: "Morality is basically the fruit of religion and . . . it was dependent upon it. Man's concept of the Deity has everything to do with what is taken to be the norm of morality."[61] Idowu proceeds to demonstrate the close relationship between religion and morality. He observes that the Yoruba "do not make a ny a ttempt t o s eparate t he t wo; a nd i t i s i mpossible f or t hem t o d o s o without disastrous consequences."[62]

Kofi A. Opoku supports Idowu's claim when he writes:

> Generally morality originates from religious considerations and it is so pervasive in African culture that the two cannot be separated from each other . . . what constitutes the moral code of any particular African society--the laws, taboos, customs and set forms of behaviour--all derive their compelling power from religion. This morality flows out of religion and through this the conduct of individuals is regulated and any break of the moral code is regarded as evil and punishable.[63]

J. O. Awolalu and P. A. Dopamu make further reference to the role of divinities as intermediaries in maintaining the moral order. They argue that "in maintaining the society, God has brought the divinities into being. They act both as His ministers in the theocratic government of the world and as intermediaries between Him and man. Through these functionaries, God gives society cohesion and persistence."[64]

Idowu presents the God Olodumare (Perfect Judge, the Pure King) as the ultimate source and guardian of human morals. Hence, the Yoruba focus on character, for "good character" is the essence of Yoruba ethics and the sure protection against the bad things in life.[65]

The main components of good character among the Yoruba are chastity before marriage, kindness, hospitality, truth, and rectitude, among others. Bad or evil moral conduct is condemned and punishable by retributive justice brought upon the offender and his or her offspring.[66]

African scholars generally agree with Idowu's analysis of African morality. However, John Mbiti goes a step further. He argues that what lies behind the concept of moral "good or evil" the nature of the "relationship" between individuals in any is given society or community. For example, witchcraft and evil magic are morally evil because they destroy relationships. In fact, Mbiti refers to the practitioners of these crafts as "the very incarnation of moral evil" because they destroy relationships, undermine the moral integrity of society, and act contrary to what custom demands.[67]

The list of "do's" and "don'ts" in studies of African morality is long. However, it is essential to note that these morals have to do with the other person's welfare or livelihood. It is what one might call "an ethic of the other." Mbiti puts it succinctly:

> The essence of African morality is that it is more 'societary' than 'spiritual'; it is a morality of 'conduct' rather than a morality of 'being'. This is what one might call 'dynamic ethics' rather than 'static ethics', for it defines what a person *does* rather than what he *is*. Conversely, a person is what he is because of what he does, rather than that he does what he does because of what he is. Kindness is not a virtue unless someone is kind; murder is not evil until someone kills another person in his community. Man is not by nature either 'good' or 'bad' ('evil') except in terms of what he does or does not do.[68]

This is indeed a dynamic ethic. One might also call it an ethics of praxis or an other-directed ethic.

Uka adds that "ethics in an African traditional society is communal ethic not an individualistic ethic. It is an ethic concerned with the welfare and moral tone of the community."[69] He also refers to it as "an ethics of shame not of guilt" because if relationships are not hurt, and if there is no discovery of a breach of custom, then something is not "evil" or "wicked" since there is no shame involved.[70] In sum, Uka captures the essence of African morality when he says "African traditional morality therefore, could be described as prescriptive, societary, teleological, communitarian and 'legalistic'. Indeed it is a morality of conduct rather than a morality of being. It defines what a person does rather than what he is."[71]

One might ask how such a strong sense of morality is regulated. Research shows that African morality is enforced through social institutions like the family, age-grade, and secret societies. There are also formal methods of teaching morals such as through myths, legends, fables, folktales, riddles, proverbs, songs, and story-telling. In most of these, goodness always triumphs over evil. Such means of communication not only have a didactic purpose, but a recreational purpose as well. Long before technological advances, story-telling was one of the means of entertaining children in Africa. There are also taboos or prohibitions whose main purpose is to ensure social harmony and acceptable moral conduct by declaring certain things, habits, behaviors, or manners of speech prohibited. In some cases, a bad or evil consequence is attached to a taboo in order to make it decisively effective. As Uka puts it, "Most of the folktales and fables are put in songs in which virtuous persons are honored with praises and commendations and with rights and privileges, while persons of mean character are condemned without reservations. These methods of communicating moral values equally assist in enforcing them in traditional African societies."[72]

Since moral regulations are so prevalent in African society, one might also ask how one manages to remember them. This is actually complicated by the fact that African religion has no sacred scriptures, written history, or founder. Everything is handed down through oral tradition. According to Mbiti, Africans have an innate sense of good and evil because "the morals are normally written down in their mind and conscience, through the long period of their upbringing and their observations of what other people do and do not do."[73]

One essential point to understand in terms of African morality is the idea of causation. Most, if not all Africans believe that an evil deed like death is always "caused" by someone or something. There is no "accident" or "chance," but always an agent. A person dies in a car crash because someone *caused* it to crash, either a witch, a bad spirit, or an aggrieved ancestor spirit. Therefore, there is technically no natural death or evil because it is all caused or willed by someone or something. And even if natural evil might be justified, people always say that natural evil is present because immoral agents exist, and these are evil because they do evil deeds.[74] Hence, it follows that when someone dies or when misfortune befalls a community, people always first ask "why" it happened rather than "how" it happened. Moreover, people are known to consult spirit mediums, traditional doctors, ancestors, or even God to determine why something happened, even if it is clearly a case of drunken driving. People will ask, "Why this time?" Mafico echoes the same point.[75]

From this survey, it is clear that in African traditional society, religion and ethics go hand in hand. They are two inseparable sides of the same coin. Religion and ethics function to provide a harmonious social order. If any problems confront the community, people come together and attempt to determine why an event happened and try to do something about it. If it is deemed that the ancestors are angry with the community, people usually propitiate them with beer, libations, or asking for forgiveness.[76] In such times of crisis or need, people usually employ their other-directed ethic to take care of, and provide for, the needy members of the community.

Coping Mechanisms

From the "communitarian" or "societary" nature of African ethics as shown above, it follows that when a problem like poverty confronts a society, community members draw upon their traditional ethic and take care of one another. Africans basically cope with poverty and other problems through their families and a variety of other social support systems or mechanisms.[77]

The Family and Poverty

The African family is the nucleus of society. It is a closely-knit unit in which the members assume responsibility for one another, especially parents for their children and children for their parents as they age. In the larger context of society, the young look to the elders for nourishment, wisdom, instruction, and knowledge. The elders look to the young for protection, caring, and the continuation of the family name. This relationship is mutually beneficial.

I therefore agree with Iliffe's assessment that because of the lack of institutions and organizations to take care of Africa's poor, "families were and are the main sources of support for the African poor."[78] He adds that the intimate connection between poverty and family structure which has been neglected by European historians may be Africa's chief contribution to the comparative history of the poor.[79]

Iliffe sees the lack of family support as a major cause of poverty. Conversely, the existence of a family greatly reduces a poor person's chances of being destitute. This is clear from his analysis of poverty in the Islamic tradition in Africa. He notes that some of the very poor (or destitute) were "unfortunate individuals who lacked family care." These, like the poor in Christian lands, survived through institutional means of support like charity and individual generosity.[80]

Due to a lack of institutions in colonial Africa, Iliffe argues, most poor people survived by the care of their own families or by their own means. "Because institutionalized provision was limited, the care of the incapacitated poor fell chiefly on families and neighbors."[81]

Iliffe's historical survey of the African family and poverty is convincing. It is true that in the late nineteenth century and early twentieth century, large families were considered not only a source of wealth but also a status symbol. This was so because of the economic viability of such a family constitution at a time when land was plentiful and labor scarce. However, by the late twentieth century, this was no longer true. Because land was scarce and labor plentiful, a large family could certainly mean poverty.[82] As we begin the 21st century, I think Iliffe's thesis still stands, but it needs to be modified. Because of the many causes of poverty reviewed, large families today are more likely to be poorer than smaller ones. However, in some cases, large families can be an advantage. This is especially the case in those African countries where diseases like AIDS/HIV threaten to wipe out entire villages. At least with a large family, one may have some hope of assistance from a (n extended) family member if other family members are deceased. In addition, the many crises of modern Africa threaten not only to bring structural and conjunctural poverty together, but also to turn conjunctural poverty into structural poverty.

Although in a few instances families have neglected their poor due to prevailing circumstances, I largely agree with Iliffe's argument about the importance of the African family in the fight against poverty. This is especially true for families in rural areas where they have owned land (and had access to other support systems like communal care). On the other hand, families dwelling in an urban setting face greater challenges of landlessness, overcrowding, unemployment, crime, and above all, detachment from their traditional roots. The significance of the family was highlighted by Zimbabwean President Robert G. Mugabe, who in 1986 declared:

> Surely, we must all long for that day when there will be no orphanages because all Zimbabweans will have renewed and rededicated themselves to the sacred traditional values of the extended family that sustained succeeding generations of our founding fathers.[83]

This point is underscored by Mafico, who argues that "Africans, even nowadays, would not dream of sending their parents to old people's homes where they will feel both lonely and neglected by family and society."[84]

Social Solidarity and Communal Responsibility

One other coping mechanism of the poor is through an elaborate system of social relations. As noted above, Africans are a very socially-oriented people. They live in closely-knit societies where the values of social solidarity and communal responsibility are deeply entrenched. Yet some significant differences exist between a rural and an urban population in the face of poverty. In rural areas people are more communal, know each other by name, visit each other at will, do things together, and explore how they are related. In towns and cities, one may not even know or talk to his or her next-door neighbor. The situation may change, however, as more families migrate to urban areas. In this case, people will hopefully resume their traditional social relationships. In the meantime, this is not yet the case since cities are normally associated with the breakdown of morals as well as the breakup of the traditional family. Consequently, if one is faced with dire poverty, however, he or she is likely to retreat to the rural areas rather than be a beggar in town, or be forced to resort to a life of crime. This would greatly compromise the African's sense of traditional morality.

Roger C. Riddell and Peter S. Harris describe this situation with reference to Southern Africa. They argue that rural-urban links among low-paid workers enable sub-PDL wage earners to survive. Because of their low wages, they rely on rural areas or their dependents may live in the rural area for some time. The links with the rural areas are "maintained as a method of providing social security where the state provides none."[85]

This quest for social security becomes an obstacle for Riddell and Harris as they try to determine the necessary conditions for PDL to be effective. One of their four conditions, that "there are no economic obligations beyond the basic nuclear family," proves to be inapplicable to low wage-earners in Southern Africa. The ideals of social solidarity and communal responsibility in African society are basically problematic to their intention. Hence, they declare, "In African society where responsibility for relatives extends beyond the nuclear family, and in Rhodesia with its serious unemployment problem, it is highly likely that a wage-earner will have to support those other than his immediate dependents."[86]

While decrying poverty and the social evils it leads to, Riddell and Harris continue to notice the strong social ties of poor Africans. They conclude, "poverty leads to an encouragement of temporary urbanization where workers identify with an urban industrial life during their employment but maintain rural links as a means of social security."[87]

Mutual Support, Sharing, and Caring

The values of mutual support, sharing, and caring are consistent with the African's sense of responsibility to the other. They enhance his or her ability to fight against poverty. Charity, generosity, kindness, and almsgiving, among others, are some of the ways Africans take care of one another in the midst of poverty. In the religious milieu of Africa, generosity and almsgiving are considered to bring people nearer to God and also to avert calamities, or even to avoid hell.[88]

Among the Shona people of Zimbabwe, similar values are expressed in proverbs or wise sayings handed down through oral tradition. For example, people often forgive a poor person's debt by saying, *kureva chikwereti kumurombo kunema Mwari* (to claim a debt from a poor person is [tantamount to] scorning God). This saying also has a variant which reads: *Chadyiwa nomurombo chadyiwa nashe* (what has been eaten by a poor person has been eaten by a chief). This saying pleads for a poor person not to be pressed to pay his or her debt. The plea is strengthened by reference to God.[89]

Other sayings extol the virtues of hospitality and mutual sharing. For example, the saying *zuva rimwe haripedzi dura* (one day's stay does not empty a granary) is also variously rendered as *mweni haaendi nedura* (a guest does not carry away a granary) or *zuva rimwe hariodzi nyama* (one day does not spoil meat). The explanation and application of this proverb is that "to feed a passerby will never exhaust the larder." Hamutyinei and Plangger add that "this proverb is used in all situations where stinginess is deplored but hospitality encouraged and praised."[90]

A proverb like *kandiro kanopfumba kunobva kamwe* (a small dish of food goes where another one comes from) means "one good turn deserves another." While people are expected to reciprocate a gift, the Shona use this proverb "to refer to a person who, in his days of prosperity, turned a deaf ear to the needs of his neighbour, but in his time of need goes to the neighbour for a favour."[91]

Finally, a few more proverbs address the state of poverty itself. For example, the proverb *nhamo urimbo, inonamira* (misery is like bird-lime; it sticks), is also rendered as *urombo hahudzingwi ngetsvimbo* (poverty cannot be chased away with a hunting club). This proverb means that "misery of some sort is part and parcel of life. You cannot simply shake it off or chase it away. Industry and skill can often overcome it."[92] Proverbs like *kupfuma ishungu* (to be rich is to be ambitious) or *kupfuma kunowanikwa nedikita* (riches are gained by sweat) and *nzara makavi, inosvuurwa* (hunger is like fiber; it can be removed) express the Shona's confidence that poverty can be overcome by hard work.[93] According to Iliffe, during periods of famine in Zimbabwe, people rarely starved to death.[94]

In some cases community leaders like chiefs, kings, queens, or other authority figures are expected to be benefactors of the poor. In Zambia, the chief is expected to feed the poor, the outcast, and the stranger. In Uganda's kingdom of Bunyoro, the coronation oath included promises to treat poor and rich equally, and to care for orphans.[95] I. Schapera notes that among the Tswana people of Botswana, the chief is the executive head of the tribe who "must protect the rights of his subjects, provide justice for the injured and oppressed, and punish wrongdoers." Moreover, "The Chief himself acts as 'upper guardian' of all widows and orphans, and should see to it that they are properly cared for."[96]

Although colonialism introduced formal schools, hospitals, and churches in Africa, Iliffe argues that there were not enough institutions to take care of the needs of the poor. This means that most people were still needy. One can only speculate how much the break-up of traditional life and support systems adversely affected the poor, or how much it benefited them. The lack of resources (or exploitation of resources) may also have contributed to the problem of poverty in Africa. But it is undeniable that colonialism did not solve all the problems of the poor. In light of this situation, people still felt compelled to alleviate the plight of the poor.

Some people rose to the challenge and offered of themselves selflessly. The most notable example is that of Jairos Jiri of Zimbabwe, who founded the Jairos Jiri Association. Jiri started taking care of the elderly, blind, and infirmed in his home. By 1967 the Association was caring for handicapped Africans of all kinds. Jiri's work and charitable efforts on behalf of the poor earned him international recognition. Iliffe agrees that "he was certainly the continent's most famous African philanthropist."[97] Others like Emperor Haile Selassie of Ethiopia established the Haile Selassie Welfare Trust in 1947. Its aim was "to promote education, to combat disease, to care for the young, the orphaned, the sick, the old and infirm, to establish hospitals, schools and ecclesiastical seminaries, to rehabilitate delinquents."[98]

Due to the lack of institutions for the incapacitated poor, many continued to depend on their families, relatives, and neighbors. In 1944, Lucy Mair completed a study on the welfare of British colonies, in which she addressed the issues of education, labor, and health. Her observations are revealing. She writes, "there are no uncared for children where the strength of African conceptions of kinship is unimpaired."[99] Mair also notices the strength of African support systems and declares that "most Africans will do far more for a distant relative in difficulties than many Englishmen would do for a close relative."[100] In this way, Mair explains why welfare was not needed in rural areas.

Although, for the most part, Africans took care of each other, not everyone was sympathetic with the plight of the poor. This was largely due to the distinction made between what Iliffe terms "the deserving poor" (like orphans, the aged, blind, and handicapped) and the "undeserving poor" (like beggars and unemployed able-bodied men and women). In Ghana, on the eve of independence, beggars were referred to as "a public nuisance" that discredited the new government. Others voiced opposition and claimed that some were real beggars who were infirmed and poor and needed government sympathy and support, especially from a government that claimed to be socialist.[101]

Other Survival Techniques

While there were a few social institutions and organizations intended for the relief of poverty in colonial Africa, not everyone benefited from them. As a result, some of the poor were forced to survive by independent means. The condition of the poor also depended on society's attitudes toward them.

A case in point is the attitude of the Igbo of Nigeria toward the poor. Iliffe reports that the Igbo concealed their poverty for attitudinal reasons:

Igbo concealed their poor. Whereas the rulers of Rwanda and Burundi deliberately emphasized differences of wealth and power, and whereas an Ethiopian court or a Hausa town attracted the poor into the open and made their numbers visible, the few institutions by which Igbo provided for the poor were designed to disguise their condition in a society where equal opportunity was the prevailing ideology and poverty was considered shameful.[102]

It is also reported that the Igbo killed twins as unwanted babies because they were considered unnatural. Their mothers were made outcasts and impoverished. Elderly women were accused of witchcraft and faced the same fate. Some diseased children were also abandoned.[103] Thus, Iliffe concludes, "Even by African standards, Igbo markedly lacked institutional provision for the poor . . . Yet where social welfare was concerned, concealment was the rule.[104]

This situation contrasts with Yoruba attitudes toward poverty. Although the poor existed in Yoruba land, they were busy taking care of themselves. The destitute were few because "the wealth of opportunities for independent survival was a distinctive feature of poverty in Yoruba land."[105] Because of the many self-help projects of the Yoruba, child beggars, crime, and prostitution were absent from the Yoruba poor.

In yet other cases, the poor survived by their own ingenuity. In cases of severe famine, the poor have survived by eating wild fruit, roots, or berries. Some work in exchange for food. Others focus on prevention of poverty by stocking up food supplies or growing drought resistant crops. During one of nine famines in colonial Zimbabwe, famine relief was issued on credit, to be repaid later.[106]

Since poverty continues to exist in Africa, some countries like Zimbabwe at independence attempted to deal with the problem by calling for a more just and equitable social order, or by empowering the poor through income-generating projects, cooperatives, self-reliance, and economic structural adjustment programs.[107]

This research shows that by a myriad of ways, the African poor have managed to survive poverty. They rely primarily on their families, as well as traditional support systems and indigenous ingenuity.

Socio-Ethical Dimensions

This study of African perspectives on and attitudes toward poverty generates several socio-ethical implications for understanding the subject of poverty. A number of issues that are ethically and socially relevant to the fight against poverty can be identified.

As discussed above, the values of strong family ties, social solidarity, and communal responsibility that are so much a way of life for African people are a great a sset i n l ight o f s ocial p roblems. T he l ess fortunate m embers o f s ociety (especially the structural poor whose poverty is due to personal circumstances) have the assurance and confidence that someone will always take care of them. When a community spirit embraces all members, it is much easier to deal with problems no matter how insurmountable they may seem to be.

Mutual support, sharing, and caring for one another are communal values which a healthy society should strive to achieve. To uphold these values means to promote the welfare of others. Such altruism can work toward the benefit, and indeed betterment, of the community as a whole.

These ethical models have many dimensions, all of which promote the existence of a more just, humane, and equitable social order. For example, inherent in these socio-ethical models are the values of generosity, selflessness, community, equality, justice, and many others. A society built on these principles is likely to be better, more just, and more equitable than one devoid of these norms.

Without arguing for a utopian society, it is nevertheless apparent that a society that is both socially and ethically conscious is a better off community and a more desirable one. Such a society, though struggling, maintains a sense of dignity. It is therefore not surprising that with widespread traditional social support systems, the African poor have managed to survive generations of grueling poverty in a society where institutional supports were inadequate. The research shows that it was not a massive dose of outside aid or colonial intervention that saved the Africans from poverty.[108] Instead, relief came from their own internal resources, which arguably can never be diminished. Such resources, though seemingly ineffective to the economist, go a long way towards confronting a particular social problem.

The African model for dealing with the problem of poverty is therefore one which is primarily familial in nature. It emphasizes the strength that families exude when they confront a problem together. In addition, the model is societal or communal. It draws strength from traditional systems of social organization. Moreover, this model is altruistic or other-directed. It is primarily concerned with the welfare of the other at the expense of the individual. Finally, this model is ethical because it calls upon human beings to do what is right or pleasing and to avoid what is wrong or displeasing. Doing what is right is measured by how it affects others.

I shall now proceed to briefly compare and contrast these perspectives and models with a study of biblical material. Our study of poverty in Africa will shed some significant light on biblical materials.

Poverty in Biblical Context

Turning our attention to the biblical picture, we are immediately made aware of the prevalence of the subject of poverty in the Bible. Research indicates that the problem of poverty was one that people struggled with in biblical times as well. Therefore this problem is not only peculiar to Africa. By focusing our attention on the biblical picture, we may be able to draw some useful models and paradigms relevant to the subject of poverty in Africa.

Although biblical historians believe that Israel did not set out to write objective history, but rather history from the perspective of her faith in God, nevertheless, that history is candid and not necessarily a record of her greatest achievements. Some of the nation's sins and failures are recorded. Israel managed to take a self-critical look at herself and dared to bare her soul on the pages of the sacred text. It is with such honesty and integrity that we should confront our problems in Africa.

To understand the problem of poverty in the Bible, one need not only engage in etymological studies. Due to the fact that language changes over time, etymology alone can be misleading or at least lead to root fallacy. For a better understanding of words and terms relating to poverty one needs to combine etymology with an examination of the context and usage of terms.109

An examination of poverty in the Bible indicates that the subject is prevalent in the biblical text. This problem exists in the Hebrew scriptures (Old Testament), the intertestamental period, and the New Testament. In the Hebrew Bible, this subject is addressed in all the three parts—the Torah, the Prophets, and the Writings.

In general, poverty in the Old Testament denotes a lack of material resources and economic goods, as well as political and legal powerlessness and oppression.[110] In her book, *Bible of the Oppressed,* Elsa Tamez writes, "For the Bible, oppression is the basic cause of poverty . . . . the oppressor steals from the oppressed and impoverishes them. The oppressed are therefore those who have been impoverished, for while the oppressor oppresses the poor because they are poor and powerless, the poor have become poor in the first place because they have been oppressed. The principal motive for oppression is the eagerness to pile up wealth, and this desire is connected with the fact that the oppressor is an idolater."[111] Other theologians such as Thomas D. Hanks join Tamez in this contention.[112]

While different Hebrew terms are used to refer to poverty and the poor (e.g., *'ebyon* = the beggarly poor; *dal* = the poor peasant farmer; *mahsor* = the lazy poor; *misken* = poverty is better; *rash* = political and economic inferiority; and *'ani* = the injustice of oppression),[113] the most predominant use is that of the term describing poverty caused by oppression (*'ani/'anawim*). At the very least we can see a connection between the causes of poverty in both Africa and the Bible.

In the legal sections of the Bible ancient Israel wrote legislation intended to ameliorate the suffering and exploitation of the poor, or the concentration of power and resources in a few hands. Historically, laws are written to address specific problems and issues. Implicitly, ancient Israel's laws sought to provide justice for the poor who would otherwise have been victimized. Therefore, specific measures were taken to ensure the protection of the poor and most vulnerable people in society—widows, resident aliens, and fatherless minor children. Consequently, the law stated that during harvest, something had to be left behind for the benefit of the poor (Deut 24:19-22; Lev 19:9-10, 23:22) and charity toward the needy was to be practiced. In addition, institutions such as the Fallow/Sabbatical Year and Jubilee Year were put in place. During the Year of Jubilee, all debts were cancelled, property returned, and debt slaves freed.

The most challenging and yet inspiring evidence of Israel's self-critical consciousness comes from the prophetic tradition. A glance at 8th century Israel reveals two groups of citizens existing in one country—one basking in the sunshine of prosperity (that is, the rich and the ruling upper class), and the other existing at the nadir of poverty and merely struggling to survive (that is the peasant class and the powerless). Upon this scene the great prophets of ancient Israel appear and make their memorable remarks. At the risk of ostracism, they fearlessly expose the corruption, oppression, bribery, exploitation, cheating, and stealing they saw going on in the nation. Robert Gnuse describes the situation in this way:

Though prophets saw themselves as messengers of Yahweh rather than as spokesmen of oppressed classes in a struggle of rural poor against rich urban

oppressors and a despotic king, their message is as virulent as any marshaled by modern social critics, and it has been the inspiration of modern reformers and social critics. The rich, powerful classes of Samaria and Jerusalem were accused of oppression, which defied the will of Yahweh. Prophets were advocates of the dispossessed and exploited against the injustice perpetrated and perpetuated by the wealthy. The prophets argued passionately for the benefit of the weak and hurled wrathful curses against the great and rich.[114]

A reading of the prophetic books reveals the passion with which they criticized the injustices of their times. Consider the following sample:

> "But let justice roll down like waters, and righteousness like an everflowing stream" (Amos 5:24).
> "Hear this, you rulers of the house of Jacob and chiefs of the house of Israel, who abhor justice and pervert all equity, who build Zion with blood and Jerusalem with wrong! Its rulers give judgment for a bribe; its priests teach for a price, its prophets give oracles for money" (Micah 3:9-11). "He expected justice, but saw bloodshed; righteousness, but heard a cry! Ah, you who join house to house, who add field to field, until there is room for no one but you, and you are left to live alone in the midst of the land!" (Isaiah 5:7-8 :)
> "Thus says the Lord: Act with justice and righteousness, and deliver from the hand of the oppressor anyone who has been robbed. And do no wrong or violence to the alien, the orphan, and the widow, or shed innocent blood in this place"(Jeremiah 22:3).

Because of their outspokenness, some of the prophets were ostracized. They became "peripheral" prophets because they went against the system and challenged the establishment. Yet we still remember their immortal and haunting words. They attacked what they viewed as the basic cause of the problem.

One biblical scholar, Leslie Hoppe, states it categorically, "Poverty just does not happen; it happens because people make it happen."[115] Conversely, he argues, "People have created poverty; they ought to be able to end it."[116] These maxims apply both to the biblical context and the African context. Genuine repentance, self-renewal, and reform are needed to accomplish this task.

The biblical context demonstrates that in addition to the many measures taken to prevent poverty, charity was one of the most important ones. This becomes an extensive debate in the Intertestamental period when the rabbis debate each other about the nature of such charity and its effects. The debate spills over into the New Testament with Jesus confronting the problem of poverty in his time. Some of his pronouncements such as the requirement to give one's possessions to the poor before becoming a disciple, or the hardship of the rich to enter the kingdom of God, are also memorable and instructive.

Some Tentative Solutions and Conclusion

From our foregoing discussion, we may ask what can be done about the problem of poverty in light of biblical evidence and African realities. A number of approaches may be identified. One way is to attack the root of the problem and the other is to address its. Our research demonstrated that Africans (and their supporters) must work for political, economic, and social reforms. We must also support those countries that have fledgling democracies. Human rights, property rights, the rule of law, and other democratic principles must characterize good government. In addition, African governments can promote practical and technical skills development for the majority of the citizens.

As the biblical record shows, charity is another solution, but it ought to be given with caution. One way is not to patronize the recipients thereby destroying their sense of self-worth. An awareness of the politics of the country or region as well as its needs may assist in deciding how best to use such aid. Aid should also be directed to those who will ensure that it arrives to help people in need. The greatest statement on charity comes from the Jewish scholar, Maimonides, who stated that the best charity is that which helps the poor dispense with charity.[117] This corresponds to the Chinese proverb that states: If you want to feed a man for a day, give him fish; if you want to feed him for the rest of his life, teach him how to fish. The best form of foreign aid is that which is appropriately channeled and intended to help the poor become self-sufficient. This ensures their dignity and self-worth.

Another way is to work closely with NGOs or African governments in implementing economic structural adjustment programs that are suitable to a particular people's needs. These programs may fail if they are ill conceived or under-funded.

Investment in the African peoples themselves is another solution. This may be done in a number of ways such as creating income generating projects in rural areas, forming co-operatives, teaching agricultural skills to small farm owners, offering competitive prices for goods, teaching school graduates particular trades or equipping them with the skills to start their own businesses. In this way job seekers will be transformed into employers.

Yet another way is to invest in the extended family. Iliffe's study demonstrated that the African poor survived chiefly by means of their families. In addition, they survived by engaging in all forms of trade and jobs requiring minimal skills. In some cases they survived by their own ingenuity and perseverance. These are lessons we can use again.

We can also implement the "Ten Commandments" drafted by Ayitteh.[118] In addition, A fricans sh ould l earn f rom t heir p ast g lorious h istory a nd h ow t heir traditional instruments of government functioned. This is essentially a return to our roots.

By the same token, Africans should also learn from their past mistakes and avoid them in the future. As in the biblical witness, Africans must heed the prophetic voices for repentance and renewal and seek to reform themselves and their systems of government.

Finally, we should realize that Africa is a great continent with a great history and culture. This fact should not be overshadowed by the crisis of poverty, or by those who seek to obliterate this reality through misrule, self-aggrandizement, or mismanagement of the economy. As Proverbs 2:9 eloquently states, "then shalt thou understand righteousness, and judgment, and equity."

Endnotes

1. This chapter is a revision of part of the author's dissertation. See "Perspectives on the P roblem of Poverty in Traditional Africa and in Ancient Israel," Th.D. diss., Boston University School of Theology, 1997, chap. 2.

2. *The Economist,* 14 September, 1996, 68.

3. See George B. N. Ayittey, *Africa in Chaos* (New York: St. Martin's Press, 1998); idem, *Africa Betrayed* (New York: St. Martin's Press, 1992).

4. Ayitteh, *Africa in Chaos,* "Foreword," xi. She adds, "after independence, most Africans w ere d enied t he v ery f reedoms t hey s truggled s o h ard for f rom c olonial rule. Tyranny is rampant in Africa . . . . Violations of human rights are committed with impunity on the continent, with the worst offense occurring under military dictatorships. But most of A frica's ' liberators' did more than oppress their people. They mismanaged their national economies and looted national treasuries for deposit in overseas bank accounts." Ibid.

5. See Medact and the World Development Movement. "Deadly Conditions? Examining the Relationship b etween Debt Relief Policies and H IV/AIDS." 2000. Database   On-line.   Available   from   Internet, http://www.globalissues.com/Geopolitics/Africa/AIDS.asp.

6. In Zimbabwe the life expectancy rate is expected to be reduced from 61 to 33 years in the same period.

7. Karen Stanecki, chief of health studies, U.S. Census Bureau.

8. *The Associated Press,* Sunday, April 18, 1999. The *AP* reported 1200 AIDS deaths a week in Zimbabwe.

9. "Deadly Conditions? Examining the Relationship between Debt Relief policies and HIV/AIDS," A Report by Medact and the World Development Movement. Internet source: http://www.globalissues.com/Geopolitics/Africa/AIDS.asp, 3.

10. Douglas Ensminger, "The Complexities and Consequent Neglect of Agricultural Development," in *The Causes of World Hunger,* ed. William Byron (New York / Ramsey: Paulist Press, 1982), 55-63. The other factors are: male-oriented education which neglects w omen's contributions in agriculture, lack of production resources for small farmers, view of the poor as acceptable in developing countries, favoring of commercial farmers by agricultural organizations, and inability to reduce rodents, insects, etc.

11. Ibid. 57.

12 Reginald Herbold Green, "Sub-Saharan Africa: Poverty of Development, Development of Poverty," Discussion Paper 218, Institute of Development Studies [IDS] (Brighton, England: University of Sussex, 1986), 1-42, especially, 5. See also Donald Crummey and C. C. Steward, eds., *Modes of Production in Africa: The Precolonial Era* (Beverly Hills: Sage Publications, 1981); and Ghai Dharam and Samir Radwan, eds, *Agrarian Policies and Rural Poverty in Africa* (Geneva: International Labour Office, 1983).

13. Stanlake J. T. Samkange, *African Saga: A Brief Introduction to African History* (Nashville, New York: Abingdon Press, 1971), 141. Other Empires of West Africa were: Kanemu-Bornu, Hausa States—Oyo, Benin, Ashanti, and Fante (148-162). Those of Southern and Central Africa were: Luba Kingdoms, Lunda Empire,

Manikongo Empire, Bunyoro and Buganda, Azania and Zanj, and the Rozwi Empire of (Great) Zimbabwe (163-178).

14. See George B. N. Ayittey, *Indigenous African Institutions* (Doobs Ferry, NY: Transnational Publishers, 1991.

15. John Iliffe, *The African Poor: A History*. African Studies Series 58 (Cambridge, New York, New Rochelle, Melbourne, Sydney: Cambridge University Press, 1987), 4. Iliffe also distinguishes between the structural poverty characteristics of societies with land and those without. In the former case the very poor lack access to the labor needed to exploit the land; in the latter, they mostly lack access to land or cannot sell their labor at prices sufficient to meet their needs (p. 4).

16. Ibid., 143-213.

17. Reginald Herbold Green, "Reduction of Absolute Poverty: A Priority Structural Adjustment," Discussion Paper 287, IDS (Brighton, England: University of Sussex, 1991), 1-40, especially pp. 4-8.

18. Ibid., 2.

19. Charles Elliott, "Rural Poverty in Africa," Occasional Paper 12, CDS (Swansea, United Kingdom: University College of Swansea, 1980), 6; idem, "Poverty 2000," *Study Encounter [SE]* 7, no. 3 (1971): 1-8; idem, *Patterns of Poverty in the Third World: A Study of Social and Economic Stratification* (New York: Praeger, 1975). See also Patrick Kalilombe, "Cry of the Poor in Africa," *African Ecclesial Review [AFER]* 29 (August 1987): 202-13.

20. Elliot, "Rural Poverty in Africa," 7. He adds that "the most basic form of poverty, shortage o f f ood, i s w idespread e ven i n r elatively well-endowed, ' well-developed' countries with higher than average GNP/head" (p. 10).

21. Ibid., 11.

22. Green, "Reduction of Absolute Poverty," 4-6. Charles Elliott distinguishes two groups among the absolute poor: subsistence producers and landless laborers. The former "may sell surplus produce but do not *plan* to do so. They farm as a way of life, not as a way to a cash income" [author's emphasis]. See "Rural Poverty in Africa" (11). Landless laborers have no right to land. Therefore "they depend exclusively on the sale of their labor-power" (p. 11). According to Klaus Nurnberger, "Poverty in absolute terms is marked by an income which lies below the level of basic essentials for a healthy and happy life of the family." See "What Do w e Actually M ean W hen we S peak o f Affluence and P overty?" i n *A ffluence, Poverty and the Word of God: An Interdisciplinary Study-Program of the Missiological Institute,_Mapumulo,* ed. Klaus Nurnberger (Durban, South Africa: The Lutheran Publishing House, 1978), 29. For further discussion, consult the following works: Lawrence Schlemmer, "The Two Significant Income Gaps in South Africa," in *Affluence, Poverty and the Word of God,* 49-56; Desmond M. Tutu, "H ow C an Y ou S ay Y ou Love God w hom Y ou H ave N ot S een w hen Y ou Hate Your Brother whom You Have Seen?" *Engage/Social Action [Engage]* 13, no. 11 (1985): 18-19; David J. King, *Land Reform and Participation of the Rural Poor in the Development Process of African Countries* (Madison: University of Wisconsin, 1974); Frederick Ferré and Rita H. Mataragnon, eds., *God and Global Justice: Religion and P overty in an Unequal World* (New York: Paragon House, 1985); Wayne E. Nafziger, *Inequality in Africa: Political Elites, Proletariat, Peasants and the Poor* (Cambridge: Cambridge University Press, 1988); Robin Palmer and Neil Parsons, eds., *The Roots of Rural Poverty in Central and Southern Africa* (Berkeley: University of California Press, 1977); and Kim Byong-suh, "A Sociological Understanding of Poverty: The Asian Context," in *Mission in the*

Context of Endemic Poverty, Papers of a Consultation on Mission in the Context of Poverty and in Situations of Affluence, Held in Manila, Philippines, December 10-14, 1982, ed. Lourdino A. Yuzon (Toa Payoh, Singapore: Christian Conference of Asia, 1983), 44-61.

23. Green, "Reduction of Absolute Poverty," 5.
24. Ibid., 6-8.
25. Coudere and Marijsse, "'Rich' and 'Poor' in Mutoko Communal Area"; Peter R. Fallon, *Incomes, Poverty, and Income Distribution in Rural Botswana: A Synthesis of Evidence Based on the Rural Income Distribution Survey* (Washington, DC: World Bank, 1981).
26. Elliott, "Rural Poverty in Africa," 11. These are either large-scale farmers or people who have other small businesses as well.
27. Ibid., 12.
28. Ibid.
29. Ibid., 16. However, he also points out that for many poor households in rural areas, wage employment is the second largest source of income and easily the largest source of cash income. Off-farm wages are usually higher than those of farm work (17-19). For example, a study done in Ghana and Uganda in 2000 indicated that for women in these countries, non-farm activities play an important role in yielding the lowest—and the most rapidly declining—rural poverty rates. In both countries, rural poverty declined faster for female heads of household engaged in non-farm work. See Constance Newman and Sudharshan Canagarajah, "Gender, Poverty, and Nonfarm Employment in Ghana and Uganda," Policy Research Working Paper 2367. The World Bank Development Research Group. Rural Development and Human Development Network. Social Protection Team, August 2000.
30. Ibid., 22. According to Iliffe's theory, except for aged and crippled-headed households, most categories of Green's absolute and relative poor fall into the group of the structural poor due to social circumstances. Victims of war, famine, or other natural disasters would fall under the conjunctural poor.
31. Elliott, "Rural Poverty in Africa," 24.
32. Ibid., 32.
33. See MacPherson, *Five Hundred Million Children.* Iliffe adds that some of the very poor Africans were children of poor women, unprotected women, or widows (*The African Poor*, 76-77).
34. MacPherson, *Five Hundred Million Children,* 69, 147-48.
35. Iliffe, *The African Poor,* 28-29, 87.
36. Ibid., 164-92.
37. Ibid., 192.
38. In Africa, the notion of "the family" usually goes beyond the Western conception of "the nuclear family." In fact it is what anthropologists usually refer to as "the extended family." In addition to the nuclear family, the extended family includes both maternal and paternal grandparents, uncles, aunts, cousins, nephews, nieces, in-laws, etc. Festus Ambe Asana asserts that "the list of those included in the family circle is extended even further." See "Problems of Marriage and Family Life in an African Context, Viewed from the Perspective of the Christian Pastor as Counselor" (Th.D. diss., Boston University School of Theology, 1990), 33. Asana also proposes his own categories of family. He uses "immediate family" to refer to the nuclear family. "Family of origin" refers to "the group of persons with whom a wife or husband traces his or her ancestry to a common root." The term "larger family" is

used "to distinguish the household from what anthropologists have called the extended family" (8).

39. John S. Mbiti, *African Religions and Philosophy,* 2d ed., rev. and enl. (Oxford: Heinemann, 1990), 81-89. See also Emefie Ikenga-Metuh, *Comparative Studies of African Traditional Religions* (Onitsha, Nigeria: IMICO Publishers, 1987), 145-59.

40. Mbiti, *African Religions and Philosophy,* 104.

41. Ibid.

42. Ibid., 105.

43. Ibid., 106.

44. Ibid. Hence, one can only say, "I am because we are; and since we are, therefore I am" (106).

45. Ibid., 102.

46. Ibid.

47. Ibid.

48. Ibid., 103. See also A. R. Radcliffe-Brown and Daryll Forde, eds., *African Systems of Kinship and Marriage,* ninth impression (London, New York, Toronto: Oxford University Press, 1967).

49. Mbiti, *Introduction to African Religion,* 7-8.

50. "There were no inns or hotels in traditional Africa, but there were dangerous wild animals such as lions, hyenas and leopards. In search of food, or in search of work, strangers needed to find shelter at night. African traditional ethics required that one offered strangers some shelter and food." See Temba L. J. Mafico, "The African Context for Theology," *The Journal of The Interdenominational Theological Center [JIntThC]* 16, nos. 1 & 2 (1988/1989): 75; idem, "Tradition, Faith, and The Africa University," *Quarterly Review [QR]* 9, no. 2 (1989): 41.

51. Bolaji Idowu, *Olódùmarè: God in Yoruba Belief* (London: Longmans, 1962), 157. The argument that "one should be hospitable because it is right to be so" is what ethicists c all a d eontological a rgument. S uch a rguments a re "absolutist" a nd "o ne cannot argue beyond them." For further discussion of this concept, see Robin Gill, *A Textbook of Christian Ethics* (Edinburgh: T. & T. Clark, 1985), 5-6, 157-60.

52. See Mordikai A. Hamutyinei and Albert B. Plangger, *Tsumo-Shumo: Shona Proverbial Lore and Wisdom,* Shona Heritage Series: vol. 2 (Gwelo: Mambo Press, 1974), 73.

53. It should be noted that while the focus of this section is on African Traditional Religion, present-day Africa is characterized by religious pluralism. Christianity has in many cases been indigenized to suit the African context and serve the local needs of the people. Among the southern Shona of Zimbabwe, this transformation is most clearly expressed in the rise and growth of Independent Churches as demonstrated by the work of M. L. Daneel. See Daneel, *Old and New in Southern Shona Independent Churches,* vols. 1-2 (The Hague, Paris: Mouton, 1971-74); Vol. 3 (Gweru: Mambo Press, 1988).

54. Bolaji Idowu, *African Traditional Religion: A Definition* (Maryland, NY: Orbis, 1973), 75. See also Ikenga-Metuh, *Comparative Studies of ATR,* 13-23; Michael Gelfand, *Shona Religion: With Special Reference to the Makorekore* (Cape Town: Juta, 1962); John S. Pobee, *Toward an African Theology* (Nashville: Abingdon Press, 1979).

55. J. Omosade Awolalu, "Sin and its Removal in African Traditional Religion," *Journal of the American Academy of Religion [JAAR]* 44 (June 1976): 275-87, especially p. 275.

56. Idowu, , *Olódùmaré*, 5. P. A. Dopamu adds that "what Idowu says of the Yoruba is equally true of the whole of Africa." See "Towards Understanding African Traditional Religion," in *Readings in African Traditional Religion: Structure, Meaning, Relevance, Future,* ed. E. M. Uka (Bern, Berlin, Frankfurt a.m., New York, Paris, Vienna: Peter Lang, 1991), 19-37, especially p. 24.

57. Mbiti, *African Religions and Philosophy,* 1. For Dopamu, Africans are "incurably religious," and "from the womb to the grave, religion governs everything" (*Readings in African Traditional Religion,* 23).

58. Mbiti, *African Religions and Philosophy,* 1.

59. These are: beliefs; practices, ceremonies, and festivals; religious objects and places; values and morals; and religious officials or leaders. See *Introduction to African Religion,* (pp. 11-13). Mbiti also discusses where African religion is found. It is found in people's rituals, and festivals; shrines, sacred places, and religious objects; art and symbols; music and dance; proverbs, riddles, and wise sayings; names of people and places; myths and legends; beliefs and customs; and in all aspects of life, (pp. 20-30). See also Mbiti, "Where African Religion is Found," in *Readings in African Traditional Religion,* (pp. 69-75). Idowu argues that African religion was handed down in "oral traditions" and transmitted through myths; the *Odu* corpus (recitals); liturgies; songs; proverbs, adages, and epigrams. See Idowu, *Olódùmaré,* chap. 1, especially pp. 5-10. See also Ikenga-Metuh, *Comparative Studies of ATR,* 25-40.

60. See Mokgethi Motlhabi, "The Concept of Morality in African Tradition," in *Hammering Swords into Ploughshares: Essays in Honor of Archbishop Desmond Tutu,* ed. Buti Tlhagale and Itumeleng Mosala (Trenton, NJ: Africa World Press, 1987), 85-100.

61. Idowu, *Olódùmaré,* 145. T. N. O. Quarcoopome agrees with Idowu concerning West African Traditional Religion (WATR). He similarly states that "in West African Traditional Religion morality is the fruit of religion. This means that in the traditional context there is no such distinction between morality and religion because there is close relationship between religion and the moral life. The social and moral ordinances are the injunctions of God, who had himself instituted them." See *West African Traditional Religion* (Ibadan: African Universities Press, 1987), 160-61; Ikenga-Metuh, *Comparative Studies of ATR,* 243-59.

62. Idowu, *Olódùmaré,* 146.

63. Kofi A. Opoku, *West African Traditional Religion.* (Accra: FEP, 1978), 152-53. It is generally believed that God has representatives who enforce the moral order. Uka states that "the African believes not only in the Supreme God as the author and upholder of morality but also in the ancestors, divinities, or spirits as the messengers of God through which He enforces His will among men and in the world that He created." See Uka, "Ethics of African Traditional Religion," in *Readings in African Traditional Religion,* 180-94, especially p. 184. Opoku adds that these gods see to it that laws are upheld and that those who infringe them are punished (p. 156).

64. J. Omosade Awolalu and P. A. Dopamu, *West African Traditional Religion* (Ibadan: Onibonoje Press, 1972), 156. On the role of divinities, see also Ikenga-Metuh, *Comparative Studies of ATR,* 103-123. Different African societies refer to God in as many different names, most of which point to God's attributes. On the nature of the High-God of the Shona people of Zimbabwe, see the excellent book by M. L. Daneel, *The God of the Matopo Hills: An Essay on the Mwari Cult in Rhodesia* (The Hague, Paris: Mouton, 1970).

65. Idowu, *Olódùmaré,* 30-56; Ikenga-Metuh, *Comparative Studies of ATR,* 85-101.

66. Idowu, *Olódùmaré*, 144-68. Other virtues include protection of the weak and poor, giving honor and respect to older people, etc.
67. Mbiti, *African Religions and Philosophy,* 208. While Mbiti is largely correct in that witchcraft and evil magic are bad because they destroy relationships, one can take his argument a step further. These crafts can also be seen as morally good if they are used to promote a social good, such as social equilibrium and equality. However, the problem of the end justifying the means arises; a moral evil is committed as a means to a just or good end. It should also be noted that while witchcraft seems to be viewed negatively in Africa, in some parts of America, there are "good" witches who are believed to do only good things.
68. Ibid., 209 [author's emphasis]. See also Mbiti, *Introduction to African Religion,* 174-79, and E. M. Uka, "The Ethics of African Traditional Religion," in *Readings in African Traditional Religion,* 180-94.
69. Uka, "The Ethics of African Traditional Religion," 190. This is so because "whatever strengthens the life, the prosperity, the solidarity, the success of the community is held to be good and right while the things that weaken or threaten the welfare, the peace and the solidarity of the community is [*sic*] said to be evil and wrong" (p. 190). According to Mbiti, there is therefore no "secret sin" in African morality, because whatever one does or does not do directly affects other members of the community. See *African Religions and Philosophy,* 208.
70. Uka, "The Ethics of African Traditional Religion," 191. He also explains in what sense African morality is "teleological," "utilitarian," or "legalistic" (pp. 191-92). See also Mbiti, *African Religions and Philosophy,* 207-10.
71.   Uka, "The Ethics of African Traditional Religion," 192.
72. Ibid., 190. See also Mbiti, *African Religions and Philosophy,* 199-210; Idowu, *Olódùmaré*, 144-68.
73. Mbiti, *Introduction to African Religion,* 178; see also pp. 16-17.
74. Mbiti, *African Religions and Philosophy,* 209-10.
75. "The question often asked after death or an accident is not *how* it happened, because the process is clear to everyone, but *why* the accident occurred at that point in time. Why should two cars collide at that particular spot and why should mine get the worst of the head-on impact, causing a fatal injury to a relative? This is the question which defies a traditional person's rationale. In this case, only a charge of witchcraft against a jealous neighbor or relative satisfies the inquiry" [author's emphasis]. See "The African Context for Theology," 78; idem, "Tradition, Faith, and The Africa University," 43-44. See also Michael Gelfand, *The Spiritual Beliefs of the Shona: A study on Field Work among the East-Central Shona* (Gwelo: Mambo Press, 1977).
76. Daneel describes the annual ritual of *mukwerere* (rain-making ceremony) whereby the Shona go to the Matopo hills with gifts in order to ask God for rain. See *The God of the Matopo Hills,* especially pp. 55-61.
77. See Hugo A. Kamya, "The Interrelationship of Stress, Self-Esteem, Spiritual Well-Being and Coping Resources among African Immigrants" (Ph.D. diss., Boston University, 1994), 55-62. Mafico adds that "the traditional [African] family structure had a way of dealing with stress, loneliness, sickness, and death." See "Tradition, Faith, and the Africa University," 40; idem, "The African Context for Theology," 73.
78. Iliffe, *The African Poor,* 7.
79. Ibid., 8.
80. Ibid., 47.

81. Ibid., 212, 193. Iliffe also reports incidents where families did not always take care of each other, but in the majority of cases, families cared for their unfortunate members (212-13). A case in point is that of leprosy sufferers who were either shunned, expelled, or confined to leprosariums (214-29). A critique of the extended family is also given in light of cases of child abandonment, neglect, and infanticide in poor Southern African townships in the 1980s (273). However, it is important to note that these urban areas were grossly overcrowded, poor, and oppressed.

82. Ibid., 57, 260, 277.

83. *Sunday Mail* (Harare), 6 July 1986; cited by Iliffe on pp. 246, 346, n. 128.

84. See "Tradition, Faith, and the Africa University," 40; idem, "The African Context for Theology," 73. Mafico also stresses this point when he writes about the Ndau people of Gazaland in Eastern Zimbabwe. He states that "the Ndaus depend very much on the security rendered them by their children in their old age. They believe very strongly that children who do not support their parents in old age stand serious consequences. As a result of this, the Ndau children will do all they can to their parents so that they may die ungrudgingly." See "The Relevance and Appeal of the Old Testament to the Ndau People of Rhodesia, Based on a Form-Critical Analysis of the Patriarchal and Covenantal Historical Narratives Recorded in Genesis 12-35 and Exodus 1-24" (Th.M. thesis, Harvard University, 1973), 87.

85. Roger C. Riddell and Peter S. Harris, *The Poverty Datum Line as a Wage-Fixing Standard: An Application to Rhodesia* (Gwelo: Mambo Press, 1975), 15-16.

86. Ibid., 17. Klaus Nurnberger explains the difference between rich and poor in South Africa in the 1970s. He argues: "Whether on a national, regional or international scale, you will find a very disquieting phenomenon: in the centre the population remains fairly constant while on the periphery the population increases very rapidly. If you look at economic progress the picture is reversed: in the centre there is rapid industrial and commercial development, while the economy of the periphery is stagnating. In other words: *the rich remain few and grow richer rapidly, the poor remain poor and grow in numbers rapidly.*" See "The Affluent Centre and the Poor Periphery: Structural Aspects of Urban-industrial and Rural Development in Southern Africa." in *Affluence, Poverty and the Word of God,* 59 [author's emphasis].

87. Riddell and Harris, *The Poverty Datum Line,* 95. They also admit that poverty has "a negative effect on those left in the rural areas . . . and has negative effects on the white man" (pp. 95-96), citing F. Wilson, *Migrant Labour in South Africa* (Johannesburg: Spro-Cas, 1972), 198. See also Michael Hubbard, *African Poverty in Cape Town* (Johannesburg: South African Institute of Race Relations, 1971).

88. Iliffe, *The African Poor,* 144. In Christian Ethiopia, only the destitute had the legal right to receive alms and even steal in dire necessity. In fact almsgiving was part of many domestic rites. In Nigeria, a Hausa family might make a rule of leaving enough at each meal to feed a beggar (p. 45).

89. Hamutyinei and Plangger, *Tsumo-Shumo,* 75.

90. Ibid., 76. Another proverb, *kunyima mufambi kuzvipa shonhe* (to be stingy with a traveler is to invite bad luck), means "to refuse hospitality never pays" (p. 447).

91. Ibid., 82.

92. Ibid., 165.

93.   Ibid., 337-38.

94. Iliffe, *Famine in Zimbabwe: 1890-1960* Zambeziana vol. XX (Gweru: Mambo Press, 1990). Iliffe chronicles nine significant famines due to drought, but there is scarce evidence that many people died. It should also be noted that some people

adopted a defeatist attitude toward poverty as can be attested by a proverb like *murombo haarovi chine nguo* (a poor man never kills [a big animal] with skin). This proverb points to the ironical situation where the poor are always poor and the rich get richer easily. A proverb like *urombo uroyi* (poverty is [caused by] witchcraft) obviously places the blame on witchcraft whereas it might just be caused by one's laziness. In Zimbabwe, some people believe that someone can use a farming magic called *divisi* either to increase one's harvest or to decrease another person's. Sometimes people tend to blame everything on the *divisi* without considering whether or not they have worked hard or whether or not the other person has worked hard. Writing about the Ndau tribe of eastern Zimbabwe who are renowned for their medicinal abilities, Mafico says, "The Ndaus are thought to possess the most effective medicines of all sorts. If a person of another tribe wants to be prosperous, he is encouraged to go to Gazaland for medicines. The Ndaus are thought to farm by magic; to study in school by magic; to play soccer or boxing by magic, and to kill by magic. This makes the Ndaus to be greatly feared throughout Rhodesia." See Mafico, "The Relevance and Appeal of the Old Testament to the Ndau People of Rhodesia," 57. For more discussion of the Shona people, see the following books: M. F. C. Bourdillon and Meyer Fortes, eds., *The Shona Peoples: An Ethnography of the Contemporary Shona with Special Reference to their Religion*, rev. 2d ed. (Gweru: Mambo Press, 1982); Michael Gelfand, *African Background: The Traditional Culture of the Shona-Speaking People* (Cape Town: Juta, 1965); idem, *African Crucible: An Ethico-Religious Study with Special Reference to the Shona-Speaking People* (Cape Town: Juta, 1968); idem, *The Genuine Shona: Survival Values of an African Culture* (Gwelo: Mambo Press, 1973).

95. See John Roscoe, *The Baganda: An Account of their Native Customs and Beliefs,* 2d ed. (London: Macmillan, 1965), 12-13; John W. Nyakatura, *Anatomy of an African Kingdom: A History of Bunyoro-Kitara*, trans. Teopista Muganwa (Garden City, NY: Anchor Press, 1973), 194; and Apolo Kagwa, *The Customs of the Baganda,* trans. E. B. Kalibaba (New York: Columbia University Press, 1934), 15.

96. I. Schapera, *A Handbook of Tswana Law and Custom,* 2d ed. (London: Oxford University Press, 1955), 69-70, 192. In times of famine, the chief opened his granaries and people worked communally on the "chief's fields" which were then used as famine reserves (p. 95). See also Michael Gelfand and Bennie Goldin, *African Law and Custom in Rhodesia* (Cape Town: Juta, 1975).

97. Iliffe, *The African Poor,* 209, citing *Oxfam News,* August 1967 and November 1975; Federation of the Rhodesias and Nyasaland, *Public Health Report,* 1961, p. 37, n. 105.

98. Iliffe, *The African Poor,* 210-11; citing *Ethiopia Observer,* 2, 4 (March 1958), p. 151; Heyer, *Die Kirche,* p. 148, n. 113.

99. Lucy P. Mair, *Welfare in the British Colonies* (London: The Royal Institute of International Affairs, 1944), 109. Mair goes on to explain that there is no delinquency, unemployment, or destitution because of the authority of chiefs or elders, and because of a land-based economy (p. 109).

100. Ibid., 110.

101. Iliffe, *The African Poor,* 248-49.

102. Ibid., 89.

103. Ibid.

104. Ibid., 93.

105. Ibid., 86. Iliffe chronicles the many trades in which the poor were involved. Some of them were porters, cotton spinners, hair dressers, petty traders, weavers, or dyers.

Others were beggars or even ascetics whose religious piety and devotion were thought to elicit the favor of the gods (82-88).

106. Iliffe, *Famine in Zimbabwe,* 14, 30-31, 72-78; idem, *The African Poor,* 8.

107. See Canaan Sodindo Banana, *Theology of Promise: The Dynamics of Self-Reliance* (Harare: The College Press, 1982); idem, *Towards a Socialist Ethos* (Harare: The College Press, 1987); Andrew Nyathi and John Hoffman, *Tomorrow is Built Today: Experiences of War, Colonialism and the Struggle for Collective Co-Operatives in Zimbabwe* (Harare: Anvil Press, 1990); and Diana Auret, *Reaching for Justice* (Gweru: Mambo Press in Association with The Catholic Commission for Justice and Peace in Zimbabwe, 1992). See also Augustine Nebechukwu, "Solidarity with the Poor: Christian Responses to Poverty," *AFER* 32 (August 1990): 96-111; Harold Wilson, *The War on World Poverty: An Appeal to the Conscience of Mankind* (London: Gollancz, 1953; reprint, New York: Kraus, 1969); Douglas Ensminger and Paul Bomani, *Conquest of World Hunger and Poverty* (Ames, Iowa: Iowa State University Press, 1980); Gunther Linnenbrink, "Solidarity with the Poor: The Role of the Church in the Conflict on Development," *The Ecumenical Review [EcR]* 27 (July 1975): 270-75; George E. Tinker, "Blessed are the Poor: A Theology of Solidarity with the Poor in the Two-Thirds World," *Church and Society [ChSoc]* 84 (March-April 1994): 45-55; and David T. Williams, "Poverty: An Integrated Christian Approach," Journal of Theology for Southern Africa *[JThSoAfrica]* 77 (December 1991): 47-57.

108. While African governments are generally leery about accepting foreign aid because it compromises their sense of self-sufficiency, sometimes such aid is abused such that the donors in turn become worrisome about donating to African governments. For example, see P. T. Bauer and B. S. Yamey, "Foreign Aid: Rewarding Impoverishment?" *Communio* 80, no. 3 (1985): 38-40. According to Miriam Reidy, "Dependence on outside aid is not only a symptom of underdevelopment but a reason for its persistence." See "Seeking the Root Causes of Poverty and Hunger in Africa," 28. "Self-reliance" and "self-hood" are identified as the most significant goals of development. Despite this situation, it should be noted that there are many international, church, and non-governmental organizations (NGOs) all over Africa which are helping the poor in Africa today. The Chinese proverb which states that if you want to feed a man for a day, give him a fish, but if you want to feed him for the rest of his life, teach him how to fish, says it better.

109. See J. David Pleins, "Poor , Poverty" (Old Testament), in *The Anchor Bible Dictionary [ABD]*, vol. 5. ed. David Noel Freedman (New York, London, Toronto, Sydney, Auckland: Doubleday, 1992): 402-14; and Thomas D. Hanks "Poor, Poverty," (New Testament) *ABD* 5 (1992): 414-24.

110. Ibid., 402.

111. Elsa Tamez, *Bible of the Oppressed* (Maryknoll, NY: Orbis Books, 19982), 3.

112. See Hanks, *ABD* 5; *For God So Loved the Third World: The Biblical Vocabulary of Oppression.* Trans. James C. Dekker (Maryknoll, NY: Orbis Books, 1984); reprint, Eugene, OR: Wipf and Stock Publishers, 2000) 1983).

113. Pleins, "Poor, Poverty," 403-13.

114. Robert K. Gnuse, *You Shall Not Steal: Community and Property in the Biblical Tradition* (Maryknoll, NY: Orbis Books, 1985), 77.

115. Leslie J. Hoppe, *Being Poor: A Biblical Study* (Wilmington, DE: Michael Glazier, 1987), 175.

116. Ibid., 179. Hoppe adds, "Whenever the Bible uses the language of the poor, it is calling for justice and for an end to oppression" (ibid.).

117. See Jonathan Sacks, *Wealth and Poverty: A Jewish Analysis* (London: Social Affairs Unit, 1984), 5.
118. Ayittey, *Africa in Chaos,* 363-71.

LIST OF CONTRIBUTORS

David Tuesday Adamo is a Professor of Old Testament, Delta State University, Abraka, Nigeria.

Dapo Asaju is Associate Professor of New Testament Studies, Lagos State University, Ojo, Lagos, Nigeria.

Joseph Enuwosa is a Senior Lecturer in New Testament Studies, Delta State University, Abraka, Nigeria.

Knut Holter is an Associate Professor of Old Testament and Rector, School of Theology, Stavanger, Norway.

Grant LeMarquand is an Associate Professor of New Testament, Trinity Episcopal School of Ministry Ambridge, PA. USA

Ukachukwu Chris Manus is a Professor of New Testament Studies, Obafemi Awolowo University, Ile-Ife, Nigeria.

Madipoane Masenya (ngwana Mphalhlele), Professor of Old Testament, Department of Old Testament, University of South Africa, South Africa.

Dr. Oyeronke, Olajubu, Senior Lecturer, Department of Religions, University of Ilorin, Ilorin, Nigeria

Friday Udoisang is a Lecturer at Harvester Theological College, Warri, Nigeria.

Robert Wafawanaka is an Assistant Professor of Old Testament Studies, School of Theology, Virginia Union University, USA.

Gerald West, is a Professor of Old Testament, University of Kwazulu-Natal, Pietermaritzburg, South Africa.

INDEX